PROFILES AND RECORDS

Profiles and Records of Achievement

A Review of Issues and Practice

Edited by
PATRICIA BROADFOOT

HOLT, RINEHART AND WINSTON
London · New York · Sydney · Toronto

Holt, Rinehart and Winston Ltd: 1 St Anne's Road,
Eastbourne, East Sussex BN21 3UN

British Library Cataloguing in Publication Data

Broadfoot, Patricia
 Profiles and records of achievement: a review of
issues and practice.—(Holt Education)
 1. Schools—Great Britain—Records and
correspondence
 I. Title
 371.2'7   LB2845.7

ISBN 0–03–910679–9

Typeset by Inforum Ltd, Portsmouth
Printed in Great Britain by Biddles of Guildford Ltd.

Last digit is print number: 9 8 7 6 5 4 3 2 1

Contents

14.00

9/24/86

ALBION

155696

Acknowledgements

The origin of this book was a conference held at the Bristol University School of Education in March 1984 in response to the DES Draft Policy Statement on Records of Achievement. Since that time we have seen the publication of the DES Policy Statement itself and the initiation of a programme of DES-funded pilot schemes in selected local authorities in England and Wales, the evaluation of which will be the basis for deciding the form such records should take when they are made available to every school-leaver at the end of the decade. At the same time, other important initiatives have been going on in the field of profiles and records of achievement, some of which were reported on at the Bristol University conference, some of which are reported here. Although this collection cannot hope to cover the range of existing initiatives at all comprehensively, and even less to anticipate the outcome of development work only recently begun, it is clear from the scale of the initiatives already in train that such a review of progress to date is urgently needed. I am therefore deeply grateful to all those colleagues who have helped make this book possible: the contributors themselves; the participants and speakers of the original conference who generated the ideas; the Bristol School of Education Further Professional Studies staff who made the meeting possible; and not least to all those partners in the educational enterprise—pupils, parents, teachers, advisers, administrators, inspectors and academics —I have met with in the common cause of furthering the profiles movement and to whom I owe whatever personal insights are represented in this book.

Sincere thanks to all the secretarial staff who helped make this book a reality, especially Sue Cottrell and Anne Mallitte for their unstinting efforts in collecting and typing the manuscript for this book.

Notes on the Contributors

Elizabeth Adams is an educational consultant and former general inspector for Surrey County Council. She is jointly responsible with Tyrrell Burgess for the Gulbenkian pilot project on validation and accreditation.

Neil Baumgart is Associate Professor in the School of Education at Macquarie University, Sydney, Australia. He has conducted research into education evaluation, student assessment, policy studies, higher education and education for development. His interest in profiling developed during a study leave at the University of Bath in 1984.

Patricia Broadfoot is Lecturer in Education at the University of Bristol. She has been involved with profile developments since the early 1970s. Her publications include *Pupils in Profile* (SCRE, 1977), *Assessment, Schools and Society* (Methuen, 1979), *Keeping Track of Teaching* (Routledge and Kegan Paul, 1982) and *Selection, Certification and Control* (Falmer, 1984). Together with Desmond Nuttall she is currently co-directing the national evaluation of the DES-funded pilot records of achievement schemes.

Tyrrell Burgess is Reader in the Philosophy of Social Institutions at North East London Polytechnic, where he was also the first Head of the School for Independent Study. Together with Elizabeth Adams he is responsible for the Gulbenkian pilot project on validation and accreditation.

Richard de Groot is the National Co-ordinator, Drugs Education and Training, YMCA. As a Regional Officer with the Schools Council (1978–81) he was responsible for the introduction and development of Pupil's Personal Records. He is former Headmaster of Kingswood School, Northamptonshire (1973–78) and was founder Headmaster of Shaftesbury School, Dorset (1981–85).

Alan Evans is Head of the Education Department, National Union of Teachers.

David Garforth is Director for Assessment and Profiling, Dorset Local Education Authority, and Chairman of the Royal Society of Arts Profile Committee. His publications include *Profile Assessment: Recording Student Progress. A School Focused INSET Working Manual* (Dorset County Council, 1983), *Profiling: A Users' Manual* (co-author, Stanley Thornes, 1985).

Harvey Goldstein is Professor of Statistical Methods at the University of London Institute of Education. His major interests are in the theory of assessment and testing, the application of statistical models to education systems, and the design and analysis of longitudinal studies.

Andy Hargreaves is Lecturer in Education at the University of Warwick. He is a member of the Steering Committee of the Oxford Certificate of Educational Achievement and is involved in evaluating pupil profiling within the TVEI. He has written widely on classroom studies, staff decision-making and the impact of educational policy and practice, including a book on *Educational Policy and Practice* (Falmer, in press).

Gloria Hitchcock is currently Warden of the Northavon Teachers' Centre, Bristol and County Coordinator of the South Western Profile Assessment Research Project. Formerly the Head of Careers at a comprehensive school, she is also involved in in-service education for teachers at the University of Bristol.

Anne Keane is Research Officer with the Inner London Education Authority Research and Statistics Branch. She is currently involved with the Education Support Grant Records of Achievement pilot scheme.

Jack Mansell is Chief Officer of the Further Education Unit. He has lectured and written extensively on various aspects of education, training and staff development and he has been involved in Further Education curriculum projects at home and abroad. He is past president of

x   *Profiles and records of achievement*

the National Association of Teachers in Further and Higher Education.

Peter Mortimore is Assistant Education Officer for Schools for the Inner London Education Authority. He was Director of the Research and Statistics Branch of the Inner London Education Authority for seven years until 1985.

Desmond Nuttall is Professor of Education Psychology and Director of the Centre for Curriculum and Professional Studies in the School of Education, Open University. Together with Patricia Broadfoot he is co-director of the DES-funded national evaluation of the pilot records of achievement schemes.

George Pearson is Co-ordinator (part-time) of the National Profiling Network, sponsored by the Dorset LEA and Southern Region Examination Board. He was Headmaster at Norton Hill School, Midsomer Norton, 1962–76, Examinations Officer for the Schools Council 1976–82, and Field Officer for the Schools Council 1982–84. He was a member of the FEU Study Group responsible for the Report 'A Basis for Choice' published in 1979.

Nick Stratton is Senior Research Officer at the City and Guilds of London Institute. He has produced various research reports on profiles and profile pilot schemes.

Alan Willmott is Director of Research at the University of Oxford Delegacy of Local Examinations, and is mainly concerned with the research, development and monitoring of the Oxford Certificate of Educational Achievement. After working with a GCE examining board, he spent a number of years with the National Foundation for Educational Research.

Introduction

Records of Achievement: Achieving a Record?

THE NEED FOR CHANGE

After more than a hundred years of external-exam dominated certification procedures, it appears that England and Wales are now on the brink of an assessment revolution. During the development and growth of mass educational provision there have been repeated attempts to introduce more comprehensive and relevant assessment procedures, but until recently these attempts have made little impression on the examination monopoly. Public concern about educational standards, political expediency and professional inertia have coalesced into a considerable barrier to change. In the last few years, however, major structural changes in the economy and associated policy developments have begun to erode this longstanding acceptance of the desirability of external examinations, and have stimulated instead some quite novel approaches to reporting assessment, such as graduated assessments, credit accumulation and records of achievement.

Of the range of approaches currently being explored—and they are not mutually exclusive—it is arguably this last which offers the greatest potential for change, in that it commits the educational system as a whole to an assessment strategy in which pupils are equal partners. Discussions of what the implications of this commitment might be for schools and teachers, and its potential impact on the learning process, constitute a major element in this book.

In July 1984, the Department of Education and Science for England

and Wales published a policy statement on records of achievement, which undertook that all school-leavers should be given a record of achievement by the end of the decade. The arguments for this initiative were expressed both in terms of the mutual benefit that would accrue to both students and their future employers from better means of school reporting, and also the impact that such a process would have on pupils' motivation during their passage through schooling itself. Whilst England and Wales show little sign at present of abolishing examinations of the more traditional kind at the end of compulsory schooling (that is, 16+), this initiative on the part of central government must be read as a desire to go some way towards compensating for the disadvantages and limitations of such external examinations. Whilst both politicians and the general public still cling to the notion that subject-based external examinations are a major means of ensuring quality control amongst educational institutions in a system which imposes no centralised curriculum, there is now a considerable ground swell of opinion amongst both educationists and (to a lesser extent) parents and pupils who feel that there is a need for a more comprehensive and curriculum-integrated approach to assessment. Apart from the fact that it is increasingly apparent to all partners in the education system that many youngsters will not go into employment, or if they do, that the selection will not be based primarily on exam results, there is also an increasingly explicit concern that schooling is not bringing about the outcomes it sets for its students.

The criticisms of public examinations are longstanding and now reasonably well-known, indeed so well-known that Ingenkamp (1977) expresses amazement that they are still so widely used given the overwhelming evidence against them. We know that examinations are frequently inaccurate (as a result, for example, of marker fatigue or markers' subjective preferences) and that they may not be a valid measure of what a pupil can really do (he or she has had an off day or has bad handwriting, for example). Even more fundamentally, they can only measure a small sample of educational achievements; they encourage extrinsic motivation rather than the desire to learn for its own sake; and they encourage and indeed are deeply associated with an educational process which discourages cooperation between students and emphasises individual competition. Teachers are heard frequently to complain that the existence of such external examinations narrows what they can offer to students in curriculum and pedagogy. Perhaps most important of all, in terms of communication, the aggregate examination grade may conceal vital differences between different kinds of competencies that a pupil may have acquired. He may be expert in essay-writing, for example, but poor in practical work, confident in oral work but poor in interpretation. This is the kind of information that both students and their prospective employers need to know.

Perhaps the best way of understanding the shortcomings of existing certification procedures is to conceptualise the two basic functions of assessment in education. On the one hand we have what might be called the *assessment curriculum*; the messages, overt and covert, that are conveyed to pupils about themselves, their own progress, and their developing personality, by the evaluative comments of teachers and the evaluative climate of the school in general. On the other hand, the second and distinct function of educational assessment concerns its role in *communication*, in which it acts as a bridge between the educational institution and the world outside; a function which continues—in the form of references, for example—throughout adult life. To extend the well-known criticisms of formal examinations in terms of this dual conceptualisation allows a more fundamental critic-ism to be mounted. Let us take first the difference between the intended and the actual outcomes of schooling.

The objectives of schooling are frequently conceptualised in terms of, for example, the acquisition of self-knowledge; the development of inter-personal skills; the development of maturity; emotional and moral awareness; the development of academic skills; an enthusiasm for learning; a respect for society, human rights, etc., and an overall life enrichment both in the short and long term. Whilst individual countries would want to add their own specific concerns to this list, I imagine there are few who would depart from this general educational agenda. But if we consider what our schools so often produce in practice, the list looks rather different. All too often, people do not develop self-awareness: they see no connection between education and life: their self-image and self-confidence is steadily eroded by the repeated experience of failure and condemnation, and they are en-couraged to rely on teachers to teach them rather than on themselves as learners. Entering school as active and enthusiastic enquirers, all too often they become passive and apathetic, uninterested and lacking in initiative and self-discipline. Schooling, except for the successful few, comes to be defined as a time-serving activity which has little relation to future life. Whilst this may be a somewhat extreme picture of the hiatus between the rhetoric and the reality, there is widespread evidence in both developed and developing countries that education-ists are deeply dissatisfied with the instrumental, extrinsic orientation induced by qualification inflation and excessive competition. This is little short of tragic in educational terms; it is also, ironically, highly dysfunctional in terms of the other aspect of educational assessment, namely its communication function.

In a recent publication, the British Institute of Personnel Management (IPM, 1984) sets out what it considers the definitive list of what employers look for in recruiting staff. The list is as follows:

(a)   literacy;
(b)   numeracy;
(c)   communication;
(d)   organisation of work;
(e)   working with colleagues;
(f)   working with people in authority;
(g)   analytical ability and problem-solving;
(h)   judgement and decision-making;
(i)   adaptability;
(j)   responsibility, self-awareness and maturity.

If this list is valid, and other evidence of a similar kind suggests that it is, then we are not only disadvantaging our students educationally with our very limited academic examinations, but we are also disadvantaging them occupationally, since the qualities employers apparently seek match very closely the outcomes we intend for the schooling process itself. There would thus seem to be a strong argument for reforming our assessment procedures with a view to bringing them more into line with both the curriculum and communication functions of assessment that I have identified.

THE IMPEDIMENT TO CHANGE

We are obviously, then, confronted with the question of why formal examinations (with their pernicious effects) are allowed to continue in the face of such cogent arguments against them. The short answer to this is the question of legitimacy in the selection process, and the need for objectivity to militate against bias and injustice in the allocation of life chances. Thus as far as the *attestation* function of assessment is concerned, there is an important need for face validity in the procedures used, and for reliable identification of what has been achieved (and in some cases also the identification of specific inadequacies). Linked to this is the *selection* function, which requires some basis for discrimination between candidates, a high degree of reliability, some measure of predictive validity and, above all, legitimacy which makes the whole process acceptable in society as a whole. It is because external examinations are the best means so far devised of meeting the criteria of comparability, reliability and legitimacy that they have enjoyed such continuing popularity, despite their negative effects on the learning process and their inefficiency in providing the information employers really wish to know. It also needs to be said at this point that examination-based selection has a far greater degree of validity when functioning as a gatekeeper for further academic study, and it is the expansion of educational provision into a mass competitive ladder which has more than anything highlighted this disjuncture.

A FORMULA FOR INNOVATION

There have been repeated calls in England and Wales since the beginning of the twentieth century for different kinds of recording procedure more in keeping with the future occupations of non-academic pupils, but here (as elsewhere) it has proved impossible to sell to such pupils and their parents the idea of alternative forms of assessment, when these are so evidently a second-class meal-ticket and a final elimination from the educational competition. The structural changes in the economy of this and other advanced industrial societies are, however, now making possible a genuine alternative approach to assessment which bids fair to improve both the curriculum and communication functions of assessment. The principles on which this innovation is based may be summarised in terms of the three Rs: *reinforcement* of the learning process, *respect* for learners, and *relevance* for action.

Under *reinforcement* are subsumed the curriculum functions of a new kind of assessment philosophy, which emphasises diagnosis of a student's strengths and weaknesses, conceptualises learning as an interactive process that emphasises mastery and achievement rather than norm-referencing and failure, and which regards assessment not as a bolt-on addition to the course but as one aspect of teaching itself. These principles together make up what is now receiving increasing attention as the formative function of assessment.

Under *respect* comes a concern (which is quite novel in most education systems) for open and collaborative relations between teachers and pupils, in which it is recognised that only by engaging with pupils will they come to a personal commitment and respect for their own learning. This mutual respect is taken to be the best basis for motivating both teachers and pupils.

The *relevance* dimension relates more to the communication function of assessment, and the provision of information about skills,
aptitudes and capabilities which will be useful for pupils, their teachers
and their families, and for potential consumers of such records. Thus
we are talking about an approach to assessment which is novel, both in
content and procedure, and is both formative and summative. The
content of such records was well conceptualised in the recent Inner
London Education Authority (ILEA) report on the curriculum and
organisation of secondary schools (1984), which distinguishes four
aspects of achievement:

(a)   written expression, organisation of material, memorisation and
       similar academic achievements traditionally measured in for-
       mal examinations;
(b)   practical skills, the application of knowledge, oral and inves-
       tigative skills (the application of the knowledge acquired under
       (a), only limited parts of which have traditionally appeared in
       formal assessments);
(c)   personal and social skills, communication and relationships,
       working in groups, initiative, responsibility and other such
       personal qualities not normally explicitly measured in tradition-
       al assessments;
(d)   motivation and commitment, perseverance, self-confidence
       and self-image.

It is this last element, so deeply personal, which is both the most
fundamental to present and future success, and at the same time least
often directly addressed in the educational process. However, the
extent to which schools are willing to depart from the relative security
of written exams and objective tests, and explore the possibility of new
types of assessment, makes it possible to conceive of assessing in quite
novel ways. It is for this reason that in the last few years England and
Wales, and to an even greater extent Scotland, have seen a considerable growth of interest in hitherto under-explored assessment techniques—such as oral exams and systematic observation—as well as
more radical innovations, such as graded tests and credit accumulation, student self-assessment and self-recording and, perhaps most
significant of all, teacher–pupil negotiated assessment. It is significant
of the scale and speed of the changes currently taking place that the
idea of pupil self-assessment, for example, which would have been
unthinkable to most people (and certainly to politicians) even in the
late 1970s, is in 1984 a central pivot of the policy statement on records
of achievement.

Thus, to summarise briefly what I have said so far, in England and

Wales there has been since the early 1970s a ground swell of dissatisfaction with traditional school examinations, and a corresponding enthusiasm for an interest in the development of alternative forms of assessment, variously called profiles or records of achievement. The grass-roots support for such an alternative, which resulted (in the 1970s and early 1980s) in a proliferation of individual schemes in schools and colleges throughout the country, has been sufficiently strong for it to be coalesced into government policy in 1984. Over the next three years a series of government development schemes will be both locally and nationally evaluated with a view to providing a national Record of Achievement scheme at the end of the decade. Whilst it is far from certain what the details of this procedure are likely to be, there is sufficient common ground within the schemes currently being developed to be reasonably certain that the new records of achievement will address both the assessment-as-curriculum and assessment-as-communication functions; that is, they will have a major role to play both in the process of schooling and in its summative reporting, and to this end will include the assessment of skills (intellectual, scientific, practical, etc.), subject-specific assessments, comments on personal qualities and a record of experience. The chapters by Mansell (Chapter 2) and by Mortimore and Keane (Chapter 5) give a more detailed account of these common principles. Having said this, there are deep divisions in the movement (as currently represented) about how such assessment is best pursued, who should do it, in what context, and in what format.

It is the purpose of this book both to highlight those features which profiles and records of achievement schemes typically have in common, and to elucidate the very real differences that currently distinguish different approaches. This is done in the hope that the very act of comparison will help to resolve these differences, and will strengthen our ability to identify the key issues which remain to be addressed before such records can hope to take the place of formal examinations.

One of the major divisions, which appears as a tension in many of the contributions to this book, is that between the priority given to the curriculum, as against the communication, function of the recording system. As Figure I.1 sets out, it is possible to identify a continuum between forms of recording. At one end are those which are predominantly subjective and personal, and have as their major purpose a means of facilitating pupils' understanding of themselves and their own progress, such as the PPR scheme described in Chapter 7. At the other end of the continuum the emphasis is on records which will be in some measure comparable and reliable, incorporating a measure of objectivity which allows them to fulfil some of the purposes currently

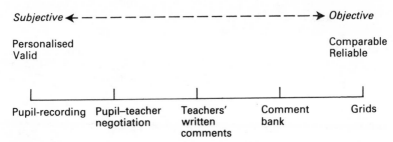

Fig.I.1 *Types of record.*

fulfilled by examinations. The City and Guilds approach which Stratton describes in Chapter 8 is more like this. Unfortunately, it is proving difficult to relate these two priorities. Early prototypes of records of achievement such as the Scottish Council for Research in Education (SCRE) profile (see Chapter 2) emphasised the comparability aspect. They provided 'grids' of descriptors of a wide range of qualities and skills against which assessments were made, usually on a four-point scale. Some of these grids were norm-referenced, and some more recent varieties emphasise criterion-referencing.

More recently still, in an attempt to get rid of the mechanistic impression such grids tend to give, considerable support has been accumulating for the idea of a 'comment bank' in which, as Evans describes in Chapter 12, teachers select pre-coded comments (from a bank of such comments) which are then processed and printed out by a computer to read as a consecutive paragraph of prose. Many other people, however, share the misgivings expressed by Andy Hargreaves (Chapter 14) that such attempts at providing objectivity and comparability in the whole range of personal and social achievement is deeply worrying, and they will tend rather to emphasise an approach which is primarily concerned with the construction of a personalised record. Indeed the distinction between the record and an assessment is critical here, in that many such exponents are in favour of pupils recording their own experience and producing a record in which the assessment element only comes in when it is read by a potential consumer. The employer must make his own judgement of the pupil in reading through what the pupil has written. Some compromise between these two extremes is increasingly to be found in the concept of negotiated records, in which teachers and pupils regularly discuss the pupil's progress, and in the course of these discussions, set targets for the next set of learning objectives. These targets may be academic, social, or personal. As Burgess and Adams suggest in Chapter 6, it is envisaged that such a formative procedure would extend throughout a particular course and terminate in a more summative document, which contains only that information which the pupils themselves wish to have included. Figure I.2 gives an example of what such a record might look like.

Although those concerned with developing profiles and records of achievement have come a long way towards conceptualising the kind of alternative assessment procedure they feel would be appropriate in the changing educational context, it is equally clear that there are many deep divisions within this movement and decisions still to be made about the organisation of such a procedure. As I have suggested, we need to decide between a norm-referenced grid approach, a pre-specified criterion checklist, or a free comment format. We need to decide on the kind of evidence to be used—for example, formal tests, traditional marking, teacher observation or pupil self-assessment. We need to decide on the content — which skills, which achievements, which dispositions, which feelings. We need to decide who is going to make the record—the student alone, the teacher alone, or both together. We need to decide whether all or only some of the school curriculum will be assessed in this way, and perhaps most important of all, we will need to decide whether there is to be a national record of achievement, or whether we can continue to allow individual institutions or local authorities to devise their own procedures. The technical and conceptual problems raised by such questions are explored at length in the chapters by Baumgart (Chapter 4) and by Nuttall and Goldstein (Chapter 13).

The experience documented in the various chapters of this book is intended to provide some of the evidence needed for us to begin to find answers to these questions. In addition, the development work of the last few years has added enormously to our understanding of the issues involved in records of achievement. Such understanding is arguably the most crucial achievement to date, since until we have learned to ask the right questions, we cannot hope to profit fully from the work currently taking place. The organisation of this book reflects this interaction between theory and practice which has become characteristic of the profiling movement.

Part 1, 'Personal perspectives', sets out the roots of the movement and the vision that transformed one or two isolated development initiatives into what is now a major policy commitment.

Part 2 is entitled 'Putting ideas into practice'. It describes seven different development initiatives from the point of view of their progenitors, and allows the reader a vicarious share in the agony and exhilaration of development work.

Part 3, 'Critiques', provides the dash of cold water necessary if

PERSONAL PROFILE SUMMARY

NAME ....   FORM ....

My interests and leisure activities

I spend a lot of time with my family especially at weekends and when they go out. I do not spend so much time with my school friends out of school except for sports. I like playing tennis and I am in the school team. I also like cycling of which I do a lot with my brother in the immediate district. I sometimes play hockey in the school team but I do not really enjoy it. My relaxation usually involves either tennis, cycling or reading, which I greatly enjoy. I help my family quite a lot and sometimes my next door neighbours who are OAPs with gardening. This I also enjoy. My hobbies include cactus growing (I am a junior member of the National Cactus and Succulent Society) and stamp collecting. I spend some of my free time on these when I feel in the mood. I also like walking long distances across country (not on roads). I enjoyed the Peak District trip due to this. I liked being with my friends during that as I think it added to the enjoyment. Swimming is another sport I like but I am not very good.

My experiences of work

I prefer mental work involving numbers than almost anything else. I enjoy maths and the mathematical side of physics and chemistry. I enjoy all the sciences because I think they are interesting and relevant to what I will probably do for a living. I am thinking of training to be a doctor which also involves hard physical work. I like this in the form of grasscutting, tennis, cycling, some hockey, housework and swimming. My mechanical skills are not very good, neither do I really enjoy that sort of thing. I quite like creating things such as in art, but again I am not very good. I need to be given one or several ideas before I can start. Most of my work involves reading and writing and listening how to do something before I start. I do not really enjoy planning or organising for large groups, but I usually plan ahead for myself.

My character, personal qualities

I am usually a quiet person, both at home and at school, but if I say something which I think is right I will argue my point. I am quite active when the weather is nice to be out in, in the way of sports. I am careful both in what I do and what I say so that I do not upset anybody. I try not to take large unnecessary risks which put either me or anyone else into danger. I am not a good leader and I do not really like being a leader in social circles but I think many people follow (or try to follow) my example in academic subjects such as maths. I try to be co-operative to everybody if they ask me to do something which I think it is possible for me to do but I do not really like joining in large groups. I always persist in finishing everything it is possible for me to do. I attach quite a lot of importance to appearance and try always to be clean and neat, though not always fashionable. I always try to be reliable and never late unless I can help it. I always keep my word, especially where I am asked to keep a promise.

g.1.2 *Example of summary record.*

enthusiasm is to be most effectively harnessed.

Already, many serious concerns have been identified by existing development work. We must be careful that we do not overlook others that might prejudice the successful fulfilment of the vision described in Part 1. It would be wrong to ignore the major professional, technical and philosophical issues which have yet to be resolved if profiles and records of achievement are to become an enduring and positive part of the educational process. Equally, there are few people currently involved in working towards this goal who doubt that such concerns can be resolved given the necessary goodwill and enthusiasm. In reporting the experience of some of these people, this book presents a challenge to the educational world as a whole.

PB
Bristol 1985

REFERENCES

ILEA (1984) *Improving Secondary Schools: the Report of the Hargreaves Committee.* London: ILEA.

Ingenkamp, K. (1977) *Educational Assessment.* Slough: NFER.

Institute of Personnel Management (1984) *Schools and the World of Work: What do Employers look for in School Leavers?* London: IPM.

PART ONE

Personal Perspectives

The movement to develop profiles and records of achievement is now so diverse and complex that it is sometimes difficult to disentangle the various issues involved. Part 1 has been designed to introduce the reader to some of the origins of the profiling movement and the way in which it has developed from these early beginnings. The first three chapters have been written by people personally involved in early development work who are now in a position to reflect upon their experience over a number of years. The fourth and final chapter in this section is quite different in kind, since it relates the thoughts of an outsider coming new to the contemporary educational scene in England and Wales. It is hoped that, together, these four 'personal perspectives' will introduce the reader to the main themes of the book.

1

Sowing the Seed: Pupil Profiles, Research and Policy in Scotland[1]

PATRICIA BROADFOOT

One of the earliest and best known profiling schemes was developed in Scotland in the mid-1970s. It is described in detail in a volume published for the Scottish Council for Research in Education in 1977, entitled Pupils in Profile. *Whilst the scheme never achieved widespread implementation in schools, it was extremely influential in bringing the idea of profiling to a wide audience both in the United Kingdom and internationally and has had a profound effect on later developments in the field. The context for this early initiative and its significance for subsequent events as described in this chapter provide both an historical and an analytical introduction to the book as a whole.*

—Editor

No area of social life is more redolent with value judgements than education. Indeed its huge call on the public purse and the supreme responsibility of being formally charged with guiding the development

---

[1] This article appeared in its full version in 'Pupil Profiles, Research and Policy: A Parable for Our Times', in Dockrell, W.B. (ed.) *An Attitude of Mind: 25 years of Educational Research in Scotland*, published by the Scottish Council for Research in Education in 1984. I am grateful to the SCRE for permission to reproduce it here.

of the next generation should make education a major focus of political discussion. As it is, politicians must be chained to their seats for 'set-piece' debates in Parliament,[2] the more politically 'sexy' issues of finance, defence and international relations seducing the attention of both elected and permanent officials from the mundane matters of the classroom. The result of this state of affairs is that, all too often, educational practices are instituted or allowed to continue without the value judgements on which they are based being held up to scrutiny. Public examinations provide a classic example in this respect, the assumption being that they motivate pupils and maintain standards whilst offering the fairest basis for selection. This has justified an extremely expensive, divisive and often counter-productive practice for nearly a century in the face of consistent research evidence substantiating such criticisms (see, for example, Ingenkamp, 1977).

As early as 1911 the Consultative Committee of the English Board of Education rehearsed the first of many arguments in favour of the provision of a school certificate rather than formal examinations for all but the most academic pupils. The argument was reiterated in 1943 by the Norwood Committee, in 1947 by the Secondary Schools Examination Council and in 1959 in the Crowther Report. But the arguments and evidence put forward were powerless against massive public pressure, which led to a proliferation of rather than a reduction in the number of examinations in the 1950s and 1960s. Similarly in Scotland, the provision of universal secondary education in 1945 was followed in 1947 by the seminal Advisory Council Report on Secondary Education, in which it was recommended that the distorting effects of external examinations on the secondary school curriculum could be removed by the provision of internal examinations as the basis for a School Certificate for 'non-Highers' candidates. But the group leaving certificate of four or five passes—normally equated with successful completion of secondary education—was retained. As recently as the 1950s, when all pupils were obliged to be in school until they were fifteen, it continued to be gained by less than 10 per cent of the age group. Two out of three pupils admitted to certificate courses were unsuccessful. The alternative 'Junior Leaving Certificate', more on the line of the Advisory Council recommendations, which was run on a county basis and administered by individual schools was of little value as it had no national currency and was in content a pale imitation of, rather than a genuine alternative to, the School Certificate. In their report of 1955 on Junior Secondary Education, the Scottish Education

---

[2] I am indebted to J.D. Morris for this comment.

Department deliberated possible alternatives (SED, 1955). Rather than looking for ways of broadening certification to include a greater range of both academic and non-academic school achievements—of more relevance to many pupils and employers than those qualities that can be measured by formal written examinations—the Scottish Education Department chose instead to extend the scope of the traditional external examinations to a greater, but still relatively small, proportion of the year group (SED, 1959).

Thus, despite the apparent commitment of powerful groups to examination reform, it was not until the 1972 initiative of the Head-teachers' Association of Scotland that such aspirations were to be more than mere rhetoric. Why this should have been the case is a complex question.

Certainly the raising of the school leaving age to sixteen in 1972 played its part in exacerbating the long-standing problem of providing meaningful and motivating courses for non-certificate pupils who had no wish to be in school. Other, less clear-cut developments also played a part, including the spirit of democratic egalitarianism which had so characterised the policy initiatives of the 1960s and had led to relatively generous provision for educational priority areas and curriculum development. The guiding spirit of these initiatives was similar to that of the headteachers as set out in their Interim Report of 1973 (SCRE, 1973), namely a desire to deal justly with the whole range of school pupils, not just those bright or privileged children that had traditionally been the concern of secondary education. In addition, these same changes in provision (which had opened up, for all pupils, opportunities on a scale their grandparents could not have dreamed of) also served to erode the significance of 16+ examinations for selection. What Dore (1976) termed 'qualification inflation' meant that the key point of selection was increasingly seventeen, eighteen or even later, as the rapid expansion of further and higher educational provision (which was another characteristic of the 1960s) allowed the level of qualifications demanded of school leavers to become steadily higher. Whilst this trend was not particularly explicit in either Scotland or England—where the rate of early leaving was, and indeed remains, much higher than in other similarly industrialised countries—it was still sufficiently marked to affect the qualification market and thus the trend away from external examinations towards increasing the responsibility of teachers for assessment of their pupils.

Less sanguine sociologists, notably Bernstein (1975) and more recently Ranson (1984), explain these developments in terms of the need for new forms of social control in which the overt and explicit sorting of examinations, like the overt categorisation of subjects, was to be replaced by the covert 'channelling' of continuous assessment that, together with informal pedagogy and integrated studies, provides for an altogether new form of selection. The replacement of 'sudden death' assessment by benign and positive guidance has, according to some commentators, produced a form of control that the individual is powerless to resist and may indeed not even be aware of (see, for example, Foucault, 1975). Experience abroad, in countries such as France, certainly testifies to the dangers inherent in such continuous and comprehensive assessment and guidance procedures, and many teachers are well aware of this.

Whilst there may be disagreement as to the underlying explanation, it is clear that it was the particular combination of practical and ideological pressures, characteristic of the early 1970s, which provided for the first time a fertile medium in which the idea of an alternative form of certification could at last take firm root. After falling many times on barren, stony or weed-choked ground, the time was at last right for the planting of a relatively small seed to result in the rapid growth of a major policy issue. This small seed was the 'pupil profiles' project. With the support of the Scottish Education Department, the project attempted to develop and test a form of 'profile' record which would fulfil the needs identified by the Headteachers' Association for a detailed, positive and comprehensive statement covering all aspects of school life: this record was to be compiled by teachers and would be available to every pupil when appropriate. (Brief details of the procedure are set out in Appendix 1.)

A prophet is rarely honoured in his own land, and it has been in England, rather than in Scotland, that 'pupil profiles' have made their greatest impact. Part of the reason for this was certainly the activities of the Dunning Committee, whose report 'Assessment for All' came out in 1977, almost simultaneously with the research report *Pupils in Profile* (SCRE, 1977). The Dunning Committee's radical proposals for reforming 16+ certificate examinations in Scotland all but eclipsed the issue of profiles in the welter of more general feasibility and development studies to which it gave rise. Despite the not dissimilar activities of the Waddell Committee (1978) in England and the mass of development work initiated by the Schools Council on a new basis for 16+ examining, England has been much slower in instituting major change in the system of public examinations at 16+. Hence the enthusiasm for profiles, as teachers desperately search for some more meaningful goal for their pupils than that provided by the public examination corset.

The movement is much wider than this, however. The new needs of the burgeoning further education sector have fuelled the growth of profiles as nothing else could have done. Largely free of the constriction of historical tradition, it is this sector of the education system which is most free to design novel assessment procedures which will reinforce its equally novel curricular goals. Thus, as Mansell describes in Chapter 2, it is in the new MSC initiatives—notably the Youth Training Scheme (YTS) and Technical and Vocational Education Initiative scheme (TVEI)—as well as in the more traditional City & Guilds and Royal Society of Arts (RSA) courses, that profile assessment is becoming a characteristic feature. Typically the tutor, often in collaboration with the student or trainee, keeps a detailed record of progress in all areas pertinent to the course—usually some combination of basic skills, personal attributes and work successfully completed. Thus whilst the establishment interests of the Government and the universities give (at best) a guarded welcome to profiles as a useful alternative form of certification (DES, 1984), they are simultaneously fuelling the growth of such profiles in their increasingly reactionary support of an outmoded examination system.

But even if England could look forward to a completely redesigned system of 16+ certification, on a scale similar to that proposed by the Dunning Committee in Scotland, and a rationalisation of post-sixteen provision in schools and colleges similar to that proposed in the *16–18s in Scotland: Action Plan* (SED, 1983), it would still lack the necessary central control to put these into practice. As it is, official circles are very far from making such a commitment. The result is a form of guerrilla warfare, in which a motley collection of educational personnel are storming the ramparts of tradition in that characteristically English way which Fowler (1981) has so aptly termed 'anarchic incrementalism'. Thus just ten years after the inception of the 'pupil profiles' project, schools, colleges, local authorities and training boards up and down the country are designing novel and idiosyncratic 'records of achievement', most (if not all) of which acknowledge the influence of the Scottish research (Balogh, 1982).

One of the strengths of what has been termed the 'disease dissemination' model of research and development is the scope it provides for those infected with a particular enthusiasm to exercise their own creativity. Whilst the basic principles of the Scottish 'pupil profile' system are still recognisable in most of the current initiatives—comprehensive, detailed and positive statements compiled by teachers, available to every pupil as appropriate, and covering all aspects of school life—the expression of these principles now takes many different forms, as this book demonstrates. The SCRE Profile Assessment System would now be referred to as a 'grid-style', 'tick-the-box' type profile, and whilst the provision of positive behavioural descriptors on the final report was intended to minimise the disadvantages of an essentially norm-referenced assessment, many of the more recent profiles have been designed to give much greater scope to qualitative, pupil-initiated records and assessments more on the lines of Don Stansbury's influential RPE (Record of Personal Experience) and the equally influential 'Personal Achievement Record' of Evesham High School. Other schools, wishing to combine the maximum degree of informativeness with the minimum of clerical work, have opted for criterion checklists and comment banks in which, as in the traditional item bank (and often with the aid of a computer), descriptors are selected from a bank of available comments to build up a verbal profile. More and more profiles are quite lengthy collections of different sorts of record combined together as a dossier. Increasingly, too, they are explicitly committed to giving pupils an overt role in the process of assessment and recording (FEU, 1984).

But whilst the details of individual profiles vary and the future of the movement as a whole is far from clear, the spirit on which it is based seems now to be securely incorporated into professional ideology. This initiative thus provides one of the rare examples in which it is possible to point to the quite explicit impact of research on practice. The combination of professional, official and research expertise in the 'pupil profiles' project was not exceptional, but it was crucial in giving the initiatives credibility among all the major interest groups in Scottish education. It was the bringing together of teacher-defined need, research council development work and government support which provided a unity of concerns almost unique in the history of attempts to reform school certification. This combination was further strengthened by the inclusion of other interests, notably those of employers, training boards, teacher unions and further and higher education, on the Headteachers' Working Party that guided the development work.

Last but not least was the admirable Scottish respect for evidence. If the 'pupil profiles' project was the first major development study in this area, it also remains the only study which has gone beyond mere 'mapping' to challenge empirically the assumptions on which profiling is based. Do teachers distinguish between the different characteristics of a pupil, between the elements of attainment in a subject? Do they agree in their assessments of cross-curricular basic skills? Are such profiles a useful basis for pupil guidance? In the flurry of publications and development activity that currently surrounds the profile movement, research that examines the fundamental assumptions of profiles has until recently been conspicuous by its absence. Although the Schools Council has initiated several studies in this area, as has the City & Guilds of London Institute (see, for example, Goacher, 1983;

Stratton, Chapter 8), these have been small-scale in relation to the mass of development work now being undertaken. As was the case with progressive education and open-plan schools, curriculum development, integrated science and mixed ability teaching, the idea itself has been sufficiently timely for its apparent merits so to commend it to the educational world that neither policy-makers nor professionals have subjected it to formal research scrutiny until it promised to become incorporated into practice. The same promises to be the case with profiles. We still do not know how this kind of assessment will affect pupils, how teachers will make their assessment, what to do about comparability and many other questions of this sort. Although this situation is now changing with the institution of, for example, national and local evaluations of the DES-supported pilot schemes, and other major research projects such as that being conducted by the South Western Examinations Board in association with the University of Bath, there is still no English study comparable to that done in Scotland in the mid-1970s. The lack of hard data on crucial issues such as comparability and practicability also means there is still a danger of the original spirit of profiles being distorted into the inspiration for a form of certification which will be available only to the 'less able'. It goes without saying that any third-best certificate of this kind is likely to be at best irrelevant and at worst counter-productive, even if its only purpose is social control.

But this is already to enter the realm of speculation. They who sow the seed cannot know to what use the fruits of their labour will be put. It may be that the current fashion for profiles in England represents the seed that fell on shallow earth so that it sprang up too quickly and was scorched and burnt. Meanwhile the good seed is still growing. When it ripens will be the time not simply for a plethora of new record cards, but for a fundamental change in educational priorities of a depth and intensity not seen since the institution of universal secondary education in 1944/45.[3] It is quite possible that the profiles movement is merely the harbinger of changes in the organisation of educational provision so fundamental that curriculum, pedagogy and evaluation in the schools of the future will no longer be recognisable for what they were. This is no millennial cant. In an age of microcomputers, biotechnology, mass structural unemployment and nuclear threat, the assumptions which provided the foundations for our present system of schooling are inevitably changing. Moves towards a more individualised, collaborative curriculum are already apparent in further and

---

[3] 1944 in England, 1945 in Scotland.

higher education, and are closely tied to the provision of assessment initiatives, such as graded tests and qualitative records, which free the evaluation of progress from any group comparison. The kind of coordinated change in curriculum and assessment that Burgess and Adams describe in Chapter 6 becomes every day a more urgent proposition, as rapid technological development makes it both necessary and feasible.

The 'pupil profiles' project did not create this climate; nor was it determined by it. But the interaction between understanding and action, vision and commitment that it represents has been replicated several times in more recent assessment initiatives in Scotland, including the provision of a common system of examining for *all* sixteen-year-olds and the creation of a unified system of modular accreditation for all non-advanced further education. England and Wales perhaps have something to teach Scotland about the power of sheer enthusiasm to bring about change pioneered at the grass-roots. Scotland can in its turn teach England and Wales some of the benefits that cental leadership and coordination, vision and commitment can bring. Whilst the various countries have different ideas about what procedures are most likely to bring about radical change, I have argued in this chapter that they share a common vision and have much to learn from each other.

REFERENCES

Balogh, J. (1982) *Profile Reports for School Leavers*. Harlow: Longman.
Bernstein, B. (1975) *Class Codes and Control*, vol. 3. London: Routledge & Kegan Paul.
Department of Education and Science (1984) *Records of Achievement: A Statement of Policy*. London: HMSO.
Dore, R. (1976) *The Diploma Disease*. London: Allen & Unwin.
Scottish Secondary Teachers Association Education Committee (1969) *Report on Examinations*. Edinburgh: HMSO.
Further Education Curriculum Review and Development Unit (1984) *Profiles in Action*. London: HMSO.
Foucault, M. (1975) *Surveiller et Punir*, Paris: Gallimard.
Fowler, G. (1981) 'The changing nature of educational politics in the 1970s', in Broadfoot, P. et al. (ed.) *Politics and Educational Change*. London: Croom Helm.
Goacher, B. (1983) *Recording Achievement at 16+*. Harlow: Longman.
Ingenkamp, K. (1977) *Educational Assessment*. Slough: NFER.
Ranson, S. (1984) 'Towards a new tertiary tripartism: new modes of social

control in the 17+', in Broadfoot, P. (ed.) *Selection, Certification and Control*. Lewes: Falmer Press.
Scottish Council for Research in Education (1973) *Headteachers' Association of Scotland Working Party on School Assessment Interim Report*. Edinburgh: SCRE (mimeo).
Scottish Council for Research in Education (1977) *Pupils in Profile*. London: Hodder & Stoughton.
Scottish Education Department (1955) *Report on Junior Secondary Education*. Edinburgh: HMSO.
Scottish Education Department (1959) *Report of the Working Party on the Curriculum of the Senior Secondary School*. Edinburgh: HMSO.
Scottish Education Department (1983) *16–18s in Scotland: An Action Plan*. Edinburgh: HMSO.
Waddell Committee (1978) *School Examinations*, vols. 1 and 2. London: HMSO.

2

Records of Achievement and Profiles in Further Education

JACK MANSELL

One of the earliest advocates of profiles, Jack Mansell, has been directly instrumental in their development in a wide range of further education courses. His influence on thinking about profiles and the educational issues involved has had an even wider impact. It is therefore appropriate that this second chapter should constitute an attempt by the author to distill some of the acquired wisdom of more than ten years' involvement with profiling, in order to identify some of the main themes and issues with which this book as a whole is concerned.

—Editor

There are many different types of student assessment record, some of national and others of local design. There is some confusion as to the relationship between records of achievement and profiles. A Schools Council viewpoint (1981) is that a record of achievement might include a profile which delineates a few personal qualities and some basic skills. An MSC publication (1981), in describing various ways in which trainees might record their own experiences and progress, suggests that such records can contribute towards a profile.

In my view, whether a profile subsumes a record of achievement or vice versa is perhaps not so much a matter of principle as of design. It is possible to have a student/trainee record, in the form of a comprehensive log or diary of activities spanning several months, and a number of schemes include this feature. Sensitively monitored by a tutor, trainer or supervisor, the construction and discussion of that record is, for both 'teacher' and 'learner', a valuable exercise. To what extent it is used by careers officers or potential employers will depend not only on its content, format and bulk, but also on the pressures under which the reader is working. As a basis for interviewing, the discussion of a diary or log-book has probably no equal; as a basis for initial screening in a highly competitive labour market, it is less likely to be used. Conversely, a student/trainee record comprising a single 'progress sheet' or a short report may well be suitable for a summary assessment after discussion and as such could be a valid contribution to a profile.

It seems unnecessary, then, to force through a definition as to whether records of achievement and/or progress are more or less comprehensive than profiles; in the context of this contribution, I hope to concentrate on a description of the characteristics and aims of student profiles. From the outset in further education, we have described individual student profiles as records of achievement, constructed in part or wholly by responsible tutors and/or supervisors collectively or individually, involving a measure of student/trainee participation and, hopefully, accompanied by counselling and guidance (FEU, 1981).

Another characteristic of the student profiles we adhere to is that they are meant for public consumption. They are not confidential reports, the contents of which are kept from the subject. Student profiles or records of achievement are documents constructed by professional teachers or trainers, in conjunction with their students, describing as accurately and succinctly as possible the knowledge, skills and experiences of an individual relative to a particular curriculum. They are meant to be read in their final (summative) form by (amongst others) employers, parents, and education and training personnel. In the formative stage they are a common focus of concern between teacher and taught, a basis for face-to-face discussion and reflection, and an opportunity to appraise the suitability and pace of the learning programme.

CERTIFICATION

A major plank of Further Education Unit (FEU) policy is that the record of achievement or student profile will not get the status it deserves unless it either comprises the certificate itself or is an integral and major part of the certification process. We were forced to admit in *A Basis for Choice* (FEU, 1979) that 'The attraction of nationally accredited examinations for young people, parents and employers cannot be denied . . . public recognition will inevitably be based as much on some form of nationally approved certification as on the quality of the curriculum . . . Such certification would in turn have to be based on a nationally approved system of assessment'. Thus not for the first time was posed the problem of linking internal assessment to national certification, this time via a profile. We would maintain, however, that the benefits of profile records apply to all learners, and that the issuing of profiles only to those who could not obtain more conventional certificates would be undesirable.

Examples of how a profile becomes an essential part of the certification process are provided by some Royal Society of Arts (RSA) and City & Guilds of London Institute (CGLI) courses (see Stratton, Chapter 8). These schemes have been in action for several years and the emerging 17+ Certificate of Pre-Vocational Education (CPVE) is also committed to the issue of a profile as a record of achievement.

CURRICULUM-LED STUDENT PROFILING

For a common curricular framework, the format of the profile/record should be standard, for unlike many personal log-books, profiles are meant to be comparable if they are related to a common curriculum. This is not necessarily the same as being competitive. A basic principle of student profiles is that if they are recording a wide and diverse range of assessments of knowledge, skills and experiences they cannot then be aggregated (conflated) into a single grade. All of us are better at some things than others; the range of experiences and the tasks attempted by the student/trainee may well be unique to that person (e.g. the job-specific skills developed through work experience). Common core skills (such as literacy and numeracy) can be the subject of conventional tests and these should be appropriately recorded. The application of these skills to real-life (or well simulated) situations, however, may be much more important, although more difficult to assess. Such assessments nevertheless deserve to appear on the profile/record of achievement.

Thus profiles or records of achievements, if they are worth using, should comprise a wide and diverse range of assessments, not necessarily amenable to aggregation, averaging or the other reductionist techniques of educational measurement. Profiles which merely comprise a series of test measurements on scales which can be statistically processed (and few of these can) are not the subject of this chapter. There are well known batteries of aptitude and personality tests which produce profiles based solely on test scores. Such profiles require skilled and specially trained interpreters; these too are not the subject of this chapter because they are not related to a curriculum. This chapter is about recording *curriculum-led* student assessment, and it follows from this that the quality of the profile is related to the quality of both the curriculum and the individual assessments. A poor-quality curriculum in terms of content, design or implementation is not likely to produce a useful profile, however accurate the assessments appear to be. Similarly, poor-quality assessments based on well-designed curricula are also unlikely to produce worthwhile profiles or records of achievement.

QUALITY AND ASSESSMENT

The concept of quality related to curricula and assessment, of course, begs many questions. An analysis of what constitutes high-quality curricula is beyond the scope of this chapter, and ultimately that requires an analysis of needs and how they are met. The quality of assessment, however, requires at least a brief discussion. By assessment we mean generally a recorded judgement resulting from any testing situation, from a personal subjective observation, or from any mix of these. The testing situation may range from well-validated objective tests, scored by using an interval scale of measurement, through problem and essay-type tests, assignments, etc., scored on less statistically advanced scales, to judgements based on observation, dialogue or interrogation, scored impressionistically, some by the students themselves. The nature of the curriculum may require all or some of these and the result will be a collection of the consequential assessments. The validity and reliability of each assessment are matters of individual and professional appraisal, and such appraisals cannot always be separated from the nature, design and implementation of the curriculum.

The quality of the profile is thus a function of these individual appraisals, the totality of which is indeterminate. Not all profiles therefore are automatically of high quality, but because they are not to be conflated, at least all their constituent assessments are recorded, and can be identified and if necessary appraised separately. In this way it can perhaps be claimed that profiles are less able to obscure error than are conventional uni-dimensional examination grades. On the other hand the overall reliability of a profile, comprising as it must a collection of smaller assessments, is seen by many as a technical weakness. This is an under-researched aspect of educational measurement. Nuttall and Goldstein, in Chapter 13, review this aspect of profiles and conclude that the inclusion of graded test results within profiles may increase their statistical reliability. Macintosh (1982), however, maintains that we should worry less about reliability and emphasise more the professional validity that teachers add to assessment when they are included in the process. This approach, coupled with procedures such as those suggested by Dockrell (1982), goes some way towards justifying profiles in technical terms, but does nevertheless leave unanswered some of the conceptual problems raised by Baumgart in Chapter 4.

PASS, FAIL AND COMPETENCE

We cannot afford to eschew the grading of competency, however defined. We must have some way of distinguishing between the competent and the incompetent. Profiles and records of achievement allow this distinction to be made at a very specific level without a blanket rejection of the student. It is thus possible, for example, to have a poor performance in some aspects of mathematics, to be better at reading, to be good in dealing with other people and to be outstanding in some manipulative skills, all without being rejected as a total failure. Any teachers who hope to use profiles merely as a means of avoiding, at any level of specificity, the connotation of incompetence are not being realistic and in the long term do not help their students. To indicate failure and remain supportive is a difficult but vital task for any teacher, and the whole concept of formative assessment by profiling and its necessary link with counselling, as explained above, is to assist the teacher in the carrying out of this task.

RESERVATIONS

There do remain reservations about profiling and records of achievement. Some of these disappear if it is realised that they are not offered as a universal solution to the many problems embedded in our examining systems; others will disappear if it is understood that a profile or record of achievement must be related to the nature of the curriculum under consideration.

Some remaining reservations are concerned with complexity and status. These overlap to some extent, but generally we are concerned with the complexity of the task confronting teachers and others who complete profiles, together with the interpretation of, and the importance attached to, profiles by employers and other 'consumers'.

There is no doubt that the completion of student profiles and records of achievement in the way that is described above is a demanding task. Profiles should be formative as well as summative. They are thus invariably associated with a variety of course work assignments as well as terminal tests, all demanding different assessment techniques. Profiles require face-to-face tutorial sessions to be organised by teachers on a regular basis with individuals and small groups of students (if the latter are to participate). If profiles are to be part of a national certification system, they should be subject to external guidance and moderation. Two years of piloting *A Basis for Choice* (FEU, 1981) confirmed these difficulties. There is evidence (FEU, 1983) that computer-aided profiling is of some assistance, and the complexities of format and vocabulary are proving amenable to simplification.

Other difficulties, however, will not be resolved without some re-allocation of teachers' time. This calls for a re-appraisal of teaching priorities, strategies and timetabling. We cannot have student/trainee self-assessment, tutor assessment and counselling, the re-setting of individual targets and mutual evaluation of experiential learning, without time being allocated for these things to happen. Unlike conventional examination marking, many of the processes described above require the presence of the student or trainee and/or sometimes the presence of other members of the staff team. Yet whilst many (not all) teachers see assessment as a key part of their overall job, fewer identify it as an integral part of the learning process worthy of competing for time hitherto allocated to 'instruction'. Assessment, like preparation, is a duty more often than not carried out after-hours, and frequently outside the school or college. Profiling does not really allow this differentiation between assessment and teaching. In effect, assuming the curriculum demands it, profiling reminds us that we probably spend too much teaching-time on information processing (a job that after all can increasingly be accomplished by the sensitive application of computers) and too little time reflecting with our students on the learning experiences to which they have recently been exposed. Recording achievement, with student participation, forces assessment into the learning process, and this requires the confidence of teachers and their managers to re-allocate classroom time to tutorial time, provided always that the aims of the curriculum are being served.

CONSUMERS

Much of the initial support for profiles arose out of the inadequacy of the information presented by conventional examination results. These are invariably given as a series of cryptic symbols, such as Grades 1–5, or *Fail, Pass, Credit* and *Distinction*, alongside equally cryptic descriptions of subject coverage. These symbols are then used by the consumers (employers and further and higher education) with great weight and rigidity, whether or not they are fully understood. Student profiles are capable of giving much more information about the skills, knowledge and experiences obtained by the student. Mention has already been made of the invalidity of attempting to conflate a profile/record into a single aggregated grade. This, together with the rather obvious fact that if more information is needed then a larger piece of paper is required, makes the interpretation of the profile a more complex procedure. There is no real evidence that two or three pages of A4 is proving unmanageable for the consumers; rather the opposite. A CBI reaction (1980) to *A Basis for Choice* was supportive of the profile, provided that it was presented in terms 'which are meaningful to employers as a whole as well as to college staff and the students themselves'.

At the present time a considerable amount of activity is being aimed at attempting to ensure that profile data is meaningful to employers. A significant contribution in this area is the survey carried out by Wood of the Institute of Personnel Management (1982). This survey included the sending of a completed profile to almost 2000 IPM members. Of those who responded, over 90 per cent considered the profile a useful aid to selection, and over 80 per cent considered that the profile would have either as much or more importance than examination results. Whilst such rhetoric is often not borne out in reality, it does look as though student profiles and records of achievement (up to a certain length) are likely to be acceptable and meaningful to employers, provided they are readily comprehensible and offer some evidence of consistency of standards.

It also appears from this and other surveys (see, for example, SCRE, 1977) that many employers are willing to give high status to profiles relative to examination results. This is obviously encouraging and will reassure the many teachers who are now involving themselves in this work. Equally important will be the status given to profiles by the education system itself. But whether the profiles are intended for employment or education, the point made above cannot be over-emphasised: the quality of the profile is related to the quality of the curriculum. Profiles are not merely devices which allow the recording of assessments hitherto largely ignored; they should also be regarded as favouring, if not actively supporting, new curricular ideas. Thus whilst it is gratifying to have on record ministerial support for a more rapid development of records of achievement in schools, it would be regrettable if the potential of profiling to liberate the curriculum were neglected.

EXPERIENTIAL LEARNING

There is, for example, a ground swell of support for experiential learning (i.e. learning acquired from work, life and other experiences) to be recognised as accreditable. The necessity for young people to participate in certain learning experiences is written into the common core of CPVE and an increasing number of other programmes. There are also the MSC experience-based youth training programmes, notably YTS. For adults, better access to skill training will rely on some form of 'portfolio' assessment, recording acquired skills, knowledge and experience. The potential of the profile to provide an adequate base for the recording of these experiences and skills is now recognised and Hills (1982) has described a joint MSC/CGLI log-book profile project which commenced in September 1981. The recording and accreditation of experience-based learning is obviously the basis of other projects as well, and an enthusiastic argument for its large-scale adoption has been constructed by Evans (1981).

TO HUMANISE AND ENRICH

Ultimately, however, the argument for profiles and records of achievement is an educational one in the broadest sense. That is to say, it is about helping individuals to develop the knowledge, skills and experience they individually possess by helping them to reflect upon and record their own progress. As Rowntree (1977) has said:

'Whatever the span encompassed, a profile and especially one that includes narrative analysis, helps *humanise* the reporting response. Even the simplest of profiles differentiates the student from other students who share the 'same' total but 'add up differently' from him. The thrust is from the nomothetic to the idiographic; dividing the students out from one another like the opening out of a fan—not with a view to classifying them or ranking them in order of preferability but, ideally, with a view to showing that each is in a class of his own . . . thereby the recipient of the report is being put into a new and more human relationship with the assessors and the assessed. (p. 236)'

REFERENCES

Confederation of British Industry (1980) *Education and Training Bulletin*, August.
Dockrell, B. (1982) *Profiles in Preparation*. London: FEU (*Profiles*).
Evans, N. (1981) *The Knowledge Revolution*. London: Grant McIntyre.
Further Education Curriculum Review and Development Unit (1979) *A Basis for Choice*. London: FEU.
Further Education Curriculum Review and Development Unit (1981) *Vocational Preparation*. London: FEU.
Further Education Curriculum Review and Development Unit (1983) *Computer Aided Profiling*. London: FEU.
Hills, J. (1982) *Profiles in Training*. London: FEU (*Profiles*).
MacIntosh, H. (1982) *A 17+ Package: A View from the School*. London: FEU (*Profiles*).
Manpower Services Commission (1981) *Trainee Centred Reviewing*. London: HMSO.
Rowntree, D. (1977) *How Shall We Know Them?* London: Harper & Row.
Schools Council (1981) *Records of Achievement*, Newsletter 37.
Scottish Council for Research in Education (1977) *Pupils in Profile*. London: Hodder & Stoughton.
Wood, S. (1982) *Profiles in Recruitment*. London: FEU (*Profiles*).

3

A Network of Profiles

G. PEARSON

The third chapter is by another of the long-standing and widely influential commentators on developments in the field of profiling. As a former headmaster and Schools Council examinations officer, George Pearson has been well placed to monitor the growing interest in profiles and records of achievement. Here he outlines some of the early features of the movement's development, focusing in particular on the key role played by the Schools Council before its demise in 1983. Increasingly evident in this historical analysis is the tension between the pattern of local initiatives, which have characterised most of the movement's history, and the now growing need for some kind of central coordination to provide for more than local acceptability. The relative contributions that official policies and unofficial 'networking' might make in this respect are a major theme of this chapter.

—Editor

We are told by G.K. Chesterton that the 'rolling English drunkard made the rolling English road'. And certainly the present-day network of roads, while owing much to Roman national initiatives and latter-day national motorways, arose from a confusion of local needs; it evolved from paths and tracks and various cul-de-sacs into a system which can now be shown on a map.

So, perhaps, will the various local profile initiatives be gradually linked into a national system. What appears to be needed at the present time are signposts and short notes for travellers from which, gradually, more useful maps will emerge; out of local needs and experience will come the highways of the future.

The DES Statement of Policy (July 1984) on Records of Achievement seeks the establishment of agreed principles, but as yet a central information base is lacking. Until recently this function was the responsibility of the Schools Council for the Curriculum and Examinations, and in some measure profile reporting was encouraged by its efforts between 1980 and 1983.

This chapter describes one such attempt to produce a map of existing developments. Following a brief review of the history of profile initiatives, it discusses a rapidly developing information exchange network which seems likely to provide at least one way of overcoming the excessively fragmented nature of initiatives to date.

A profile is not a new method of assessment; it is a method of reporting assessments. It is the naming of parts. It is a record of information about a pupil, which may be presented in a variety of ways. Profile reporting therefore is not new; the description of a student's achievements subject by subject is a crude profile, as is the time-honoured reference, however much blurred the outline of the person may be. Recent activities have served to add precision to the profile and to extend its usefulness.

THE HISTORICAL CONTEXT

The wider interest shown in profile reporting during recent years has largely stemmed from dissatisfaction with examination results, which are shown as a single grade, as a worthwhile summary of a student's success. The profile form was seen to be the means of describing a wider spectrum of achievement than examinations normally cover; it could embrace personal qualities and describe skills not directly assessed by public examinations. In addition a profile was more likely to provide 'feedback' information to motivate and guide both teachers and pupils in the educational process.

So it is not surprising that work on profiles in Scotland during the early 1970s (see Chapter 1 and SCRE, 1977) was largely due to the absence of examinations appropriate to pupils of an ability range served by the CSE in England and Wales. In England and Wales the voices of employers, puzzled by the curriculum of schools and wishing to emphasise specific basic skills and durable personal qualities, gave support to the wider assessments promised by profiles.

Meanwhile a pioneer attempt to motivate pupils and to enhance qualities valued more often, or more explicitly, in society at large than in the timetabled curriculum of schools, could be seen in the work carried out in Swindon in the early 1970s. The Record of Personal Achievement (RPA) had considerable impact upon pupils too often labelled 'less able', yet it was in no sense a profile of discrete qualities; it might produce an in-depth record of an individual's experience—a self portrait—but it was rarely considered useful by busy employers when work was plentiful (Swales, 1979). But just as the thinking behind the Scottish scheme was to be deeply influential in the development of subsequent 'grid-style' profiles, so the thinking behind the RPA helped to inspire two separate, but related, later initiatives—the Record of Personal Experience (RPE) and the Pupils' Personal Recording scheme described by Richard de Groot in Chapter 7.

Amid such conflicting purposes it is not surprising that the profile scene became one of confusion, of local needs being served, with one school seeking solutions to its own problems and another school adopting a profile leaving report without much regard for its curricular implications; of some employers seeking this skill and that quality above all, while others sought another set.

In the late 1970s, most schools had their eye on the changes being proposed in external examinations, and local education authorities generally held back from promoting profiling schemes. The politicians who had tended to echo the views of employers in seeking to make the 'hidden curriculum' more open now began to promote a new curriculum consensus in schools. Meanwhile the establishment of the Further Education Unit encouraged a new cohesion of provision in further education.

THE CONTRIBUTION OF THE SCHOOLS COUNCIL

This was the educational context in which the Schools Council planned its research programme on profiles. The Council had already commissioned an evaluation of RPA, the report of which was published in 1979 (Swales, 1979). Following this it was decided that Programme Five, inspired by the Council's examinations team, should include a three-pronged survey into profiles and profiling. A major survey into school leavers' records (Balogh, 1982) was followed by an investigation into the profile reporting of examination results (Harrison, 1983) and a large-scale inquiry into the way employers and other users considered examination results and other forms of reporting.

The survey of schools in England carried out by Jan Balogh during 1980/81 confirmed how few in number were the schools which provided any form of 'profile' leaving record. Fewer than 100 schools (less than 1 per cent of all secondary schools) offered anything more than a structured testimonial, and scarcely 25 school profile reports appeared to meet the four basic criteria proposed by the Council's staff, namely that a profile was to be non-confidential; was to be available to all pupils irrespective of ability; was to include assessments of cross-curricular skills and some personal qualities; and was to be in a structured format common to all pupils in the one school. (Among the pioneer schools so identified were Evesham High School, Helston School and Comberton Village College.)

The Department of Education and Science were sufficiently impressed by the implications that profile reporting appeared to have for curriculum change that the School's Council Examination team was requested to accelerate its work in that field. Accordingly Brian Goacher was commissioned by the Council to promote the development of school leaving profiles. This was done in twenty or so schools in Suffolk, Liverpool and the Inner London Education Authority during 1981/82, and the report was published in 1983 (Goacher, 1983).

Meanwhile the Schools Council Programme Two helped finance a research exercise in Wales, in association with the Welsh Joint Examinations Council (WJEC) and the Schools Council Committee for Wales. A two-year feasibility study was organised, whereby two dozen schools during 1981/82 piloted four model profiles. The models used were based upon work done at Brynmawr School, Gwent, at Evesham High School, Worcestershire, and in the Further Education Unit of the DES. The outcome was a discussion paper published in 1983 (Schools Council Committee for Wales, 1983) which commended the framework of a 'national' profile to the WJEC (see Evans, Chapter 12). Other Programme Two activities also looked at different aspects of profile reporting—in reports to parents and in the profiling of particular subjects. The Council also gave a grant to a group of schools in eight southwestern counties to enable them for two years (1981–83) to pioneer a new version of RPA under the title 'Pupils' Personal Recording' (PPR). As de Groot describes in Chapter 7, this scheme was intended to introduce the idea of personal recording across a full ability range and to provide a view from the pupil as a useful segment of a record of achievement. This work continues.

At the same time, interest in profiling was growing rapidly in the further education sector. In 1979 the Further Education Unit published *A Basis for Choice*, the report of a study group on post-sixteen pre-employment courses, which recommended that profile methods of recording the assessment of students should be developed. *A Basis for Choice* found favour also among those seeking new objectives for sixth-formers, and profiling procedures devised by the City and Guilds of London Institute (CGLI) in conjunction with the FEU began to influence thinking in schools.

The Schools Council and the FEU had thus in their publications 1981–84, formed linked but isolated profile bridgeheads. But in January 1984 the Schools Council came to an unfortunate end. In its place the Secondary Examinations Council, set up in 1983 and briefly accorded the chance to monitor profile developments, was diverted from such tasks by the pressure of work in overseeing syllabus criteria and new forms of assessment for the GCSE.

The other successor body to the Schools Council, the School Curriculum Development Committee, has not been expected so far to engage in the widespread exchange of profile information.

ENTER THE DES

The vacuum created by the demise of the Schools Council was filled as far as profiles were concerned by uncharacteristically direct intervention on the part of the DES. In its draft statement of October 1983 and its policy statement of July 1984, the DES expressed a wish for more work on records of achievement and to this end it had financed nine pilot schemes in local education authorities (LEAs) throughout the country (DES, 1984). In December 1984 the DES announced financial support for the OCEA initiative, involving Somerset, Oxfordshire, Coventry and Leicestershire; the WJEC; the Inner London Education Authority; Suffolk; Essex; Dorset; Lancashire; Wigan and the East Midland Group of Northamptonshire, Nottinghamshire, Lincolnshire and Derbyshire. Several of these areas have yet to decide whether they will invent their own records, adapt others, or try existing schemes. A national steering committee will oversee and monitor these pilot schemes for a period of three years. The DES hopes to establish guidelines for the introduction of records of achievement in all schools, perhaps by the autumn of 1988. It has also established a team of national evaluators, who will report to the national steering committee,

charged with drawing national guidelines for records of achievement in the light of the insights generated by the pilot schemes.
Outside these areas there are, in addition, a rapidly increasing number
of schools, LEAs and other agencies which are experimenting with
profile schemes; a few have several years of experience behind them,
while others are in danger of 're-inventing the wheel' in a variety of
shapes, widths and weights, and some are not always certain of the
load the wheels (or the profiles) have to bear.

Meanwhile the scope of profile reporting has been greatly extended.
It has encouraged the movement towards modular courses, credit
accumulation and 'staged assessment', the profiling of examination
results (which depends on a restructuring of syllabuses), and the
development of graded tests, all now being investigated in a number of
subjects. Moreover profiling, which began as a display of basic skills
and qualities, now has to take account of the need to discriminate
within each student's achievement if not between students. It is the
composition of the record of achievement which now invites discussion
and clarification. Meanwhile, other schemes will continue. Until 1988,
'all flowers may bloom together'.

Throughout the country there is a considerable degree of goodwill
and a desire that the aims of the DES should be achieved. This is
apparent in the contributions to this book. In recent years numerous
initiatives have been generated at local, regional and national levels in
both secondary and further education. This has fostered a growing
body of experience and expertise, serving a variety of needs.

Already informal exchanges have taken place between practitioners, and some of the current pilot projects have published discussion
papers and newsletters in order that experiences may be disseminated.
However, there is a great deal of practice that is still taking place in
isolation, and there are likely to be many more local schemes which
will emerge in the next few years.

There is clearly much to be gained from the establishment of a
formal network for the exchange of information, experiences and
expertise. It is essential that good practices are shared, especially with
the growing number who will be undertaking similar work before the
end of the decade. Many groups, both large and small, have expressed
an interest, and the DES have stated in informal discussions that there
are many advantages to be gained from the establishment of such a
network.

THE PROFILING NETWORK

Accordingly, in November 1984, the Dorset Education Authority and the Southern Regional Examinations Board, which had already initiated a research and development project in the field of profile assessment and records of achievement involving 24 institutions within the county of Dorset, took steps to establish a 'National Profiling Network' (Garforth, 1984).

Both bodies were well aware of the variety of profiling experience; of schemes serving very different purposes; of schools working in isolation and often in ignorance of much that already occurred in other parts of the country. Nevertheless, membership of this network has grown faster than originally expected, and by 1 June 1985 it had acquired over 200 members. By November over 75 schemes had been described.

The network aims to locate and briefly describe upwards of a hundred distinctive experiments, to promote the use of a common language by its draft glossary of terms and to maintain a bibliography of useful books and leaflets. It will provide an answering service chiefly in the style of a directory; major enquiries will be referred to the practitioners.

The network will respond to the needs of the members and will constantly review the services offered, modifying and extending as appropriate. The quality of the service will in large measure depend upon the participation of the members and their ability to provide accurate, useful and up-to-date information on present or planned practice and on the difficulties encountered and the solutions found.

It may be that this National Profiling Network will have a limited life. At the very least it will provide signposts to the major practitioners, point to more regularly used paths (and vehicles) and encourage the creation of national profile maps by the travellers themselves.

CONCLUSION

At the time of writing (May 1985) it would appear that the hundred or so institutions which are actively pioneering profiling schemes range from single schools (perhaps thirty with distinctive formats), through consortia of three or four neighbouring schools, to large-scale projects where as many as two dozen schools are loosely linked. The profiling process, while it is now usually available, if not required, for all pupils, differs in its purposes from school to school: some are still content with a summative record intended primarily for employers' use, others dwell upon the value of dialogue to motivate pupils and teachers in a formative sequence. Some schools are busily identifying parts of a subject and planning 'subject profiles'; others are seeking ways of distilling the pupils' own experiences and self-assessments into a conscious self-image.

In all there are probably as many as a hundred or so schools with involvement of a year or more in some form of profiling and there are another hundred or so, now nominated by the new consortia, actively preparing for profiling in 1985/86. There remain the great majority of secondary schools—well over 90 per cent—aware no doubt of the profiling movement but as yet largely untouched by it. The technical problems of assessment are being investigated by a growing number of researchers and teacher-coordinators; more sensitive tutoring is being encouraged in more and more schools; the delicate balance required for a summative record (if it is to be no more damaging than a low examination grade) may yet be achieved in more cases. But the fears of the bulk of the teaching profession, that the teachers will lack the time, the resources and the self-confidence to do justice to the pupils, have yet to be translated into a firm commitment and into a new sense of priorities which could bypass the cries for more time and more resources.

Those schools with years of profiling experience are the first to admit how they have needed to develop and extend their work. They have profited from their own mistakes and the errors of others. And it is significant that one of the first actions of those schools nominated as part of the new DES-funded projects is to survey what has happened already. They can learn much from the pioneers, and especially where some of them are taking their own experience with them into the bigger schemes.

Profiling—as education—is essentially a one-to-one process: local commitment is vital. But understanding of profiles, the succession of summative statements as well as the 'final' leaver's record requires national publicity and national guidelines, an accepted glossary of terms and a broad recognition of the limits and limitations of any summative statement. For profiles to have any value beyond the process of education they need to have a currency that is generally recognised and the backing of some professional body, be it a local education authority or an examination board, to provide for consistency of standards. A multiplicity of profiles could prove fatal to widespread understanding, and thus acceptance, of this new approach.

Profiling, like horses, is for courses (the courses of education) but the profile, be it of a subject or of a collection of skills or of personal characteristics, needs a commonly recognised format. Yet, like the human face, the profile must be recognisably individual as well.

The network of profiles may have trunk roads and main roads (A1 nationally) and secondary roads (B roads for local use) and even narrow roads with passing places. A few footpaths may also be needed for sanity and progress. The network must enable the user to choose according to needs: a map with recognised main roads and some conventional signs can only aid the traveller. In the same way, developers need a highway code setting out some broad, basic principles which all can adhere to, whether their vehicle is a juggernaut or a push-bike. It remains to be seen whether this fine balance between conformity and diversity can be achieved in practice amongst the many different types of scheme currently being developed.

REFERENCES

Balogh, J. (1982) *Profile Reports for School Leavers*, Schools Council Programme 5. Harlow: Longman.

Department of Education and Science (1984) *Records of Achievement: A Statement of Policy*. London: HMSO.

Further Education Curriculum Review and Development Unit (1979) *A Basis for Choice*. Report of a study group on post-sixteen pre-employment courses. London: HMSO.

Goacher, B. (1983) *Recording Achievement at 16+*, Schools Council Programme 5. Harlow: Longman.

Harrison, A. (1983) *Profile Reporting of Examination Results*, Schools Council Examinations Bulletin 43. London: Methuen Educational.

Schools Council Committee for Wales (1983) *Profile Reporting in Wales—a Discussion Paper*. London: Schools Council Committee for Wales.

Scottish Council for Research in Education (1977) *Pupils in Profile*. London: Hodder & Stoughton.

Swales, T. (1979) *Records of Personal Achievement: an Independent Evaluation of the Swindon RPA Scheme*. London: Schools Council.

Garforth, D. (1984) 'National Profiles', *Times Educational Supplement*, 27 October.

4

An Outside Observer's View of Profiles in Britain

NEIL BAUMGART

In this fourth and final chapter of Part 1, Baumgart gives his outsider's personal perspective on the profiling movement as he has studied it in Britain. Writing with the advantages of hindsight and an outsider's detachment, Baumgart identifies some of the generic themes in the development of profiles and how these are embodied in particular initiatives. The various themes identified in the chapter—conceptual, ideological, technical, practical and accountability—provide a useful summary of the issues raised in Part 1 and a conceptual focus for the more detailed accounts which follow.

—Editor

The word 'profile' has been used over a long period in the literature on measurement and evaluation in education to describe the presentation of an individual's achievements or characteristics on multiple dimensions. The *first* thing that strikes an outside observer, then, is that the term has taken on a particular meaning in Britain in recent years in respect of reporting students' academic and other achievements and personal qualities, particularly at the time of leaving school. Thus, in this context, a profile has been defined as 'a systematic, comprehensive description and assessment of a pupil's academic and non-academic achievements, attributes and interests, set out in a format easy to interpret both by educational and non-educational users, and issued at the end of the student's period of secondary education' (Assistant Masters and Mistresses Association, 1983, p. 2). The term has also been used more narrowly to describe disaggregated reporting of examination results (Harrison, 1983), but popular usage corresponds to the broader definition above.

Secondly, an outside observer is impressed by the extent of the support which the profiling movement has commanded. The support is evident at the national level, where the Government has issued a policy statement on records of achievement (Department of Education and Science, 1984) and has supported a number of studies into the development and evaluation of schemes of reporting; it is evident in the initiatives of various examination boards (for example, Oxford Delegacy of Local Examinations, 1983); and it is evident at the school level (see Chapter 3), where teachers look optimistically towards assessment-led curriculum reform.

This breadth of support has to be understood in the context of the long-standing dominance of the systems of public examinations. Thus, the GCE Ordinary ('O') level, catering for about 20 per cent of 16-year-olds, was introduced in 1951, and CSE examinations, catering for a further 40-plus per cent of this age group, have been offered since 1965. Following a report of the Waddell Committee in 1978, the Government has decided to replace these two examinations with a new joint GCSE examination to be instituted in 1987, and in which seven levels of awards or grades are to be based on explicit, nationally valid, grade-related criteria.[1]

Advocates of profiling have cautioned that the new 16+ examinations amount to little more than tinkering with the old system rather than providing a genuine restructuring. Thus, they point out that the GCSE will still leave a significant proportion of the age group without any certification on leaving school (see, for example, Burgess and Adams, 1980). Moreover, public examinations based on academic achievement are seen to reflect narrow objectives of schooling and to give no incentive for, or recognition to, the development of personal and social skills (Broadfoot, 1984). The use of profile reporting is seen

---

[1] Efforts now going into the formulation of these grade-related criteria via the work of the Secondary Examinations Council closely parallel the attempts in Queensland to define criterion-referenced grades under the Review of School-Based Assessment (ROSBA). However, in England the attempt is to provide national grade-related criteria while in Queensland the criteria are formulated at the school level.

to have the potential to give adequate recognition to the full range of cognitive, affective and psychomotor objectives of schooling; to provide more useful information to students, employers and other users because of the disaggregated nature of the information; and to increase the motivation of students and the morale of teachers by focusing on short-term, well-defined goals in which students are able to experience success.

The diversity of practices occurring under the label of profiling is the *third* feature readily evident to an outside observer. Accounts of the history of the profile movement over the last decade as provided by Balogh (1982) or Broadfoot (1984) provide some explanations of the diversity. The description of the movement by Broadfoot (1982, p. 68) as 'an ad hoc one, equivalent to the little ships of Dunkirk' seems particularly apt, since several local initiatives preceded developments now occurring at the level of examining boards.

Two of the several examples of initiatives in profiling described in this book, each quoted sufficiently often to stamp it as a seminal contribution, emphasise the diversity of schemes. The first example is the work of the Scottish Council for Research in Education (1977) over several years on the development, trial and evaluation of profile-style reports (see Chapter 1). The Scottish 'Pupil Profile' was intended to be accommodated within existing assessment and certification practices in Scotland and called for ratings by teachers on a range of basic skills, subject achievements and personal qualities. Ratings were essentially norm-referenced and made on four-point scales patterned as a 'grid', but scale points were also anchored to descriptive labels evolved through work with participating teachers.

Of a very different ilk was the 'Record of Personal Achievement' (RPA) developed by Don Stansbury (1980) and his colleagues at Swindon. The RPA placed the onus on the student to record events, achievements and experiences in descriptive fashion with a teacher or other adult having a role in validation, but not in assessment per se. Swales (1979) provided an independent evaluation of the Swindon RPA scheme which has proved a stimulus for several other initiatives in personal reporting (see Chapter 7). Such schemes seek to capitalise on the intrinsic motivation underlying learning focused on the individual's needs and interests, but at the same time to provide insights into the work accomplished both through the substance of the written accounts of activities and through their organisation and presentation. In these respects, personal recording bears some similarity to the use of contract grades in some secondary schools in the USA, particularly where teacher–pupil negotiation is used to arrive at an a priori explicit statement of intended outcomes.

A *fourth* aspect of profiling very evident to an outside observer is the strong base of support which the movement has had in the further education sector. This is not surprising since curricula in technical and further education are frequently concerned with the acquisition of multiple, well-defined skills, and a profile format facilitates reporting in this case. Mansell, chairman of the Further Education Curriculum Review and Development Unit (FEU), became a strong advocate of profiles (Mansell, 1981) and FEU publications (1979, 1982) made important contributions to the debate. Of particular importance was *A Basis for Choice* (FEU, 1979) which reported the findings of a study group into post-16 pre-employment courses and gave strong support to pupil profiles, particularly for basic abilities. By the time a second edition of this publication appeared in 1982, it was able to include several examples of profile reporting schemes given trial in the further education sector following the initial report. Further impetus to the use of profiles in further education came through the support of agencies such as the City and Guilds of London Institute (CGLI) and the Royal Society of Arts which found their work in validating pre-vocational courses was greatly facilitated by the use of profile reporting. Both these developments are described in detail elsewhere in this volume.

A *fifth* feature of the profiling movement is the emergence of a number of what Broadfoot (1984) termed 'macro-initiatives'. Mansell (1982) was careful to advocate that profile schemes in further education had to be part of formal certification and to be nationally approved if they were to achieve their purposes. In the schools sector, there is an indication that profiling is beginning to emerge from its diverse beginnings and to receive attention at the system level. While a Schools Council review of existing practices in profiling (Balogh, 1982) revealed numerous schemes in isolated schools (see also Chapter 3), examples of more recent initiatives at the system level are the proposals by the Inner London Education Authority for a 'London Record of Achievement' and the development of the 'Oxford Certificate of Educational Achievement' (OCEA), both of which are described in this volume.

It is significant, however, that in the macro-initiatives in the schools sector, profiles are seen as an *adjunct to examination results and test scores* rather than as a substitute for them. Perhaps this is a key to the breadth of support that the movement has attracted. As Nuttall and Goldstein argue in Chapter 13, 'the intention seems to be that profiles should become a dominant element in assessment (in pre-vocational courses), while in schools there seems to be a recognition that public exams will remain the dominant element for some time to come' (p. 111).

Finally, in spite of the breadth of support for profiles mentioned above, the outside observer is soon made aware of a number of criticisms. One major concern is that assessment in the affective domain leaves open the potential for social control as discussed in a later section. Also, some authors (for example, Murphy, 1984; Stevenson, 1983) have warned that criticisms of one set of practices do not justify the implementation of another set without adequate research and evaluation. Thus the impetus given to profiling by the concern that public examinations do not adequately measure attainments across the curriculum, should not be interpreted as an acceptance of profiling without critical appraisal. In their excellent overview of the current state of profiling and a discussion of the associated technical difficulties, Nuttall and Goldstein warn that 'too ready acceptance of a technically weak system will ultimately be counterproductive when its deficiencies become apparent during use'. Their warning also refers to another, increasingly popular component of records of achievement, which is variously referred to as graded objectives, graded tests or graduated assessments (see Chapter 13 in this volume).

GRADED OBJECTIVES

The literature on profiles inevitably overlaps that on graded objectives and graded tests.

Graded tests are designed to measure achievement on a series of progressive levels, hierarchically ordered so that mastery at one level is required before progression to the next.

Harrison (1982) has reviewed the use of graded tests, which have attracted considerable recent attention, initially through the movement known as Graded Objectives in Modern Languages (GOML) (Harding, Page and Rowell, 1980). The principles underlying the GOML movement were formulated in opposition to the proposals for new public examinations at 16+. By noting the use of graded tests in music, dance and physical education, developers of various GOML schemes scattered throughout England and Wales have devised graded sets of task-oriented objectives for language learners, with achievement of the objectives measured via corresponding criterion-referenced tests. Although considerable differences exist across GOML schemes, a common feature has been the emphasis on functional use of language, presumably perceived by learners as meeting their immediate needs.

Evaluations of selected schemes (for example, Buckley *et al.*, 1981; Freedman, 1982) have identified as outcomes high levels of student motivation and increased student demand for further study in the language.

Concerned in particular with the need to devise a means of providing evidence of achievement in mathematics by lower-attaining students, the Cockcroft Committee (Department of Education and Science, 1982) also recommended a study into the development of 'graduated' tests. They saw the need for 'the tests to be criterion-referenced . . . [where], in order to succeed at any level, it was necessary to achieve a high mark'. They thus stressed the motivational value of having children attempt tasks in which they had a reasonable chance of success, and they indicated that schools could include 'a record of achievement in the tests as part of profiles which they provide for the benefit of employers and those concerned in further education'. Financial support by the Government for research and development on graded tests in mathematics, as recommended by the Cockcroft Report, has given further impetus to movements for graded objectives. For example, in addition to the G-component work (graded assessment—see Chapter 9) in mathematics, science, languages and English within OCEA (Oxford Delegacy of Local Examinations, 1984), the Midland Examining Group based in Cambridge has a project on graded objectives in French, English, mathematics, science, and craft, design and technology; the University of London School Examinations Board (1984) is working on graded assessments in the same subjects; and Jones (1984) reports on a project in health education.[2]

The dominant approach in the more recent developments on graded tests and graded assessments seems to be towards criterion-referenced tests, often ordered hierarchically. There are many possible reasons for this—the influential criticisms of Rasch scaling (for example,

---

[2] The work being undertaken on graded objectives and graded tests in England is similar in many respects to the developmental work being carried out within the Education Department of Western Australia (Hill, Mossenson and Tognolini, 1984). However, there are notable differences. The research branch of the department in Western Australia has relied on the calibration of item banks using Rasch scaling techniques, and has endeavoured to provide tests spanning several years of schooling. Thus Tests of Reading Comprehension (TORCH) comprise 14 Rasch-calibrated tests to cover years 3 to 10. This vertical coverage approach is seen to facilitate 'the introduction of a unitized curriculum and vertical timetabling to allow students, regardless of age, to select units from across the total range of units offered within schools' (Hill, Mossenson and Tognolini, 1984), in line with recommendations of the *Report of the Committee of Inquiry into Education in Western Australia* (Western Australia, 1984).

Goldstein, 1979); the graded test developments having occurred within local authorities where breadth of curriculum is not an issue; and the philosophy (made explicit in the Cockcroft Report and identified as important in GOML schemes) that tests should measure predominantly what students know and understand rather than what they fail to comprehend.

As in the case of profiling, many issues relating to graded objectives remain unresolved. The final section addresses what appear to an outside observer to be some of the major unresolved issues underlying the use of profiles and graded objectives in England. The discussion is organised under five categories—conceptual, ideological, technical, practical and accountability—which briefly introduce some of the major issues which are dealt with at greater length in other chapters in this volume.

UNRESOLVED ISSUES IN PROVIDING PROFILE REPORTS FOR SCHOOL LEAVERS

Conceptual issues

One conceptual problem is the *relationship* between formative and summative profiles. In the literature on profiles, clear conceptual distinctions are made between formative and summative profiles, but it is a dubious assumption that the latter can be compiled through some simple aggregation or condensation of the former. Formative profiles, like regular school reports, provide diagnostic feedback to learners and parents, and provide a basis for dialogue between student and teacher on ways to facilitate future learning (Black and Dockrell, 1980). In contrast, summative profiles, while issued to students, are intended to have a wider public audience, including employers and those in institutions of further education, and to serve the purposes of certification.

Nuttall and Goldstein (Chapter 13) note that the purposes underlying these two types of profile may often be in conflict. How reliant should a final assessment be on cumulative records and interim reports? If formative profiles contain descriptive accounts of work accomplished throughout a course, they should be important and objective sources for the compilation of a summative profile. The difficulty lies in their evaluative component since students (and teachers, for that matter) will have diagnosed problems, modified expectations and altered behaviour on the basis of feedback from formative profiles. A further problem is that terminal objectives and hence terminal assessments often require students to integrate and synthesise earlier fragmentary learning, and in this sense also a summative profile might be expected to be more than 'the sum of the parts' from earlier formative profiles. These problems have often been faced where continuous assessment is practised, and provision for a final piece of work, whether through external examination or school-based assessment, contributing substantially to summative evaluation, is a wise option. The relationship between formative and summative elements needs to be addressed and made explicit in institutional and system-level policies on grading.

A *second* source of conceptual confusion is the distinction made between profiles and records of achievement. Some see the former being evaluative but the latter only descriptive, much like the distinction between a reference and a curriculum vitae. Thus

> The major differences between a profile and a record of achievement (as the Government defines it) are important. The latter (i) lists only a student's successes and does not seek to be a comparative assessment, (ii) is not to be used as a reference. A profile presents a total picture, balancing strengths and weaknesses; an achievement record is a portrait which registers weaknesses only tacitly.
> (Assistant Masters and Mistresses Association, 1983, p. 2)

Macintosh (1982) similarly quotes the distinction made by the Educational Resource Unit for a Youth Opportunity Programme at Jordanhill College between a *report*—'a judgement which outsiders can take as evidence'—and a *record*—'evidence on which outsiders can make judgement'. However, some see 'profile recording' as involving both description and judgement (Harris, Bell and Carter, 1981) and Mansell (1982) noted that, for records of achievement and profiles, it was not clear which subsumed which.

Conceptually, measurement and observation should be kept distinct from evaluation, and it is generally held that a sound principle of evaluation is to complete one's description of a characteristic or event before passing judgement upon it. There is a case for including in a school leaver's report some descriptive records, as in a curriculum vitae. Some such records could be compiled by the student and verified by the institution. However, in the present writer's view, if a school leaver's report is to have salience with users, it will also need to contain a professional evaluation of the student's summative attainments. Such an evaluation should be clearly distinct from reported measures or observations, the criteria for the evaluation should be explicit and the evaluation should be interpreted in language understood by those who will use it. By analogy, an investor seeking advice from a stockbroker requires an assessment of investment potential, not just a description of profitability. A patient requesting a medical report from a doctor may appreciate a description of observations and measurements made but also expects an assessment of state of health. In each case, the client would expect the criteria to be clear and the assessment made in meaningful terms. It is doubtful that a summary like 'C+' would suffice.

A *third* source of conceptual confusion concerns the roles of norm and criterion referencing with respect to profiles and graded tests. Nuttall and Goldstein (Chapter 13), noting that criterion referenced assessment is commonly advocated here, draw attention to the dependency on normative information in establishing cut-off points in criterion referenced assessment. They also note that, although the focus on a specified domain required by criterion referenced assessment is consistent with the ideal of the profiles movement to relate assessment closely to the curriculum, attempts to achieve comparability across curricula have led to the development of so-called 'context-free' assessments. This, Nuttall and Goldstein rightly argue, was 'an inbuilt contradiction'. Hence, to reflect faithfully curriculum objectives and also to achieve sufficient comparability across curricula, profiles might need to include both centralised and localised elements. They then conclude that 'whether the assessments are norm referenced or criterion referenced is secondary' although, in the context, one suspects they are warning against the exclusive use of criterion referenced assessments.

Black (1984) is concerned about a similar problem but for a different reason. He argues that, historically, the attributes inherent in criterion referenced assessment (namely, information on an individual's attainment with respect to a well-defined domain enabling decisions of mastery or grading) make the model attractive because of the consequences for pedagogy. That is, application of criterion referenced assessment provides clear goals, permits ready identification of the achievement of those goals, yields realistic expectations and hence enhances the motivation of students and the professional satisfaction of teachers. Black notes that these features are still most readily achieved in diagnostic (or formative) assessment since the domains remain small and specific. But in applications requiring large-scale domains (as is the case for summative profiles and graded tests), the desirable pedagogic features are likely to be compromised by the problems of scale.

Black raises a number of speculative implications following his analysis—for example, that summative profile evaluations might be conveyed in specific domains selected for their relevance to the user; or that graded tests might be designed to yield formative rather than summative profiles.

In summary, the disaggregated nature of profiles and the hierarchical structure of graded objectives both suggest an application for criterion referenced assessment. However, for several reasons, such an approach will not always be appropriate.

A *fourth* and fundamental conceptual issue relates to the theoretical underpinning of educational achievement. Focusing on a criterion referenced approach to evaluation, Meskauskas (1976) sought to identify different models defining mastery. He differentiated between 'continuum' models and 'state' models. In the former, mastery is described as a 'continuously-distributed ability or set of abilities' with the criterion for identifying *masters* being defined by an area at the upper end. Christie and Forrest (1981) extended the idea to include several points on the continuum defining particular levels of competence. State models, on the other hand, are characterised as an all-or-none achievement of the specified content domain, at least in the absence of measurement error.

Meskauskas then argued that these different conceptions of mastery could lead to quite different ways of defining standards. A continuum model is appropriate where a task can be conceptualised as having different levels of proficiency: the function of the measurement is then 'to estimate with the best possible accuracy what the individual's proficiency level is and whether it exceeds a given minimum level of competence or not'. But given a situation where learning tasks are ordered in hierarchical fashion so that success at one level is a prerequisite for study at the next, Meskauskas argued that the state model is more appropriate. In discussing Emrick's (1971) mastery testing evaluation model as an example of a state model in which a test comprises questions based on a homogeneous content area, Meskauskas concluded that a summative examination would comprise several sub-tests covering a number of tightly defined skill areas, and that results should therefore be reported as a profile. For convenience, we might label this as a 'meta-state' model.

Approaches to setting standards under a continuum model require some method of locating a passing score, corresponding to an optimum standard of performance. Various methods of determining passing scores have been suggested in the literature and these are usually classified into two categories. One possibility is to use experts, competent in the subject area and knowledgeable about the abilities of students who will study the course, to judge the test and to determine an *absolute* passing score. A second possibility is to select a target group of students as a standardising group and to use their test performance to infer a *relative* minimum pass level. Glass (1978), in a seminal paper within a special issue of the *Journal of Educational Measurement* on 'standard setting', warned against exclusive use of the former where judges set absolute standards without taking into account actual student performances. In line with suggestions by Glass, other writers (for example, Jaeger (1982) and Beuk (1984)) have proposed methods of reaching a compromise between absolute and relative standards. In the opinion of Christie and Forrest (1981), the model which characterises British public examinations is also such a compromise. They argued that the content domain is clearly enunciated, the chief examiners have developed a fairly accurate sense of threshold levels but that final cutting scores can still be modified on the basis of subjects' performance.

Of what relevance is a consideration of the theoretical underpinning of achievement measures? Consider as an example the differences between *graded tests* (as used in the GOML schemes or as envisaged by the Cockcroft Report) and the proposals for *grade-related criteria* within the new 16+ examination, where an attempt will be made to define explicitly the criteria for each of seven levels of achievement in each subject. There are similarities— both will rely on some aspects of criterion referencing such as domain specification and the determination of standards; and both require some form of hierarchical ordering. But there are also major differences.

At least as developed in the GOML schemes, the use of graded tests suggests a state model, or rather what we called earlier a meta-state model. Multiple skills are defined for each level and the expectation is that most students who opt for the testing will achieve mastery of the objectives. Competence in some skills (say, reading or writing) does not compensate for failure to achieve mastery in others (say, listening and speaking). Success at one level is prerequisite to entry to the next but the skills are not necessarily cumulative. That is, as in the case of moral development, what is appropriate behaviour at one level may be replaced by different behaviour at a higher level.

In contrast, the determination of grade-related criteria assumes a continuum model. The specification of criteria is an attempt to clarify levels of competence along this continuum. Test elements will normally be aggregated since the content will be seen as relatively homogeneous and often related to a single trait.

Other examples are not difficult to find. The often-cited example of a driving test assumes a state model of achievement. The domain comprises a range of sub-skills, some practical and some theoretical.

Mastery must be demonstrated by success on all sub-skills. A weak practical performance is not compensated by excellent knowledge of road rules and lack of competence in one sub-skill (say, parking) is sufficient to deny passing status.

Interestingly, in contrast to the graded tests discussed above, the work in Western Australia (Hill et al., 1984) assumes a continuum and, indeed, a single latent trait. This may be partly a function of the subject areas (reading, mathematics), although one could speculate about the influence of the Rasch scaling procedures adopted. Harrison (1982) raised the general question of whether the principles underlying graded tests, presumably ones related to hierarchical structure, could be transferred to other subjects, for example, where a modular approach to the curriculum is feasible. If the work so far undertaken within the G-component of OCEA is a guide, curriculum elements can be perceived as modular but achievements within an element can be hierarchically ordered. For example, the English curriculum is divided into a number of features (including 'reading for information', 'talking in groups', 'reading stories, plays, poems'), but achievement criteria within elements of a feature are ordered from 'first steps', to 'development', to 'competence'. If it is necessary to divide a whole curriculum into a number of ordered levels of mastery (as in GOML schemes or music examinations), the meta-state model described above would seem to be more flexible and more pedagogically sound than a continuum model. Thus, in order to progress from one level to the next, a student might be expected to show competence in each of a number of features, but the features themselves might only be loosely associated or even independent. Schematically, one might think of a student progressing through a series of ordered plateaus (levels). But to progress from any one plateau to the next, the student might be expected to climb (or show competence in) each of several towers (features) with ordered tasks within them.

In contrast, if the purpose of an assessment is to describe how well different students have accomplished the same set of tasks, then a continuum, norm referenced model would seem to be more useful in defining and grading levels of quality of performance.

Ideological issues

As noted earlier, support for profiling in Britain was founded on a concern to recognise the attainments of those students who have traditionally not received examination certificates and to recognise accomplishments beyond those measured in formal examinations. A number of writers (for example, Balogh, 1982; National Union of Teachers, 1983; Willmott, 1984) have noted the need for profiles or records of achievement to be issued to students of *all* levels of attainment, and this indeed is government policy. One argument is that restricting records of achievement to non-GCSE students would deprive other students of the broader recognition provided by the records (Willmott, 1984), although Swales (1979) noted in his evaluation of RPA that the higher-achieving students were dubious about the virtues of personal records. But another argument is that a division into GCSE certificates for one group (possibly further sub-divided into distinction and merit awards holders) and records of achievement for another would perpetuate existing elitist practices. Thus Broadfoot (1982), noting the French experience with 'dossiers scolaires', argues that such a 'half-way house may prove to be more deadening and divisive than the status quo'. Of course, even when records of achievement are issued to all students, while they remain an adjunct to examination certificates, divisions will still be apparent (Hargreaves, 1985). Incorporating examination results within the overall record of achievement (as in the OCEA) is one strategy to minimise the divisions.

Other writers have warned that records of achievement and profiles, far from accomplishing egalitarian ends, may by their very nature create divisiveness. Thus Spooner (1981, 1983) perceived profiles and cumulative records as resulting in a further undesirable emphasis on assessment. Stevenson (1983) cautioned that the purpose of profiling could be restricted or diverted by the demands of users. In particular, he noted the tensions which sometimes exist between employers and educators over their different perceptions of the role of schools. Hargreaves (1985) similarly questions whether records of achievement can simultaneously satisfy 'two of the dominant, publicly proclaimed purposes' of pupil motivation and employment selection. He argues that some activities of students, which warrant recognition if motivation is to be enhanced, will not be valued in selection for employment. On the other hand, if records of achievement are restricted to activities, skills and attitudes valued in selection for employment, the result could be to 'depress motivation still further' among less able pupils. Johnson (1984), writing on further education, expressed concern about the influence on the curriculum per se of the requirements of profiling. Thus, although profiles are intended to reflect attainment across the curriculum in a more adequate way than external examinations, Johnson claimed that a focus on an objectives-based curriculum, particularly with respect to attitudes and values, was an insidious way of regulating behaviour. Thus there is a fine line between the potential of profile reports to recognise attainment across the curriculum and their potential for an undesirable level of social control, a point which is explored in some depth in Andy Hargreaves' chapter (Chapter 14).

Technical issues

As noted earlier, Nuttall and Goldstein (Chapter 13) provide a very comprehensive account of the technical difficulties raised by profiles and graded tests, and readers are referred to their chapter. The section above on conceptual issues also touched on a number of unresolved technical problems.

School-based assessment, provided it is carried out by teachers with a modicum of training in student assessment, is likely to yield a fairly valid measure of classroom learning experiences. The value of such assessment for formative evaluation is not in question, but where a summative evaluation is required—as in a school-leaver's report—the problem of comparability across classes, across schools, across subjects or simply across profile elements looms large. Even under external examinations supported by years of experience in various modes of moderation, teachers are well aware of the difficulties of achieving comparability of standards. These difficulties are likely to be compounded when profile reporting with school-based moderation comes to be used more widely and, at the very least, extensive in-service work for teachers will be required.

Australian school systems have tended to use statistical moderation widely in an effort to achieve comparability across schools, across subjects and between internal and external assessments. Such techniques have been viewed with suspicion in England, and the research of Nuttall, Backhouse and Willmott (1974) documents the difficulties of achieving comparability of standards between subjects. The Australian Capital Territory Schools Authority has had to investigate charges of sex bias in an aptitude measure used for moderation purposes (Adams, 1984) and the New South Wales system has recently decided to abandon adjustments across subjects at the matriculation level intended to allow for different candidatures. Difficulties of this kind would be greatly magnified if statistical moderations were applied to profile reports with their multiple measures and small numbers of students.

The requirement to assess qualities other than academic achievement also raises a host of technical issues. The lower reliability of attitude measures is well known, and the attempt to assess values and skills across different contexts is fraught with difficulties. Where several teachers are asked to rate students on particular characteristics, in the experience of the writer, the law of averages is well demonstrated as disparate ratings sum to yield moderate values.

Practical issues

By their very nature, graded objectives imply individual progress through the curriculum. One major practical difficulty is that, organisationally, schools are not well placed to adapt in this way (Harrison, 1982). This is particularly true of Britain where the lock-step system is so entrenched that levels of schooling are still labelled according to the age of the student cohort (for example, 16+). Not surprisingly, then, some of the GOML schemes have continued to test students as a group, regardless of their readiness for the criterion measure (Her Majesty's Inspectorate, 1983). Pennycuick (1984) notes the implications of the use of graded tests for changes in classroom organisation, and concludes that some form of vertical timetabling warrants consideration, in spite of the obvious logistic difficulties.

The review by Harrison (1982) stressed the conviction and effort of teachers as key ingredients in the success of the GOML schemes. Nuttall and Goldstein (Chapter 13) warn that this high level of teacher commitment could reflect their professional satisfaction stemming from the opportunity to be involved in curriculum innovation and in the assessment of their own pupils. They therefore speculate that, if because of the technical requirements for reliability and comparability, teachers need to forgo some of this freedom, some of this professional commitment might be dissipated. In similar vein, Pennycuick (1984) speculated that 'large-scale schemes developed by examination boards might not necessarily be as successful as those developed locally by groups of teachers'.

But the dilemma is that public acceptance of different reporting schemes is likely to be higher if these different schemes follow similar patterns of style and presentation. Parents in a given locality will want local certificates to have national currency which will only be achieved if employers and other users perceive sufficient commonality across certificates to make valid comparisons. Those Australian school systems which have moved from external examinations have had to contend with a decline in credibility of certificates derived from school-based assessments. For related reasons, school-based curriculum offerings at Years 11–12 have attracted low enrolments when in competition with centralised curricula, even when the former have been designed specifically to meet local needs.

A further practical problem associated with profiling schemes is the additional workload for teachers. The taxing, recurrent problems of keeping cumulative records and then interpreting and reporting these in summary form will be exacerbated in the initial stages by the need to engage in staff development work related to new ways of assessing and reporting. Although it has been demonstrated that electronic systems of data storage and retrieval can minimise the workload (Maxfield, 1983), the use of computers might be perceived by some critics as sacrificing professional judgement for administrative efficiency.

A further potential source of tension in implementing summative profiling is the relationship between teacher and student. Teachers rightly perceive their role as guides, counsellors and cooperative learners. It is a role readily reinforced by conjoint submission to external examinations and one consistent with the diagnosis and remediation inherent in formative profiling. However, it rests uneasily with the judgemental role required in the compilation of summative profiles. Possible conflict might be defused if a viable system of teacher–pupil negotiation can establish realistic a priori goals for particular students, but as Broadfoot suggests in her paper (Broadfoot, 1984) on 'the affective curriculum', how far this is a real possibility for schools has yet to be subjected to systematic study.

Accountability issues

Accountability can be described on a number of levels, but discussion here is confined to broad concerns about schools being accountable to their clients and to a tax-paying public. In recent years, governments have seen fit to encourage public accountability of schools through systems of national assessment, such as the Assessment Performance Unit (APU) in England, or the National Assessment of Educational Progress (NAEP) in the United States, or the Australian Studies in Student Performance (ASSP). An evaluation of the last of these (Power et al., 1982) has noted its limited utility for both system-level policy decisions and for identifying students in need of remedial help. Is it possible, then, that administrators or politicians will see in profiling and graded tests ready-made opportunities for system monitoring, and that this will undermine the educational benefits for particular pupils and schools?

To date, the rhetoric on profiling has not canvassed issues of system monitoring and major concern on accountability has focussed on meeting the needs of individual students. In the Australian context, the media-fed public concern about standards in schools has been triggered by interpretations or misinterpretations of the results of national testing (Power et al., 1982). However, such concern is not mirrored to nearly the same extent in the result of surveys in which the public has been asked to give opinions about the schools 'they know best' (Baumgart et al., 1979). It has been argued (Baumgart and Power, 1983) that the best form of public accountability of schools is one in which schools are answerable directly to their clients and the local community they serve. Provided the other issues raised above can be resolved, the profiling movement will have taken a significant step in this direction.

CONCLUSION

This review of current issues in the profiling and records of achievement movement in England and Wales has focused on both the potential and some of the problems inherent in such a major assessment initiative. It is often easier for an outsider to be detached from the hurly-burly of policy-making and development and to bring to bear the experience of a quite different set of assumptions and prejudices characteristic of another educational system. But whilst the particular solutions favoured by individual countries may differ, the pressing needs to which they are increasingly having to respond are common to many, if not all, of the industrialised nations, a situation which makes such international comparisons of particular relevance.

REFERENCES

Adams, R. (1984) *Sex Bias in ASAT*. Melbourne: Australian Council for Educational Research.

Assistant Masters and Mistresses Association (1983) *Profiles and Records of Achievement: an introduction to the debate*. London: AMMA.

Balogh, J. (1982) *Profile Reports for School Leavers*. York: Longman for Schools Council.

Baumgart, N. et al. (1979) *Survey of Public Opinions about Schools in New South Wales*. ERIC document ED 201 046.

Baumgart, N. and Power, C. (1983) 'Grading schools—what do we expect and how do they rate?', in Shannon A. (ed.) *Educational Expectations—Promise and Performance*. Melbourne: The Australian College of Education.

Beedle, P. (1983) *A Survey of Employers' Opinions about Final Profile Reports*. London: CGLI.

Beedle, P., Stratton, N. and Veasey, J. (1983) *A Survey of Vocational Gatekeepers' Opinions about Profile Reports*. London: CGLI.

Beuk, C.H. (1984) 'A method for reaching a compromise between absolute and relative standards in examinations', *Journal of Educational Measurement*, **21** (2) 147–52.

Black, H.D. (1984) *Whither Research on Criterion Referenced Assessment?* Paper presented to 10th Annual Conference of British Educational Research Association, Lancaster, September 1984.

Black, H.D. and Dockrell, W.B. (1980) *Diagnostic Assessment in Secondary Schools*. Edinburgh: Hodder and Stoughton for Scottish Council for Research in Education.

Broadfoot, P. (1982) 'The pros and cons of profiles', *Forum* **24** (3) 66–9.

Broadfoot, P. (1984) *Profiles and the Affective Curriculum*. Paper presented at the Sociology of Education Conference, St. Hilda's College, Oxford, September 1984.

Buckley, M. et al. (1981) *Graded Objectives and Tests for Modern Languages: an Evaluation*. London: Schools Council.

Burgess, T. and Adams, E. (ed.) (1980) *Outcomes of Education*. London: Macmillan Education.

Christie, T. and Forrest, G.M. (1981) *Defining Public Examination Standards* Schools Council Research Studies. London: Macmillan Education.

City and Guilds of London Institute (1984) *Basic Abilities Profile*. (Information leaflet.)

Department of Education and Science (1982) *Mathematics Counts* (the Cockcroft Report). London: HMSO.

Department of Education and Science (1984) *Records of Achievement: A Statement of Policy*. London: HMSO.

Emrick, J.A. (1971) 'An evaluation model for mastery testing'. *Journal of Educational Measurement*, **8**, 321–26.

Freedman, E.S. (1982) *Evaluation of the East Midlands Graded Assessment Feasibility Study for the Year 1979–80*. University of Leicester, School of Education.

Further Education Curriculum Review and Development Unit (1979) *A Basis for Choice*. London: FEU.

Further Education Curriculum Review and Development Unit (1982) *Profiles. A Review of Issues and Practice in the Use and Development of Student Profiles*. London: FEU.

Glass, G.V. (1978) 'Standards and Criteria'. *Journal of Educational Measurement*, **15** (4) 237–61.

Goacher, B. (1983) *Recording Achievement at 16+*. York: Longman for Schools Council.

Goldstein, H. (1979) 'Consequences of using the Rasch model for educational assessment', *British Educational Research Journal*, **5** (2) 211–20.

Harding, A., Page, B. and Rowell, S. (1980) *Graded Objectives in Modern Languages*. London: Centre for Information on Language Teaching and Research.

Hargreaves, A. (1985) 'Motivation versus selection: a dilemma for Records of Personal Achievement', in Marland, M. and Lang, P. (ed.) *New Directions in Pastoral Care*. London: Blackwells.

Harris, N.D.C., Bell, C.D. and Carter, J.E.H. (1981) *Signposts for Evaluating. A Resource Pack.* London: Council for Educational Technology, Schools Council.

Harrison, A.W. (1982) 'Review of Graded Tests'. Schools Council Examinations Bulletin 41. London: Methuen Educational.

Harrison, A.W. (1983) 'Profile Reporting of Examination Results'. Schools Council Examinations Bulletin 46. London: Methuen Educational.

Her Majesty's Inspectorate (1983) *A Survey of the Use of Graded Tests of Defined Objectives and their Effect on the Teaching and Learning of Modern Languages in the County of Oxfordshire.* London: DES.

Hill, P.W., Mossenson, L.T. and Tognolini, J.S. (1984) *Educational Testing in Western Australia: Recent Developments and Future Prospects.* Paper presented to the 10th Annual Conference of the International Association for Educational Assessment. Perth, Australia, June 1984.

Jaeger, R.M. (1982) 'An iterative structured judgment process for establishing standards on competency tests: theory and application', *Educational Evaluation and Policy Analysis,* **4**, 461–75.

Johnson, P. (1984) 'Examine and control', *Times Educational Supplement,* October 26, p. 18.

Jones, A. (1984) 'Developing approaches to assessment of health education'. Paper presented to 10th Annual Conference of British Educational Research Association, Lancaster, September 1984.

Macintosh, H. (1982) 'Profiling: a discussion paper', *Coombe Lodge Report,* **14** (3).

Mansell, J. (1981) 'Profiling must be a better way', *Education,* **157** (22) 479–80.

Mansell, J. (1982) 'A burst of interest'. In Further Education Curriculum Review and Development Unit, *Profiles. A Review of Issues and Practice in the Use and Development of Student Profiles,* pp. 4–9. London: FEU.

Maxfield, B. (1983) *Computer Aided Profiling.* London: FEU.

Meskauskas, J.A. (1976) 'Evaluation models for criterion referenced testing: views regarding mastery and standard setting', *Review of Educational Research,* **46** (1) 133–58.

Murphy, R. (1984) 'Educational assessment: changing the face and facing the change'. Paper presented to 10th Annual Conference of British Educational Research Association, Lancaster, September 1984.

National Union of Teachers (1983) *Public Profiles: a Discussion Document.* London: NUT.

Nuttall, D.L., Backhouse, J. and Willmott, A.S. (1974) 'Comparability of standards between subjects'. Schools Council Examinations Bulletin 29. London: Evans/Methuen Educational.

Oxford Delegacy of Local Examinations (1983) *Oxford Certificate of Educational Achievement Newsletters 1 and 2.* Oxford: Delegacy of Local Examinations.

Oxford Delegacy of Local Examinations (1984) *Oxford Certificate of Educational Achievement Newsletters 3 and 4.* Oxford: Delegacy of Local Examinations.

Pennycuick, D.B. (1984) 'The development and impact of graded tests'. Paper presented to 10th Annual Conference of British Educational Research Association, Lancaster, September 1984.

Power, C. et al. (1982) *National Assessment in Australia: An Evaluation of the*

Australian Studies in Student Performance Project. ERDC Report 35. Canberra: AGPS.

Queensland Board of Secondary School Studies (1978) *A Review of School-Based Assessment* (Professor E. Scott, Chairman).Brisbane: BSSS.

Scottish Council for Research in Education (1977) *Pupils in Profile.* Edinburgh: Hodder and Stoughton for SCRE.

Spooner, R.T. (1981) 'Wielding the profile as a weapon of destruction', *Education,* **157** (10) 213–14.

Spooner, R.T. (1983) 'A celebration of success or an advertisement of inadequacy', *Education,* **162** (2) 29.

Stansbury, D. (1980) 'The Record of Personal Experience', in Burgess, T. and Adams, E. (ed.) *Outcomes of Education.* London: Macmillan.

Stevenson, M. (1983) 'Pupil profiles—an alternative to conventional examinations?', *British Journal of Educational Studies,* **31** (2) 102–116.

Swales, T. (1979) *Records of Personal Achievement: An Independent Evaluation of the Swindon RPA Scheme.* London: Schools Council.

University of London School Examination Board (1984) *Graded Assessments Newsheet* No. 2. London: University of London School Examination Board.

Western Australia (1984) *Education in Western Australia.* Report of the Committee of Inquiry into Education in Western Australia, Chaired by Mr K.E. Beasley, Perth.

Willmott, A. (1984) 'Letter to editor', *Times Educational Supplement,* October 26, p. 16.

PART TWO

Putting Ideas Into Practice

The chapters in this part of the book have certain characteristics in common. All of them set out the rationale for profiles and/or records of achievement as agreed within a particular development initiative; all of them give at least some indication of how these ideas might be put into practice. Beyond this common framework, the chapters describe a range of very different types of initiative. There are descriptions of schemes involving local authority, exam board or other kind of consortium support; schemes which draw their inspiration from the work of a few committed individuals; and schemes which are being pioneered by individual schools and even subject departments. The principles and organisation of the various approaches described are equally heterogeneous. Indeed the intention behind this section is to provide as much variety as possible in the various accounts, in order that the rich diversity—which is as characteristic of the profiles movement as are its common concerns—should be clearly apparent.

5

Records of Achievement

PETER MORTIMORE
ANNE KEANE

In this first chapter in Part 2, Mortimore and Keane reiterate some of the central arguments for records of achievement and, in so doing, sound the keynote which the very different schemes described in subsequent chapters have in common. Building on the experience of some years' involvement in the development of profiling schemes in ILEA, Mortimore and Keane describe briefly the initiatives currently being pursued to institute records of achievement within the authority.

—Editor

Introduction

'. . . Most young people leave school after 11 or more years of education with no comprehensive record of their educational achievements.'

This quotation is not from a radical critique of the education system but from the recently published statement of government policy on records of achievement (DES, 1984). It highlights one of the most serious problems facing secondary school teachers: how to record and acknowledge the achievements made by pupils in the course of their school careers. Up to now, in most schools, results of public examinations, in some cases supplemented by an open testimonial, have had to suffice. For the small proportion of pupils who have obtained a high level of success in public examinations the situation was tolerable; for the majority who do not, and especially that proportion who are not entered for such examinations, it is clearly most unsatisfactory.

In a minority of schools, profiles such as the Record of Personal Experience, developed by Stansbury (1980) or the log-book Record of Personal Achievement, pioneered by Michael Duffy (1980), have been implemented to fill this gap, but for the majority this has not been the case. Now as a result of a rising crescendo of criticism from teachers and others concerned with education, this problem has been recognised officially.

The Secretary of State for Education, Sir Keith Joseph, in a speech to the 1984 North of England Education Conference, reiterated some of the criticisms of the curriculum and of the system of public examinations that teachers have been making for a number of years. The statement on records of achievement followed on the heels of his speech. The public purse has since been added to the exhortation of Government: one of the categories of the special education support grants for 1985/86 has been designated to pay for a set of pilot schemes of records of achievement. Just before the end of 1984, eight proposals worth over two million pounds were approved from a list of applicants that included the majority of local education authorities in the country.

In this chapter we will attempt to say why records of achievement based on pupil profiles are valuable. We shall go on to make some suggestions as to their form and how they might operate. Finally, as a way of linking the discussion to specific policy developments, the initiatives currently being pursued within our local education authority will be noted.

WHY ARE RECORDS OF ACHIEVEMENT VALUABLE?

We believe the opportunity to develop records of achievement should be grasped because it provides the possibility of bringing together two aspects of learning: assessment and recording. Such a system provides an opportunity for assessment of learning and development on a much wider basis than the traditional 'academic' areas currently assessed by GCE or CSE examination boards. As regards recording, such a system could bring together feedback from assessment, traditional school reports and testimonials.

In order for the potential values of records of achievement to be maximised, schemes need to be carefully designed to include a number of other characteristics. The most important of these are listed below.

1. Process and outcome

One of the most telling criticisms of current public examinations is that they are concerned only with the outcome of learning. Pupils generally spend five years in secondary schools prior to any formal assessment. For many, the first results of this are received after the pupil has left school. Of course secondary schools have their own examinations—usually held annually—but the value of these will vary according to both the experience of the teachers and the ability of the pupils.

In contrast, records of achievement are concerned with the continuous process of learning. All routine assessments that take place can be used as a basis for pupils, not only to analyse their progress, but also to look ahead and plan a programme of future learning.

2. Success rather than failure

Examinations such as the GCE 'O' levels, which are targeted on approximately 20 per cent of the population, have a failure rate of about 50 per cent of the entries: half the pupils entered experience failure. Unlike these examinations, records of achievement are geared to success. Whatever the level of achievement, success can be celebrated. Furthermore, success does not have to be solely in matters academic. Practical work, oral work, experience outside school (such as part-time employment or hobbies) can all be recorded. Although the emphasis is on success, this does not mean the record has to be restricted to a bland acceptance of mediocrity. One of its purposes is to highlight where achievement has been limited, but to do so in a positive way.

3. Active involvement of pupils

Records of achievement are quite different from traditional assessments and school reports in that one of their key components is to be the involvement of pupils in the evaluation of their own learning. The term 'negotiation' is sometimes used to express the quite different relationship that can be developed between teachers and taught. In some ways, this relationship is much more like that found in primary schools whilst, in others, it resembles the norm of the further education college.

4. Active involvement of parents

Parents have an important role to play in the assessment and planning of learning, and the record of achievement will provide a much firmer and more comprehensive basis for teachers and parents to discuss and review a student's achievements and progress. In addition, parents could be given an opportunity to make their own contribution to the record of achievement in the way of commenting on the evaluations of staff and student or supplementing information about achievement and activities outside the school. In this way it is hoped an effective dialogue can take place between all partners and facilitate the process of learning and the level of achievement.

5. Guidance and counselling

Involving pupils in a scheme based on learning processes is not easy. Some pupils are likely to prefer a much more passive role. In order to encourage the change, and to support and guide pupils in these tasks, teachers need to devote some of their time to working with individuals. This is time consuming and, as such, involves some rethinking of priorities, but the benefits are likely to be considerable.

6. Validation

Any move from externally-managed assessments towards school-based systems raises questions of validity. The degrees of bias, favouritism and differential expectations have been well documented and, even in 1. above, the limits of internally-managed assessment were noted. Clearly it is essential to ensure that every effort is made to establish systems that are valid.

It may be that the support of external agencies, such as examination boards, is needed to approve assessors, monitor their performance and accredit achievement. The DES-funded pilot schemes, hopefully, will provide guidance on this and many other issues.

WHAT FORM SHOULD RECORDS OF ACHIEVEMENT TAKE?

As yet there are no agreed 'models', though in some schools and further education colleges developments—in the form of local profile schemes—have been undertaken. Two examination boards, the Royal Society of Arts and the City and Guilds of London Institute, have each developed profiles. The Manpower Services Commission has adopted the use of profiles in the Youth Training Scheme and has recommended their use in its Technical and Vocational Educational Initiative. The joint board responsible for the pilot scheme of the new Certificate of Pre-vocational Education have requested that a profile be adopted as a means of recording the progress of students.

It is evident, however, from the very varied formats of the records of achievement currently being developed in schools and colleges, many of which are described elsewhere in this book, that quite different styles are possible. Those that have been adopted include an open reporting sheet in which both teachers and pupils enter comments on the basis of agreed criteria; a matrix grid of skills and subjects in which assessors tick the appropriate box; the selection of a suitable ready-written comment from a bank of possible responses; the ticking of a series of items on a checklist, and the ticking of a selected 'step' on a hierarchically designed grid.

For each of these formats, advantages and disadvantages can be listed. The unstructured open-reporting format, for example, can accommodate differences in curriculum design and teachers' individual aims, but the information is unlikely to be presented in a compact or uniform manner and may not readily be amenable to storage on a microcomputer. The use of prepared comment banks allows for greater comparability between subjects than is possible with open reporting, but there is a danger that teachers will only use the middle range comments and thus establish a norm; the range of skills covered by this style of record may also be limited by the size of document. The last format involves a hierarchically designed grid. Information is presented in a simple way and the identification of progressive steps of achievement may motivate the student to work towards the next level; it is suitable for storage on a microcomputer, thus allowing teachers' precious time to be spent in reviewing progress or in providing counselling and guidance. Furthermore, this design offers sufficient scope for local initiative in that the 'steps' can be defined by the teachers according to their aims and the distance to be covered. Flexibility to allow individual schools and colleges scope for their own developments appears to be an important consideration: much of the enthusiasm that has been generated in the development of profiles stems from their 'locally driven' nature. Teachers feel more committed to a scheme they have helped develop. The challenge, therefore, is to design a framework in which teachers—in conjunction with parents, governors and local employers—can operate. As stressed in point 3 above, since the active involvement of pupils is seen as essential, local developments should also allow pupils some share in the planning.

WHAT SHOULD RECORDS OF ACHIEVEMENT RECORD?

The format or design of a record of achievement will depend, in part, on the areas of learning to be assessed and recorded. The DES statement on records of achievement suggests that account should be taken of 'a pupil's progress and across the whole educational programme of the school, both in the classroom and outside, and possibly activities outside the schools as well'. A more detailed specification has recently been drawn up by a group of our ILEA colleagues. In their view, the following aspects of a pupil's learning need to be included.

Knowledge which refers to the acquisition of factual content and the bssic concepts of a subject. It is often tested by means of questions which require recall of relevant facts.

Understanding goes beyond acquisition of the facts and can be defined as an ability to relate the factual to the conceptual content of a subject.

Analysis can be defined as a skill which involves the examination of a collection of data in a way which requires the pupil to go beyond the presented evidence and to apply past experience as well as factual knowledge and understanding.

Synthesis involves the pupil in putting together separate elements, data, concepts or possibilities into a connected whole in the form of a system or theory. It can be the drawing of conclusions or the framing of hypotheses.

Practical skills are those which clearly involve pupils in doing things.

Some examples are: writing; drawing; assembly; organising; physical agility, and communication.

Creativity may be a skill measurable in all areas of the curriculum. It can include the use of imagination, original expression, and the inventive use of a medium or a material.

Aesthetic appreciation involves a pupil making an evaluation, assessment or judgement which goes beyond a stereotyped response. It often takes the form of criticism and may be addressed through a variety of different forms such as drama, music, painting, photography and craft work.

Cross-curricular and learning skills will include both study techniques and study processes; collecting, analysing and summarising information; communicating with others; and planning and organising one's own work.

Personal and social skills may include working in a group; showing an awareness of self and of others; initiative; taking responsibility; and working with those in authority.

Student's activities and experiences may include: membership of organisations; athletic interest; practical pursuits; musical interests; institutional responsibilities; and employment.

It was appreciated by the ILEA group that not every aspect of learning and development could be assessed and recorded without the imposition of an impossible burden on teachers and an unacceptable domination of the life of the school or college. The group suggested, therefore, that particular aspects should be chosen by relevant local people to act as indicators of a much larger population of possible items.

The final form of records of achievement will depend on the choice of particular items, but will be likely to consist of systematic assessment by the teacher and pupil of each of a number of separate but interrelated skills. These skills cannot be judged in isolation, but need to be seen within the context of learning tasks which would themselves be seen within the various environmental contexts of the classroom, workshop, activity centre or, if appropriate, the pupil's home.

HOW MIGHT RECORDS OF ACHIEVEMENT WORK?

Many important details relating to the mechanics of a system of assessing and recording achievement will depend on the styles and wishes of people in particular schools and colleges. School resources, organisation and timetabling may impose constraints on the design of a profiling system, and may themselves be affected by the implementation of such a system. Time would have to be allowed for staff to agree on those areas of learning to be assessed, their relationship to cross-curricular skills and personal and social qualities, and to define the assessment criteria. Steps would then need to be taken, by way of discussion and training sessions, to ensure that staff are familiar with the necessary procedures. Following the implementation of the system, regular sessions for pupils and teachers to discuss the assessments would have to be timetabled and organised in a way which would allow not only a review of achievements but an opportunity for pupils to evaluate their performance and to negotiate a plan for future learning.

Once or twice yearly the assessments would need to be collated and the record of achievement compiled. The time demanded by this task will be minimised if schools can develop computer programs to store assessments in an efficient and easily accessible form, and it is possible to envisage schools sending a computer-printed copy of the record to parents. Following this, it is hoped that parents, pupils and teachers will be able to come together and use the record as a basis for a constructive discussion of a pupil's progress and future learning plans and goals.

It is recognised that the implementation of a scheme to provide records of achievement to pupils may initially be time-consuming, and heads and teachers in schools whose resources are already over-stretched may be unwilling to take on the idea. It is hoped, however, that once the scheme has been established and assimilated into the timetable, and teachers are familiar with the procedures and the initial difficulties overcome, 'profiling' will demand no more time than is currently spent on keeping records, writing reports and preparing for meetings with parents.

LOCAL EDUCATION AUTHORITY INITIATIVES

As a final section to this chapter and as a way of linking some of the general issues described to specific policy, the initiatives currently being pursued within our LEA will be outlined.

Over the last few years our local authority has been monitoring developments and collecting information on profile schemes, leaving certificates and new methods of assessment, both from within its own schools and colleges and from outside. From time to time, reviews of existing systems and suggestions for schemes which schools could adopt have been prepared and published. More recently a working party of inspectors and officers has been conducting a comprehensive review of recent developments in pupil profiles. The working party has attempted to identify the critical issues including form, target groups and validation procedures. The group is currently considering the practical details and difficulties of profiling with the aim of producing material which could be recommended for use in schools. The working group have not completed their deliberations, and in any case their recommendations will need to be related to other initiatives in the authority. The following section of this chapter represents only our view of what the likely outcomes may be. It should not be taken as indicating an official account but rather should be seen as a personal view.

Ideally, in our view, two or more models should be made available to schools. Heads and teachers, however, should not be 'strait-jacketed' by a set of rigid rules as to how to operate the scheme. They should be given a framework within which they can develop a system geared specifically to their own needs and organisation.

The guidelines prepared for schools should define those areas of learning and development considered to be important components of a record of achievement, but the decision as to how these should be represented—the balance between the different components and the procedures for assessment—will need to be made by individual schools. Heads and teachers, however, will be encouraged to:

(a) employ criteria-related assessments;
(b) place achievements and experiences within an appropriate context detailing difficulties, limitations and opportunities affecting the pupil at the time;
(c) assess personal and social skills in the learning situation and in a way that reflects actual performance rather than potential capability.

In this way we hope that records of achievement will provide an objective and helpful account of a student's achievements.

According to the DES statement, records of achievement should be both formative and summative. During the student's school career the formative record will provide an ongoing annual, or twice yearly, account of achievements and positive experiences. The summative record will be that which the student is given upon leaving school and which will be taken on to employment or the next stage of education. We envisage that this document will comprise a summary statement of the pupil's achievements, knowledge, skills and personal-social qualities, and will contain a record of the results of any accredited assessments and public examinations. If the final record can be compiled in this way, there should be no reason for the school to need to write additional references for prospective employers or admissions tutors.

CONCLUSION

Earlier sections of this chapter have argued that records of achievement are valuable, and have described their possible form and operationalisation. As has frequently been stressed, much will depend on the particular needs and styles of individual schools and colleges. The pilot schemes, funded by the DES under the 1985/86 Education Support Grants, will stimulate the development of suitable methods of assessing and recording. Since these schemes will be evaluated, successful practice should be identified.

At the same time, for records of achievement to have status, they must also be widely understood and recognised. In this chapter we have described some general principles which we feel ought to inform records of achievement, principles which we hope will be incorporated as part of any *national* recording scheme which emerges out of the DES pilot schemes. Finding a balance between a desire for records which have national currency and a commitment to allowing individual schools and colleges to reflect their own priorities in their recording schemes is likely to prove a difficult and delicate task. Nevertheless, it is vital if this kind of recording is to receive sustained support from all sections of the educational and lay communities. At a time when teachers are under pressure to modify the curriculum, to develop special policies and to become involved in the appraisal of their own skills, resistance to further ideas may be felt unless the value of records of achievement is made clear. Similarly, when opportunities are severely restricted, parents and other consumers will need reassurance that such records will be useful credentials. If, however, these diverse pressures can be successfully combined, the potential benefits of bringing together all the processes of assessing and recording achievement will be considerable.

Whilst the views expressed in this chapter are personal and should not be taken to represent the policies of the ILEA, we wish to express our debt to those colleagues, amongst the officers and inspectors of the ILEA, who have been involved in debating these issues and from whom we have learned so much.

REFERENCES

Department of Education and Science (1984) *Records of Achievement: A Statement of Policy*. London: HMSO.

Duffy, M. (1980) 'A logbook of personal achievement', *Education*, Feb. 1980, p. 119–20.

North of England Education Conference (1984) Speech given by Sir Keith Joseph.

Stansbury, D. (1980) 'The Record of Personal Experience', in Burgess, T. and Adams, E. (ed.) *Outcomes of Education*. London: Macmillan.

6

Records for all at 16

TYRRELL BURGESS
ELIZABETH ADAMS

Tyrrell Burgess and Elizabeth Adams have been involved for some years in formulating and introducing an alternative approach to curriculum and reporting in the later years of secondary schooling. In this article they analyse some of the implications of the DES Policy Statement on Records of Achievement and suggest how its recommendations might be most fruitfully put into practice in the light of their own experience.

—Editor

The Secretary of State's policy statement on records of achievement (DES, 1984) represents a major initiative in improving the experience of young people at school, the standards they reach and the quality of what it is they have to show for their years in compulsory schooling. It is potentially the most important national initiative in education since the establishment of a national system of public examinations, and it offers more hope than the latter for the enhancing of educational experience and standards. This is because it is the first significant attempt to make assessment (including public examinations) *serve* rather than *dominate* the curriculum. The challenge it offers to schools is to build upon it in the interests of their students and thus of society at large. The promise of the policy will be realised only if schools are inventive in using it.

For example, if records and recording systems are to give credit for what students have achieved and do justice to their own efforts and the efforts of others, they cannot be merely another set of marks or grades added to existing practice. Their preparation must be part of a different way of organising achievement, experience and effort. If they are to strengthen students' development and motivation, they must be the outcome of programmes of work which the students have had some responsibility for establishing. The Secretary of State is explicit in hoping that a records system will itself prompt schools to change the curriculum. Similarly, the Secretary of State is clear that the document of record should provide a more rounded picture than is offered by a list of examination results, and that it should be a positive statement of achievement, not an attempt at prediction. It is thus a radical attempt to free the schools from the function they so much dislike, that of being mere selectors for the next stage, either at work or in further education. Equally welcome is the Secretary of State's insistence that records are apt for *all* students in secondary education. This is perhaps the first time that a significant innovation has been proposed in secondary schools which is not meant for a limited group—of the able, the less able or the majority. A proper record is to be available for *all* students, including those in special education. There is only one weakness in the present policy statement, and that may be inadvertent: the documents of record are to be available to all students 'on leaving school'. If the other objects are to be attained, particularly that of universality, it is clear that the records should be available to all young people at the same stage—that is, at the end of compulsory education.

WHOSE RECORD?

It is in the discussion of the content of records that the policy has the most significant implications. For example, the recognition that records will require 'regular dialogue' between students and teachers implies the establishment of personal tutorial relationships which transcend those familiar in subject teaching and 'pastoral' care. The reference to a short, clear and concise 'summary document' implies a larger body of evidence of achievement on which it is based. Such evidence will best fulfil the Secretary of State's hopes if it is itself the outcome of programmes of work which the students themselves have had a hand in creating.

The importance of students themselves making a contribution to the identification of a programme of work is reinforced by the Secretary of State's view of the elements of a recording system. In particular the emphasis on a factual account of what students have achieved and experienced and an acceptance of accounts by students themselves of what they have done suggests a new place for students in the management of their own education. The whole emphasis of the policy is away from traditional judgements of character, qualities and abilities. Indeed it explicitly accepts misgivings about such assessments. The record is to be less a set of judgements, more or less securely based, and more a factual account of things that students have done. Happily, the policy statement rejects 'ticks in boxes or number or letter gradings' (p. 6).

There is one issue which the policy statement has not yet satisfactorily resolved: that is, the place of external examination results. It recognises that external examinations are only one means of assessing educational attainment, and discusses a number of others, including internal assessment and graded tests. The statement faces the practical problem that examination results become available only after most students have left school, but it does not accept the logic of this. Records of Easter leavers must be available to them in the spring term, and summer leavers will also need them if they are applying for jobs or further education while they are still at school. The principle of universality, and the practical organisation of schools, suggests that the records should be available to all in the spring term. The results of external examinations, when available, will be additional to, and not part of, the record of achievement.

This will have an important effect on the relationship between curriculum and examinations. If the record is to include academic achievement it will concentrate the minds of both students and teachers on the course itself, its purpose, content and effect, rather than simply on the 'result'. It will encourage them to regard that result, not as the object of the course of study, but as additional evidence, to be added to that which makes up the record of achievement.

The policy statement recognises that a system of records, built up over the entire experience of secondary school, will require changes in school organisation and in the place of students within it. This includes not only the opportunity for regular discussion, referred to earlier, but also ways of involving students in the recording process. This process is to be seen not as a judgement by teachers on students but as a means of assessing both students and teachers. The statement adds that some students may want to contribute elements which are entirely their own. This cannot be effective unless the students are involved in creating their educational experience as well as recording it. The record, when produced, is to be the property of the student. If the student has shared responsibility for the programme on which the record is based, it will in reality, and not just formally, be his own.

In short, it is likely that schools will find that the objects of the new policy will be better served if students themselves are offered initiative in their own learning and responsibility in compiling their records. In particular, motivation is greatly enhanced where students exercise such initiative and responsibility. A student who has been encouraged to record and report concrete examples of his or her activities, experiences and achievements will not only better understand what he or she has done but will be better able to present and defend the record of it. If, as the policy statement proposes, the record should include accounts of experience and achievement outside school, it is only the student who can be expected to present both elements, in-school and out-of-school, as a coherent statement. A record compiled in this way would itself be evidence of what was being claimed on the student's behalf. The motivation of students and the perception of teachers would alike be enhanced by being expected to discuss together the programmes of work under consideration for school groups and individual students.

In practice this would mean that students should be made aware of the purpose and process of compiling records and should be involved in it from the beginning. They should know what positive achievements at primary level are recorded on their new secondary record. They should be offered responsibility for building up their strengths and remedying their weaknesses and should be enabled and encouraged to monitor their own progress so that, by the age of sixteen, they have experience of formulating their purposes and monitoring their achievements. Their own file of evidence of attainments could be an important basis for the 'official' record. Many schools have already found that student initiative and responsibility enhances the compilation of records and the motivation, confidence and capacities which these attest (Burgess & Adams, 1980).

INDIVIDUALISING THE CURRICULUM

Competence in managing one's own learning and recording its outcomes is itself an important preparation for the challenges of adult life. To accept this is to recognise that in education, the learners are the greatest resource. They do not come to education empty-handed, and it is only if their characters, capacities, knowledge, energies and hopes can be harnessed that education can take place at all. Their desire to learn will be enhanced if they can themselves take responsibility for their own learning. Education is a personal matter: it succeeds or fails with individuals, not with systems. The Education Acts provide that every young person shall receive an education 'suitable to his age, ability and aptitude': the time has come to take this individual promise seriously.

Hitherto, education has been a matter of classes, forms, sets and streams. The individual has been overlooked. The balance of schooling has been towards assessment, selection and grading: it has been least good at valuing and developing the unique contribution that individuals can make. There has been too much acquisition and repetition of inert knowledge, too little development of competence and capacity. A heavy price has been paid for this, in apathy and even lawlessness in school, and in dependence and frustration in adult life.

Both can be minimised by offering to all young people greater responsibility for their own learning, by encouraging them to think of their education as a solution to the problems they themselves can see and understand. As adults they will have to manage their own lives and face serious problems. The best preparation for this is managing their own lives at school. We learn throughout life: school can be a relatively safe place to learn, where people can learn from their mistakes because the mistakes need not be devastating.

THE PLACE OF PARENTS

The new policy on records also recognises the place of parents, accepting for the first time the logic of the legal position. Under the Education Acts, the duty to see that children are educated is placed firmly upon parents. The law asserts the principle (heavily qualified) that children are to be educated in accordance with their parents' wishes. Parents have tried to use this principle as a basis for insisting on choosing one school rather than another. They have not used it to influence what happens to children in the schools to which they happen to go, even though the courts have held that it is to this that the principle applies, rather than choice of school.

For their part, few schools have made serious arrangements for ascertaining what parents' wishes are. Information and opinion tend to flow from the school to the parents, through reports, open days and parents' evenings. There is little encouragement for the reverse flow. This is a pity, since it is clear that children do best at school when they have their parents' positive understanding and support for what they are doing. The question is how parents can take a real responsibility for seeing that their children are suitably educated and how their wishes can be effectively considered. The most promising solution is to make the assent of parents a part of the students' self-managed learning.

A RECIPE FOR CHANGE

In short, we believe that the Secretary of State is right in seeing that the logic of the new policy statement on records of achievement will require changes in the curriculum and organisation of schools. In particular, schools will find it necessary to develop their present practice at the 'options' stage at the end of the normal third year of secondary school. At present, this usually offers to students a choice of existing courses, leading or not leading to external examinations. Already in a number of schools this stage is made more effective by making it an opportunity for students to consider seriously their present position and in the light of this to share in planning their educational programmes. We ourselves have developed proposals which build upon this experience (Burgess & Adams, 1985).

Briefly, we believe that as they reach the age of 14 students can and should be ask to take careful stock of themselves, of their abilities, qualities and achievements, and to ask themselves what they hope to be and to be able to do in two years' time, at the end of compulsory schooling. With the help of their parents and teachers, they can then be asked to face the problem of getting from where they are to where they want to be, and the solution to this problem is the programme of education which they negotiate with the school. It is the task of the school, in this system, to respond to the agreed needs of the students themselves.

At present the organisation of schools is ill-adapted to the learning needs of individuals. Students are grouped by age and often sub-divided by ability. They are taught 'subjects' for specified 'periods'. These periods are typically quite short, and between them the students change teachers and rooms: every 35 minutes or so the school is in motion. Academic organisation is based upon these subjects, with senior teachers acting as heads of 'departments' or 'faculties'. This internal organisation is confirmed, if not determined, by the demands of external 'subject' examinations. It is hard for teachers to imagine any other kind of organisation.

In many schools the weaknesses of this kind of organisation are known. These schools typically set up a parallel 'pastoral' organisation to make sure that the individual student is not overlooked and his or her human needs are promptly met. This division of academic and pastoral care is not, however, the best solution to the school's problem.

Our proposals include new forms of organisation in schools, to enhance the responsible learning of young people. Briefly, we propose that every student should have a personal tutor, responsible for his educational progress through the school. The tutor's responsibility is educational, not simply pastoral. For this tutorial relationship to be a reality the tutor and the students in his care must have substantial time to meet and work together, so that supervision can be real and effective. We propose also that specialist 'subjects' should be organised and presented in ways that make them more accessible to individual students, as part of the students' own programmes of work. Such a reorganisation would have the effect of ending short 'periods' of instruction, minimising disruptive movement and making it possible for students to establish personal and productive relations with individual teachers.

This organisation is designed to get the best out of records of achievement, by making the records the outcome of programmes of education which the young people have planned themselves. The planning of the programme and completion of the record will take place in four stages. The *negotiation* stage will occupy the whole of the school year in which the student reaches the age of 14. The *commitment* stage will be at the beginning of the year in which the student reaches the age of 15, and there will be a *review* stage before the completion of that year. The *final* stage will be the year in which the student reaches 16. The record of achievement at 16 will be ready for the student in the spring of that year.

These proposals imply not only a new organisation in schools, but also new tasks for students, parents and teachers at the successive stages leading to the record of achievement. The alternative, however, is not the simple absence of change. The general introduction of records of achievement will mean new practices and new organisation. If these are merely additional to the existing activities of schools they may well become impossibly burdensome. Equally, without a change in the way in which teachers and students relate to each other, these new forms of reporting may well be perceived as yet another feature of an alien educational system. This can be avoided, provided schools follow through the logic of the new policy statement, making the new records the outcome of new ways of learning and teaching.

In developing new methods and practices, the schools will need external support, in terms of both resources and in-service training. This has already been recognised by the Secretary of State.

NATIONAL CURRENCY AND ACCREDITATION

When the policy statement of records of achievement was issued in July 1984, it contained a very important addition to the consultative draft issued earlier: this related to national currency and accreditation. The Secretary of State recognised that there should be as much assurance as possible about the currency, reliability and significance of the information in the records. He believed that these needs might best be met if the schools, in compiling and checking the records, were 'accredited' by an outside organisation.

The problem is not a new one. This is not the first time that official backing has been given to records of achievement. The need for such records has been a staple of official reports since the Consultative Committee on Examinations in Secondary Schools in 1911. At the same time, schools themselves have developed many different ways of recording the outcomes of education. Until now, it has not been found possible for records of achievement to command the same degree of general public acceptance as is accorded to external examinations. A similar problem attended the attempt, through secondary modern schools, to establish the 'parity' of non-academic and academic values in education. The secondary modern school experiment collapsed, partly because no way was found to give public recognition to alternative forms of achievement. The success of the present initiative on records will depend critically upon the establishment of a form of general external recognition of the worth and standing of the records of achievement of individual students and schools.

The difficulty of this task should not be underestimated. Public examinations carry conviction, at least superficially, because the syllabuses are normally created, and the examinations set and marked, by independent boards. A system of records cannot use this device, because their object is to report the outcome of programmes of work established by schools with their own students particularly in mind. For this the methods of public examinations are not apt. It is the essence of the policy statement that work on externally set syllabuses towards externally marked examinations should be only a part of the final record. The rest of the record is to be a positive statement of achievements other than those which are measurable in this way. This requires new forms of external recognition.

The suggestion in the policy statement is that records should be based on national guidelines, with a common format, common characteristics and appropriate forms of validation or accreditation. The Government's determination to tackle the problem is welcomed, but the proposed solution carries its own dangers. Foremost among these is that the national guidelines, format and characteristics, when they are identified, may come to determine what is recorded, so that the work of the schools is constrained again by records of achievement in the same way as it has been by external examinations. Too early and too rigid an application of guidelines could undermine everything that the policy is otherwise designed to promote. Fortunately there are many examples, particularly from further education as to how the danger can be avoided. The earliest was the National Certificate and Diploma Scheme, introduced in the early 1920s. The essence of the scheme was the national recognition, by joint boards of the then Board of Education and the professional associations, of local courses of technical training. The courses concerned were often specially developed for a particular local industry, or even for a local firm. The subsequent certificate, however, carried national recognition.

This principle, of giving national currency to a local initiative, has been developed in higher education since 1964 by the Council for National Academic Awards. The Council approves courses proposed by polytechnics and local institutions. Under the terms of its Royal Charter, the Council's degrees and other qualifications are required to be, and hence are regarded as, comparable in standard with those of universities.

A similar development can be seen in the recent history of universities. At one time academic standards in universities were maintained by requiring new institutions to be established as university colleges preparing students for the external degrees of the University of London. This method lost acceptability and was replaced by the well-known system of external examiners, and the new universities established in the 1960s benefited from the change. Standards in British universities are maintained, and public recognition secured, not by the external creation of syllabuses and the setting of examinations to which all work, but by acceptable external checks on the independent initiatives of university departments.

The problem, for the new policy, is to establish a framework which will accord external recognition to the work and records of individual students in schools. At the least it must create public confidence in the courses proposed, guard against accusations of bias and partiality in teachers, and support claims for activities undertaken and standards reached. The system should also accommodate the desire of the Secretary of State to involve parents, local employers and other significant persons in the community in the education of young people.

Our solution is an institutional framework which meets these objectives. It would establish, for each school, a guarantee that the students' educational programmes were worthwhile and a recognition that the records of their outcomes were reliable and dependable. It would also provide for a general, national recognition of the records of achievement produced in individual schools.

We have set out the details of our proposals more fully elsewhere (Burgess and Adams, 1985): the following is a brief summary. Our proposals provide, first, that a school's governing body should establish—from its own members and others—a Validating Board for the programmes created by the school. This would give reality to the legal position of the governors in relation to the conduct and curriculum of schools. Governing bodies themselves are better placed today to exercise these functions, since they contain representatives not only of the local education authority but also of the school's parents and teachers. Many governing bodies also include independent local people. Whatever the composition of the governing body, the Validating Board it establishes should certainly include people from industry, commerce, higher education and other local interests. The task of the Validating Board would be to receive the school's proposals for the educational programmes of students for the last two years of compulsory schooling. It would have access to the programmes as they affected individual students, at least on a sample basis. Its task would be to assert the validity of the programmes proposed in the sense of assuring students, parents, teachers and the local community that the successful completion of these programmes would represent a worthwhile education. An example of the detailed procedures of such a board is to be found in the work of the Validating Board, chaired by Sir Toby Weaver, at the School for Independent Study, North East London Polytechnic (Adams et al., 1981).

Second, each local authority will establish a local Accrediting Board for its schools or groups of schools. Accreditation is an independent and distinct process from validation and should be in the hands, not of lay people, but of professionals, including inspectors, academics and teachers from other schools. The Accrediting Board would act in the manner of external examiners, to guarantee the objectivity of the procedures used to produce records and the reliability of what was recorded. The work of such a board would reassure students, parents, teachers, employers and others that the records produced could be depended upon.

The creation of Validating and Accrediting Boards would have powerful effects on the work and standing of the schools themselves, and would go a long way towards meeting the need for accountability which Baumgart identifies in Chapter 4. This effect would be greatly enhanced if there could be established a national system of external recognition for the work of Accrediting Boards. It is in this way that general confidence in the procedures can be built up and general acceptability of records established. A central Accrediting Body, on the outcomes of local initiatives, would be a first step to creating general public acceptability for records. Local and national Accrediting Boards together form the best hope for the effective establishment of the system to which the Secretary of State is committed in his policy statement.

Believing that a framework of this kind is essential to the success of the policy for records of achievement and of the objects it is designed to attain, the authors have established a small pilot project to test the feasibility of the framework. Supported by a grant from the Gulbenkian Foundation, a number of schools in different local authorities have agreed to establish their own Validating Boards along the lines described above. It is important to emphasise that what the boards will be validating will be the initiatives and innovations of the schools themselves. The purpose of the scheme is to test whether the framework is capable of accommodating widely different activities and practices.

The authorities with schools participating in the project have for their part agreed to establish Accrediting Boards locally, and will collaborate in setting up a pilot 'National' Accrediting Council for Education.

A list of schools and authorities is given below.

GULBENKIAN PILOT PROJECT: SCHOOLS PARTICIPATING

Croydon	Haling Manor High School, Kendra Hall Road, South Croydon, Surrey.
Harrow	Whitmore High School, Porlock Avenue, Harrow, Middlesex.

Sheffield	Brook School, Richmond Road, Sheffield.
	Ecclesfield School, Ecclesfield, Sheffield.
	Hinde House School, Shiregreen Lane, Sheffield.
	King Ecgbert School, Furniss Avenue, Dore, Sheffield.
Surrey	Bishop Wand School, Laytons Lane, Sunbury, Middlesex.
Wiltshire	Malmesbury School, Malmesbury, Wiltshire.
Community home	The Royal Philanthropic Community, Redhill, Surrey.

REFERENCES

Adams, E., Robbins, D. and Stephens, J. (1981) *Validity and Validation in Higher Education* (research report and papers 1, 2, 3 and 4). London: North East London Polytechnic.

Burgess, T. and Adams, E. (ed.) (1980) *Outcomes of Education*. Basingstoke: Macmillan.

Burgess, T. and Adams, E. (1985) *Records of Achievement at 16*. Windsor: NFER–Nelson.

Department of Education and Science (1984) *Records of Achievement: A Statement of Policy*. London: HMSO.

7

Pupils' Personal Records

RICHARD DE GROOT

The Swindon 'Record of Personal Achievement' (RPA), Don Stansbury's 'Record of Personal Experience' (RPE) and, more recently, Pupils' Personal Recording (PPR) are all well-known versions of a particular type of approach to the recording and reporting of student experience which removes the teacher entirely from an assessment role. As the introduction to this book suggests, this approach may justly be regarded as one of the main influences on the profiling movement as it has developed during the last decade. In this chapter, one of the leading figures in the movement, Richard de Groot, sets out the general rationale for this approach and the particular context that allowed PPR to grow and develop into the scheme it is today.

—Editor

Prologue

In the autumn of 1973 I was just entering my first Headship at Kingswood School, Corby, at a time of major pre-Houghton strife. I found a young staff—exceptional in commitment, thin on comprehensive experience.

The school was growing very rapidly, almost doubling its numbers in four years as one more grammar school metamorphosis was accomplished. The Sixth Form 'went comprehensive' at this stage. The delayed shock-waves of the raising of the school-leaving age to sixteen hit the Fifth Year quite hard. The ready availability of homes and work created a regular influx of steel-workers to the town, bringing with them teenagers who were all too often bemused, uprooted and deeply unhappy.

Despite the unpromising context, I was eventually persuaded to try the Records of Personal Achievement (RPA) scheme pioneered by Don Stansbury. Against all the rules of good practice in educational innovation, we tried out RPA with some twenty recalcitrant teenagers. I appointed the tutor, using uncertain criteria.

In spite of making all the basic mistakes, we found that there was a change in the pupils caught up in the scheme. We could feel the build-up of positive relationships between tutor and pupil. Perhaps RPA was merely a catalyst. Whatever the reasons, we noticed more heads held high among a sector of our population who had formerly been marked by very defeatist attitudes. By the time I left Corby in 1978, the basic philosophy of RPA had made a real mark on my own thinking.

RECORDS OF PERSONAL ACHIEVEMENT

This chapter will argue that the dedicated band of teachers who created RPA in Swindon in the late 1960s had a penetration and foresight which places their work at the very centre of our educational priorities in the second half of this century.

At the physical heart of the scheme was the Record Card. The early programme included twenty-eight different card headings. Pupils inserted completed cards into a specially designed Record Book, retaining the right to remove cards if they so wished. Support materials included a diary jotter, a pupil's handbook and a card carrier as optional items. Publicity on RPA drew attention to its particular merits when used with less academic pupils in fourth and fifth years. Additionally, the completed Record Book was projected as an invaluable aid to employers selecting young recruits. Above all, the designers of the scheme saw as its role the development of personal qualities through the recording of achievement in and out of school. Throughout, emphasis was placed on personal qualities, with secondary importance attached to the development of skills and concepts.

Wiltshire Education Committee promoted the scheme within the county's schools, according to demand, and allowed the materials to be purchased by schools elsewhere. During the 1970s enquirers were advised that Wiltshire saw the following as the scheme's essential elements:

1. Emphasis on personal development.
2. A system of recording and organisation.
3. In place of a teacher assessment, the RPA provides a factual record of whatever the pupil takes a pride in having done.
4. Each item must be validated by a responsible adult who is in possession of the facts.
5. No adult can veto a truthful item which the pupil wants recorded.
6. Each item must be factual and must not contain any subjective or value judgements.
7. Items can refer to objective standards of performance.
8. Nothing should prevent a pupil who completes two years (4th, 5th) from taking away his Record Book.
9. Some flexibility concerning the actual finishing date of each set of Record Books is possible, and is a matter for each school to decide upon.
10. Pupils who take RPA may also take examinations.
11. RPA may be taken by pupils in any ability group or in mixed ability groups.

Throughout, it was stressed that the scheme was a procedure, not a course. Sadly, this fundamental point was missed by many of the schools which purchased RPA materials. My enquiries to a cross-section of some thirty schools nationally showed that RPA was not understood by many of its early users, some Headteachers having adopted the scheme in the erroneous belief that it resolved curricular gaps! It is clear that RPA was viewed by a number of schools as being somewhere between a palliative and a panacea, to be applied in suitable doses to the recalcitrant, less academic teenagers. The palliators were likely to 'teach' Personal Records to 4E on Friday afternoons; the panacea prophets sought their elusive syllabus solutions from RPA, sometimes condemning it when they came away empty-handed. Such misconceptions must not be laid at the doors of the scheme's originators. They do, however, add much weight to the arguments of those who maintain that some of this country's most important educational innovations have failed for want of planned dissemination strategies.

Fortunately, Wiltshire was able to arrange some short conferences to think through issues about philosophy and practice, and for some ten years RPA was used by schools to assist in the motivation and ultimate accreditation of school-leavers. One is left with a powerful feeling, on analysing the schemes used in the 1970s, that recorders' personal development did receive a boost wherever the scheme was given an appropriate place of honour in a school's priorities. The fostering of self-esteem is the fundamental aim of personal recording.

RECORDS FOR ALL

In 1979, working as a Regional Field Officer with the Schools Council, I convened a meeting of those interested in the development potential of RPA. The Schools Council was no newcomer to RPA matters. The Council had pondered several times over the support it might give to this uncomfortable offspring of dedicated teachers. Not only did it seem unwieldy to operate, but it also championed quite radically the rights of pupils to record on their own terms. In addition, the original group was itself somewhat divided over development priorities.

Nevertheless, the Schools Council had commissioned an independent evaluation of the Record of Personal Achievement Scheme (Swales, 1979). In 1978, the final report lay in the Council's coffers, unedited and unpublished. There had been an abundance of reasons for delays, but when the evaluation was published in 1979, some three years of development time had been kept 'on the shelf' by the Wiltshire Education Committee, since there was an understandable wish to include in the development work issues highlighted by this evaluation.

The report made an appraisal of the scheme as conceived in 1970. In broad terms, pupils' motivation was found to be extremely inconsistent. At its best, the scheme was a liberating force for youngsters who lacked the academic skills needed to gain recognition of achievement through conventional accreditation. But as already highlighted, the Record of Personal Achievement had set out to provide a prestigious alternative pattern of qualifications for school-leavers. Its pioneers were convinced that the very process of recording increased maturity and thereby employability, especially in the case of less academic pupils. It was hoped that employers would use the Record of Personal Achievement to make discriminating choices in the absence of examination evidence. In practice, nobody at the time queried the fallacy of relying solely on examinations in the first place. It is not surprising that the Evaluator stated:

'The overwhelming evidence is that RPA has not fulfilled its potential as a leaving qualification for a majority of pupils involved. Employers, with some notable exceptions, have been shown to be only marginally interested. Few asked about RPA, although some found it useful as a starting-point in interviews. However, not many schools involved the employers. Even in Swindon, where efforts were made at the start to interest employers in the scheme, the links established were not, in most cases, maintained. Many employers also did not seem to have thought out in detail the sort of personal qualities needed for the various jobs in their firms. Of course, at the time of the evaluation, the country was in a recession and jobs were very hard to get anyway. It would be interesting to see whether in a better economic climate more use would be made of RPA records in matching school-leavers' talents with job requirements. RPA appears to offer the beginnings of a formal mechanism by which this better matching could be accomplished.' (Swales, 1979)

The potential identified by the Evaluator went further than the comments on employment links. An important summary paragraph claimed:

'The potential of RPA is clear but not generally realised in the present working of the Scheme. The needs for improvements are indicated in terms of . . . teacher and tutor training, in the materials themselves, and certainly in establishing firm links with LEA services and employers, and in involving parents.'

Clearly, we were at a stage in 1979 where fundamental reappraisal was called for. Links were made with Don Stansbury, a key figure in the early days of RPA and, subsequently, the developer of Records of Personal Experience (RPE). Under the auspices of the Schools Council, it was agreed by a small group that the absolute basis of the RPA and RPE schemes lay in the promotion of personal development. The emphasis on the provision of ready-made accreditation for employers was to be reconsidered.

Above all, the targeting of RPA towards the less academic was challenged. Don Stansbury had maintained for some time the necessity of 'opening up' personal recording across the ability span. In short, we decided:

(a) that personal recording should have as its main aim the promotion of confident personal development and self-awareness;

(b) that it is invidious and illogical to regard personal recording as an educational scheme limited to certain sections of the academic population.

Within this context, the Schools Council agreed in 1980 to support a pilot development programme in south west England.

After much discussion, it was agreed that the term 'achievement' in RPA was at best superfluous and at worst misleading, as there was no attempt made to screen, to measure or to assess the file entries against objective standards. Indeed, to do so in a 'personal record' could become a contradiction in terms. Thus, Personal Records was the preferred title, from which PPR (Pupils' Personal Records) was coined as the distinguishing title for the development project.

Operationally, RPA had held national relevance, but had remained for the most part corralled within the confines of one LEA. Schools Council strategy was to take a regional initiative, and invitations to participate were issued to Avon, Cornwall, Devon, Dorset, Gloucestershire, Somerset and Wiltshire LEAs. All except Gloucestershire accepted. Oxfordshire sought involvement and this was agreed. The title RPA was phased out and PPR promoted, to emphasise the new approach. As RPA had suffered from lack of understanding at LEA officer level and at headteacher level, our development strategy responded by designing the model shown in Figure 7.1 over a two-year pilot programme (1980–82).

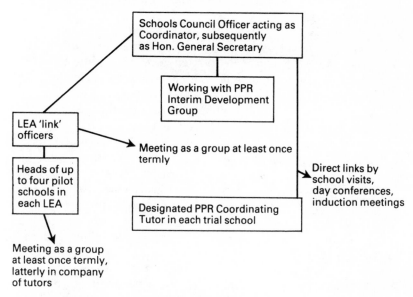

Fig. 7.1 *Development model for communication network.*

Local Education Authorities and their nominated Headteachers were invited to consider the work proposed for the development phase, and pilot schools undertook to 'subscribe' to the 'key criteria' of PPR. These 'key criteria' are set out here in full, since they represented the central element in the piloting of the new work. (Extracts are from the 1st edition of the *PPR Handbook*, by J. McNaughton and R. de Groot.)

KEY CRITERIA FOR PPR

1. The development pattern for the 1980s holds quite closely to the style of the original forms of personal recording. Experienced tutors have assisted in confirming and refining the essential ingredients. Together, these create a recipe which places with the recorder real decision-making and real responsibility.

2. Not all schools will necessarily follow the same working pattern or use identical materials for Pupils' Personal Records. The PPR development group wants to encourage local initiative, whilst assuming some important common ground. Respecting individual pupil needs and pupil autonomy within PPR is part of the developmental process. No change can be made to this principle without damaging the very heart of the scheme.

3. The foundation for personal recording is embodied in the following key criteria:

(a) *In principle, the opportunity to keep a Personal Record shall be available to all pupils*
Record-keeping is not restricted to any academic ability range. In due course, the participating schools hope to resolve issues of resources and time, making Personal Records a part of each pupil's accreditation at 16+.

(b) *Entries are pupil-decided*
The recorders use their own judgement and exercise their own choice in deciding which experiences/activities they wish to record.

(c) *Entries are pupil-controlled*
The language, style and pattern of an entry are determined, and made by the recorder in person.

(d) *Records are designed for use from the Fourth Year of secondary schooling*
The usual pattern of record-keeping will cover the last two years of compulsory education.

(e) *Record files are of good quality material and appearance*
Participating schools will take great care in using attractive, durable files and cards for all Personal Records.

(f) *Records are pupil-controlled during development and on completion*
The Personal Record is a private document during preparation and on completion, but the school accepts full custodial

responsibility for the record during preparation. Public reference and display must be agreed by the recorder personally.

(g) *Personal Record schemes are procedures, not courses*

Recorders need time from tutors for discussion and advice; but the time with an adult tutor is time spent on the growth and sharpening of the pupil's own self-definition. Personal Records are critical tools in personal education, they are not curricula in their own right.

4. Underpinning the criteria is the assumption that pupils create Personal Records because they *wish* to do so. This does not invalidate vigorous projection of the scheme by the school—to potential recorders, to parents, to professional colleagues, to the full local community.
5. The acid test of a Personal Records scheme lies in the dignity it gives to the recorder. We believe that such dignity depends on the firm application of the guidelines set out in this section.

To an established teacher, the criteria were often more unnerving than they may seem at first reading, for PPR requires the teacher to put away her red pen and to suspend her judgemental role to a marked degree, yet to give sympathetic mature guidance to young recorders. An apparent recipe for anarchy? Paradoxically, many PPR tutors (including a number who, like myself, came unwillingly to the trials) found that their professional role was enhanced by seeing each pupil's daily life from the pupil's side of the fence. That said, it is clear at once that personal recording can be sunk without trace by an uncomprehending or insensitive tutor.

The Evaluator of RPA had spoken of the importance of clear guidelines for tutors. This need was even more pressing in the PPR pilot schools, and the confident growth of tutoring skills was given a renewed standing as a development priority. Therefore, in 1981, at an early stage in the development programme, a tutors' Handbook on Personal Recording was published. In particular, Personal Recording challenges the tutor to strike a fine balance between 'just listening' and 'interfering'. This same dilemma scorched the first drafts of the Handbook. We have become increasingly convinced that personal recording—and, by implication, any recording or reporting which claims partnership between tutor and learner—requires a concentrated period of induction for any tutor, and the opportunity for shared experiences with colleagues from other schools or colleges.

The development phase, 1980–82, started with strict regional control and expanded to include fifty schools and some three thousand participants by the end of the academic year 1982/83. Particularly striking was the naturalness with which the work was adopted across the full academic range by those schools which carried out large-scale trials.

Less widespread than intended were the initiatives to involve the wider community in the pilot programme. Nevertheless, the scheme was the mainspring for Governors' discussions on accreditation, for open evenings attended by pupils, parents and employer representatives and for school reviews of reporting systems. The capacity of teenagers to talk with vitality about 'their' scheme was demonstrated when we asked for their involvement in lecture/discussion contributions to teachers' in-service programmes, in the making of a video and in explaining PPR to community representatives. Despite this the challenging realisation remains that such involvement has done no more than scratch the surface of the possible front-line contributions which pupils themselves can make in the debate on recording.

THE WIDER ARENA

Somehow, it must be possible to reconcile the current developments on records of achievement with the liberating force which personal recording has already brought to pupil–teacher roles. In 1980, when PPR was launched, the national implications of wider accreditation patterns were but a glimmer in the eye of a few radicals. The pace of change since that time is illustrated in the diagrams that follow (pp. 100–101) and they are included to underline the speed of the developments which have recently taken place. In addition, the following notes and diagrams are essential to any understanding of the place of PPR in contributing to national trends on accreditation.

In 1980, a decision had to be made whether personal recording was to be promoted as an 'alternative qualification' to public examinations. This was rejected decisively. Next, we considered whether it might become a complementary component in a new, wider range of qualifications. Nobody in the PPR Development Group doubted the fine balance needed, if pupils were to be convinced that a personal record was privately compiled and ultimately privately owned.

The following section from the PPR Handbook sets out the principles which emerged from this debate.

CREDENTIALS AT THE AGES OF SIXTEEN AND SEVENTEEN

1. The Personal Record is first and foremost a private document. It is a chronicle assembled during the two years when most young people are becoming acutely conscious of their own image.
2. The record has the potential for contributing strongly to the confident firming up of self-image. The Personal Record enables the pupil to define and to declare an identity. Compilation of entries over several months depicts attitudes, values, experiences, interests which combine to show a unique picture. There is an opportunity to carry from school a handsome individual document which is totally uninhibited by competitive factors. They have their place elsewhere.
3. The Personal Record has been valuable if it has met, however modestly, some of the potential claimed for it as an instrument in self-definition. Yet its contribution to the wider pattern of credentials cries out for development.
4. The credentials currently held by most young school-leavers are both restricting and restrictive. This suggests we should be looking much harder at the place of the Personal Record within the overall pattern of credentials. It should remain a private document, but become more widely used—at its owner's absolute discretion—as public evidence of qualities and qualifications.
5. The Personal Record may be much more likely to provide evidence of personal attributes than other forms of credentials. Above all, a carefully maintained record can present a picture which is individual and positive. Other forms of credentials all too often publicise a pupil's limitations but fail to highlight specific strengths.
6. Less academic pupils are particularly vulnerable in an educational system and in an employment arena which have developed an over-reliance on examinations. Major effort and exhortation come from schools in the quest for 'success' in public examinations. This is absolutely appropriate until the public start to over-value the currency on offer. Many a holder of CSE middle or low-grade results (and not a few GCE 'O' level candidates) will be utterly

dejected on realising that the credentials are given scant respect. If that dejection turns to alienation, society can pay a high penalty.

Figure 7.2 is an attempt to set the PPR ideas in their wider context, to illustrate the present dilemma and to suggest a path ahead. In any change, the chief beneficiary must be the individual pupil. Figure 7.2 sets out the case for a development which uses four complementary forms of credentials. No single form is seen as adequate in its own right for any pupil. Equally important, the components of the credentials will constitute a kaleidoscope whose pattern may change for an individual pupil over the years. Indeed the pupil is master of the kaleidoscope in that he or she may choose to vary the projection of the credentials to suit particular job applications or other situations, as adults so often do in their own lives.

We may choose to see credentials as analogous to items of clothing, with which a pupil is equipped on leaving school. The distinctive clothing enables—indeed obliges—the leaver to declare the tangible outcomes of compulsory education, upon which the adult world stands ready to pass judgement. Yet for too many the result is incongruous or unbecoming garments. For the pupils who leave school, as in Outline A, 'clothed' in such doubtful attire, even small progress must be crucial. At present, we concentrate too much school effort and esteem in the gaining of 'clothing' which leaves the owner as destitute and as disconsolate as the Emperor in his new suit of clothes.

Perhaps the most important decision implied in Outline C, Figure 7.2, was the separation of the Personal Record (or 'Chronicle') from the teacher-controlled skills profile. In the former, the pupil/recorder is the 'senior partner', logging private interests and experiences and using the teacher as mentor. In the latter, the pupil negotiates the recording of skill levels, but understands the teacher's role as assessor using externally-agreed standards. There would seem to be positive educational merit in keeping the two sets of credentials 'within the same circle, but apart'. In such a manner, both the rationale of personal recording and the criteria for objective skills profiling can co-exist.

LESSONS LEARNED

The teachers in each of the pilot schools came to realise in nearly every case the importance of keeping Personal Records truly *personal*. The PPR administration model required the participation of the Head in early planning meetings and the identification of a school coordinator at the outset, followed by regional induction meetings. It may be that the PPR experience is closely relevant to the wider development of records of achievement, and these comments on its administration are set down with that realisation.

In the PPR development, Headteachers were asked to avoid automatic transference of the co-ordinating role to a Deputy Head. This suggestion was made, first, because too many educational innovations are sent by reflex action along that much-burdened route; secondly, and more importantly, because personal recording offered the professional challenge for other teachers to contribute a leading role—staff development in action. Headteachers were asked to keep the following attributes in mind when identifying a coordinator:

(a) sound organising ability;
(b) the capacity to 'service' an expanding system;
(c) the capacity for listening sympathetically to young people talking;
(d) a readiness to break free during tutoring from the 'red-ink syndrome', to understand non-judgementally the priorities of activity or experience as felt by the pupil; and
(e) communicative skills of sufficient level to guide staff room discussion of personal recording.

Further, it was pointed out that the prospective coordinator's experience and standing in the eyes of colleagues could be of more importance than actual seniority.

The elements for effective implementation appeared to be the Headteacher's informed interest and publicised support for the initiative, linked to the identification of a promoting agent (coordinator) in the staff room, chosen against an agreed checklist of personal attributes.

From the direct experience of setting up PPR, it would be difficult to over-emphasise the role of the Headteacher in the provision of sound roots for an innovative programme. From twenty-one pilot schools in the first stage of PPR development, only three tutors found major hurdles in gaining colleagues' sympathetic acceptance of the trials. In two cases, the Headteacher had sent a substitute to the early Heads' Planning Meetings. In the third case, the coordinator had been selected using quite inappropriate criteria. How far the scheme can be misunderstood when these criteria are not followed may be illustrated by some remarks made about PPR by several comprehensive school Headteachers at a national conference in 1979:

Outline A
Typical picture of credentials for less academic school-leavers. The leaver and the school have conceived accreditation almost entirely in public examination terms. A confidential reference is available but the pupils have no awareness of its nature, and are often reluctant to see it within their credentials. They may prefer to use recent and not-so-recent school reports. These were prepared for home-school dialogue, and are invalid when used as credentials.

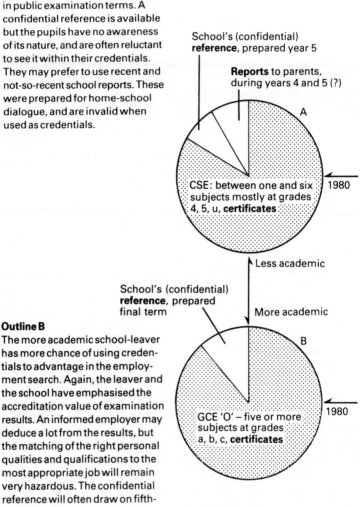

School's (confidential) **reference**, prepared year 5

Reports to parents, during years 4 and 5 (?)

A

CSE: between one and six subjects mostly at grades 4, 5, u, **certificates**   1980

Less academic

More academic

School's (confidential) **reference**, prepared final term

B

Outline B
The more academic school-leaver has more chance of using credentials to advantage in the employment search. Again, the leaver and the school have emphasised the accreditation value of examination results. An informed employer may deduce a lot from the results, but the matching of the right personal qualities and qualifications to the most appropriate job will remain very hazardous. The confidential reference will often draw on fifth-year activities alone.

GCE 'O' – five or more subjects at grades a, b, c, **certificates**   1980

Fig.7.2   *Relative importance of credentials at ages 16 and 17 — a decade for change?*

Outline C

During the 1980s, it would be quite possible to move towards a much more positive system of tangible support for school-leavers. I have anticipated that public examinations continue to play an important role. But they are presented as more equal partners in the total pattern of credentials. In this outline, the Personal Record is widely used as the pupil's own contribution to an educational contract which sees him/her as a partner rather than a client. Quite separately, the school has created an objective record of the pupil's range and depth of academic skills. The Skills Record emphasises skills across subject boundaries and does not in any way seek to judge or categorise personal qualities.

A fourth element in this Outline is a much-improved school reference, based on not less than two years of educational contract between pupil and school.

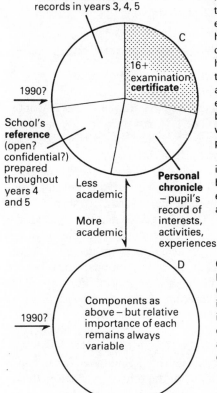

Teacher assessed **skills profile**, based on criterion-referenced records in years 3, 4, 5

C

16+ examination **certificate**

1990?

School's **reference** (open? confidential?) prepared throughout years 4 and 5

Less academic

More academic

Personal chronicle – pupil's record of interests, activities, experiences

D

1990?

Components as above – but relative importance of each remains always variable

Outline D

If the patterns of credentials of Outline C are valid for some pupils, it is logical to make them available in principle to all pupils. Many will continue to prefer to be judged, and will be judged, to a substantial degree on academic performance.

'We tried RPA but have dropped it as our ethos grew clearer and public examinations became better established . . .'

   'Records of Personal Achievement have a great deal of educational merit, but they would never work with my staff . . .'

Ironically, the advocates could be as frightening as the opposition:

'We issue every pupil with his Personal Record Book and my staff ensure that no book leaves the premises with incorrect spelling or punctuation. Our Record Books go with our reputation.'

These quotations represent a distorted view of recording—some would say, of education—yet they do illustrate the three concepts central to any appraisal of PPR, namely control, audience and the physical shape of the record.

The concepts of control (who influences style and content?) and of audience (for whom is the record created?) are bound together. PPR starts from the stand that a school must always respect authorship and identify ownership, on behalf of the pupil. It was significant that at the first exploratory conference on OCEA (Oxford Certificate of Educational Achievement) (see Chapter 9 in this volume), several PPR tutors spontaneously and cogently set out this priority. However, with proper professional care, it is possible for the completed record to serve more than one purpose. In carrying out this development, recorders and tutors have to work in mutual trust. Research in the form of pupil interviews during the pilot programme confirmed that this creation of partnership is not elusive idealism. Pupils were not easily deceived and they showed intuitive understanding of the degree to which the school promoted genuine personalisation on the one hand or the degree to which it was in business as a tightly conformist agency on the other. At the most extreme, an educational model in which public praise is restricted to certain types of academic performance, or to team achievements in approved sports will almost inevitably release in pupils a response which finds personal recording alien. It is sobering to keep in mind that records of achievement are intended for all pupils and for all types of school. As many of the other contributors to this book are at pains to stress, the spirit as well as the letter of the procedure must be right before a Personal Record can fulfil its intentions and have a place at the school's altar of achievement. A school which realises this fact and acknowledges it has already created the subtle atmosphere in which control of the record is no longer a threatening issue.

With hindsight, it is now clear that we would have been well advised to have paid more attention in the PPR pilot programme to the question of audience. It is not sufficient to state that Personal Records are intended primarily for an audience of one—the recorder. Although this is the case, it is also necessary to probe the educational process of recording if the final document is not to be useless in its owner's hands.

The attraction of personal recording must lie in the chance it gives each student to create a truly individual chronicle. This is much more than a diary, for it represents selection, review and organisation of entries, but it is every bit as private, unless the owner chooses to show it to others. The satisfaction to the recorder lies in the steady compilation of personal interests and the growing realisation that the contents are unique. 'This is me' is a more novel concept in the education world than most of us care to confess! Even the best references and records often reflect preoccupation by the adult world with ranking and sifting. These processes have their place, but they can disguise qualities of personality and achievement at least as often as they project them.

Personal recording takes a step in the direction of promoting confident self-image by a process which totally respects the individual student. At sixteen, it is not easy to talk about your *real* self. At sixteen, most of us are still absorbed in conjuring up a self-definition which is acceptable to ourselves. We are at the age of self-doubt, when emotions all too readily run the gamut from total confidence to complete self-denigration, perhaps hitting the buffers at each terminus with unnerving frequency. Add to this theory the stark fact of unemployment or the relentless grading treadmill for higher education, and it is not difficult to see how confident self-image may become rapidly eroded. Current health education priorities stress that feelings of self-worth derive in particular 'from the ability to take responsibility for our own lives, to make decisions about life-style and to function confidently in social situations' (McNaughton, 1982). In this context it should be considered that personal recording has a central relationship to health education and to social education programmes.

In acknowledging recording's relationship to health education and, through that link, to the whole curriculum, any developer of such recording is brought to the realisation that we must start from where the pupils are, from what is important in their lives. Opportunity to talk about personal interests and to be listened to matters to all of us. Newsom drew our attention to the fact that it matters particularly to adolescents, when he spoke of the growth of personal qualities and social skills (Newsom Committee, 1963). It is a great encouragement to find that same far-sighted report quoted as a preface to the Secretary of State's document on records of achievement (DES, 1984): 'Boys and girls who stay at school until they are sixteen may reasonably look for some record of achievement when they leave'.

The differences between personal recording and records of achievement represent an immediate challenge, yet they are not irreconcilable. Above all, there remains the need to keep flexibility within both systems.

PPR has realised conclusively the merits of unpressurised partnerships between adults and teenagers within our educational framework. Any adult is able to endorse an entry, confirming its accuracy but not editing or censoring. Experience shows that most students value such regular, unpressured communication between recorder and teacher, neighbour, club-leader, weekend employer—or indeed any other adult who is in a position to endorse the record card.

> 'The Personal Recording scheme is exciting and interesting. It gives you time to talk about things that have happened during the week, where we have been and so on. I think talking with people once a week gives you a break from normal lessons. The best thing in our school yet I think!'

The Fourth Year girl who made the comment above was typical of many who stressed the attraction of talking and recording from within their own evolving sphere of priorities. Two boys from the same age-group commented:

> 'I like Personal Recording—it is the sort of thing I prefer because it is all about yourself, and it is the only lesson I enjoy.'

> 'I think Personal Recording is a very good idea because you can keep a record of what you do. You don't need to show it to your teacher to have it marked.'

Some observers have suggested that PPR emerges as a 'mere' diary. A preferable term would be 'chronicle'. A diary is intended, usually, for the eyes of the writer alone; it may be written as a kind of secret confessional. Others have drawn parallels with curriculum vitae. This definition has some relevance, but curriculum vitae will be designed almost always with an audience in mind.

Further trials and evaluation will be needed before the place of Personal Records becomes wholly established in schools. The recent past has seen a heartening move away from the 'tick-in-a-box' approach to identifying personal qualities and social skills. Equally important is the rejection of 'graded assessments' for qualities such as honesty, leadership or initiative. PPR has reminded us that these qualities surface in unexpected ways at unlikely times, with no guarantee that they are constant anyway. What is needed is the documentary evidence of activities from which the reader(s) may reasonably deduce the display of interests or qualities over a period of time. At all times, judgements of personal qualities use personal yardsticks. The same piece of behaviour, if it is viewed from different perspectives, may be recorded as any of the following 'assessments':

I am tenacious
but   You are obstinate
and   He is cantankerous.
On the other hand, we can safely summarise the following objective assessments (given a constant factor—the time for meeting!):
I am early
You are punctual
She is late.
These examples bring us to the very edge of the question of 'condensed versions' of Personal Records. The arguments in favour are strong:

1. The Recorder takes stock, reviews entries and selects key items for summary.
2. Employers welcome brief analyses of applicants' strengths and experience.
3. The critical facet of recording lies in the process, not the product. Therefore, any summative document cannot damage the advantages gained during the 'journey of self-discovery' as the record is built up.

Against this might be weighed some of the lessons learnt from experience with RPA and PPR. It is neither desirable nor practicable to divorce the formative process from any proposed summative process. If a Personal Record undergoes stages of review by its author, this can only sharpen self-awareness, and makes very good educational sense. On the other hand, if the rules of the game change between creation and review, we have to consider quite specifically whether the recorder is still the principal beneficiary.

Any student creating a Personal Record over a period of two years or more determines entries, with a tutor's advice, throughout that process. The PPR pilot scheme demonstrated that students across the academic range could draw a sense of relaxed pride in watching the record grow, and in the knowledge of undisputed ownership. There were no 'hidden extras' at the end, no extraneous processes to the main programme of compilation.

Knowledge that summation is one outcome must run the risk of influencing the character and the quantity of entries throughout, as well as the role of tutor towards the end, in any chronicling process. The finished document may well have a wider value, but the primary focus on PPR must be its effectiveness as a tool for confident self-definition. It is on this factor that PPR must stand or fall. 'A balance has to be struck between emphasis on a scheme which is truly a vehicle for personal education, and emphasis on a scheme which is used in selection. The two strands are compatible, but we are in no doubt that the key to effective personal recording lies with the first strand—the record serves as a business-like tool in promoting a young person's self-image. All pupils, irrespective of academic ability, can benefit from the opportunity to assemble, to review and perhaps to project the positive elements in the picture they have of themselves. We must remember that the Personal Record is in no sense an examination and it does not employ or depend upon any variant on the idea of assessment. Equally important, it is not a form of report or testimonial. It does not contain judgements by teachers and it does not express standardised values.' This section of the original PPR rationale probably goes quite a long way to explaining the predominantly enthusiastic response of pupils who were following 'their' scheme in the pilot schools.

It is neither sacred nor immutable, but it is founded on a policy of non-intervention by adults. Thus, my reasons for caution about summative documents derive from the degree of respect we choose to accord to the notion of individuality. Personal recording has completed trial stages and has reaffirmed the value of a high level of recorder autonomy. For their part, a majority of tutors confirmed that the enforced shift in the nature of their relationships with pupils was properly educative for each side of the partnership.

> 'A great deal of productive attention is directed to many children . . . who tend to be an unnoticed sector of the school population. The role of tutor is educative to the teacher as well as to the pupil. The role is seen as one in which the function of the tutor is "to reflect like a mirror rather than refract like a prism". It brings teachers to the task of thoughfully developing a pupil's self-image' (Review by one school).

The process we are considering has at its roots a mature, mutually respecting, relaxed relationship between teacher/student or tutor/ recorder. As such, it lies at the heart of the debate on negotiated curriculum and assessment in schools. I am convinced that the potential of records of achievement lies truly in their impact on what students learn and on how that learning is carried out. Carefully managed, the change could bring a revolutionary shift in teenagers' attitudes to learning. But first, the nature of the revised learning relationship has to be understood and nurtured. It would be naive to suppose that teaching styles and relationships will change of their own volition because wider forms of assessment happen upon the scene.

My first-hand experience as a teacher is matched by the appraisals of tutors in PPR pilot schools: personal recording, as put on trial in 1981–83, enhanced social and learning situations in schools because it was non-judgemental and non-threatening. Above all, it charted a possible pattern for giving young people a greater 'say' in the depicting of their own work and interests, without surrendering the chance for influence from adults. Any attempt to summarise brings with it the risks of externally imposed priorities.

Intuitive tutor decisions have to be made constantly and at every stage concerning the extent and nature of help given to each individual. Subject teachers make these kinds of judgement nearly every minute of the working day, in response to pupils' performance. But PPR calls for the tutor to maintain razor-sharp awareness of individual need and individual response. Again, we remember that there is no absolute norm to be pursued.

Naturally, within any group of recorders the pattern of need will vary significantly. The tutor has the task of determining and applying the support needs of the individual recorder. This is the initial task, and no effective tutor can stop here. If the pattern of support becomes ossified, the recorder cannot mature. Ultimately, it is hoped that pupils move towards independence and a degree of self-reliance in recording, and as this growth takes place the nature of the tutoring should subtly alter. It should be possible to observe a gradation of support from the tutor. Gradually, as pupils gain experience and confidence, the texture of the partnership between tutor and recorder can change. It is a sophisticated weaning process.

ROUTES AHEAD

It would be valuable to research the extent to which true decision-making comes into the daily lives of teenagers in our schools, at even the most modest levels. By the very business of determining an entry, selecting a card, soliciting a validating signature and organising the placing of the entry within the main record, pupils have to take such responsibility. In secondary education, generally, we have yet to come to terms with the unpalatable fact that deprivation of decision-making chances is as unhealthy in adolescence as is deprivation of play opportunities in infancy.

If this claim has some merit, logically we must retain the working model of personal recording, as refined by the PPR pilot programme: or we must analyse step by step the implications for recorders themselves of any changes we propose. '*Festina lente*', lest the baby slips out unnoticed with the bathwater. As reinforcement of the educational advances claimed by PPR, this typical comment from a group of teachers may suffice:

'Having an unstressful talk with a teacher about personal achievement can be an important catalyst in developing better class and teacher relationships amongst those easily alienated.'

The pilot programme found negligible evidence of records being created to bait, impress, horrify or otherwise assault the sensibilities of the reader. There was virtually no report by tutors that lying was detected or suspected in the records. This is not as surprising as it may seem, for if the recorder understands the real intended audience for the finished article as being himself, then the incentive to exaggerate or to deceive never gets going.

Future modifications to personal recording may imperil its literal and figurative integrity if this evidence from PPR trials and from other schemes is overlooked. There is a danger that the elements that underpin summative reporting and its more visible importance will constrain if not choke the delicate and painstaking formative process that is at the heart of PPR. How far this is so, is a question which goes far beyond PPR and to the centre of the contemporary debate about records of achievement generally. Indeed it is one of the questions raised by nearly all the contributors to this book. In this chapter I have tried to show that the long experience and distinctive criteria of PPR can make a unique contribution to the debate.

REFERENCES

de Groot, R. and McNaughton, J. (1982) *PPR Handbook* (1st edn.).

Department of Education and Science (1984) *Records of Achievement: A Statement of Policy*. London.

McNaughton, J. (1982). *The Times Educational Supplement*, 23rd April.

Newsom, J. (1963) 'Half our Future'. London: HMSO.

Swales, T. (1979) *Records of Personal Achievement: An Independent Evaluation of the Swindon RPA Scheme*. London: Schools Council.

8

Recording Achievement: The City and Guilds Experience

NICK STRATTON

Of more recent origin than personal recording, the City and Guilds contribution to the development of the profiles movement has nevertheless been equally influential. Partly this is because unlike the two preceding chapters, the scheme has not depended solely on the goodwill of individual schools and teachers but has had the support of a major institutional infrastructure. Initially reflecting the rather different context of further education, City and Guilds development work has also had a considerable impact on schools. Many of its ideas have been incorporated into the new CPVE qualification. Having been centrally involved in this development work, the author of this chapter, Nick Stratton, is well-placed to review the progress of the last few years and to identify what seem likely to prove the major development concerns for both small and large-scale profiling initiatives in the future.
—Editor

The history of profiling at the City and Guilds of London Institute started with the Further Education Unit (FEU) and its *A Basis for Choice* curriculum, which the Institute helped to pilot (see Mansell, Chapter 2). This included a profile, and the City and Guilds general vocational preparation course (365) came out of that work as a development of the FEU's original project. The 365 course contains

	ABILITIES	EXAMPLES OF ABILITIES		
COMMUNICATION	TALKING AND LISTENING		Can make sensible replies when spoken to	Can hold conversations and can take messages
	READING		Can read words and short phrases	Can read straightforward messages
	WRITING		Can write words and short phrases	Can write straightforward messages
	USING SIGNS AND DIAGRAMS		Can recognise everyday signs and symbols	Can make use of simple drawings, maps, timetables
	COMPUTER APPRECIATION		Can recognise everyday uses of computers	Can use keyboard to gain access to data
PRACTICAL & NUMERICAL	SAFETY		Can explain the need for safety rules	Can remember safety instructions
	USING EQUIPMENT		Can use equipment safely to perform simple tasks under guidance	Can use equipment safely to perform a sequence of tasks after demonstration
	NUMERACY		Can count objects	Can solve problems by adding and subtracting
SOCIAL	WORKING IN A GROUP		Can cooperate with others when asked	Can work with other members of the group to achieve common aims
	ACCEPTING RESPONSIBILITY		Can follow instructions for simple tasks and carry them out under guidance	Can follow instructions for simple tasks and carry them out independently
	WORKING WITH CLIENTS		Can help someone to carry out clients' requests	Can carry out clients' requests under supervision
DECISION-MAKING	PLANNING		Can identify the sequence of steps in everyday tasks, with prompting	Can describe the sequence of steps in a routine task, after demonstration
	OBTAINING INFORMATION		Can ask for needed information	Can find needed information, with guidance
	ASSESSING OWN RESULTS		Can receive advice about own performance	Can seek advice about own performance

N/O = No opportunity to assess

Main Activities:

Signed ....
(Trainee/Student)

Name of Centre and Course...

Period covered by this profile (dates) – start:,...................

Fig. 8.1   *Progress profile (CGLI. Reproduced with permission).*

PROGRESS IN ABILITIES   Progress Profile

Can follow and give simple descriptions and explanations	Can communicate effectively with a range of people in a variety of situations	Can present a logical and effective argument. Can analyse others' arguments
Can follow straightforward and written instructions and explanations	Can understand a variety of forms and written materials	Can select and judge written materials to support an argument
Can write straightforward instructions and explanations	Can write reports describing work done	Can write a critical analysis, using a variety of sources
Can make use of basic graphs, codes, technical drawings, with help	Can interpret and use basic graphs, charts, technical drawings unaided	Can construct graphs and extract information to support conclusions
Can enter data into the system using existing programs	Can identify potential applications for computers	Can construct error free programs
Can spot safety hazards	Can apply safe working practices independently	Can maintain, and suggest improvements to, safety measures
Can select and use suitable equipment and materials for the job, without help	Can set up and use equipment to produce work to standard	Can identify and remedy common faults in equipment
Can solve problems by multiplying and dividing	Can calculate ratios, percentages and proportions	Can use algebraic formulae
Can understand own position and results of own actions within a group	Can be an active and decisive member of a group	Can adopt a variety of roles in a group
Can follow a series of instructions and carry them out independently	Can perform a variety of tasks effectively given minimal guidance	Can assume responsibility for delegated tasks and take initiative
Can carry out clients' requests without supervision	Can anticipate and fulfil clients' needs from existing resources	Can suggest realistic improvements to services for clients
Can choose from given alternatives the best way of tackling a task	Can modify/extend given plans/routines to meet changed circumstances	Can create new plans/routines from scratch
Can use standard sources of information	Can extract and assemble information from several given sources	Can show initiative in seeking and gathering information from a wide variety of sources
Can assess own results, with guidance	Can assess own results for familiar tasks, without help	Can assess own performance and identify possible improvements

Signed ....
(Supervisor/Tutor)

end: ....

what may be referred to as the Mark I profile, now largely superseded by development work which recently culminated in the Mark III profile (Figure 8.1). The main development work was a two-year project supported by City and Guilds, the MSC, and Oxfordshire and Lancashire Local Education Authorities (Stratton, 1983). The two-year project involved about a thousand students each year, and these were split between the training and the education sectors, with MSC training schemes on the one hand and already existing full-time courses either in further education or in schools on the other. Despite this range of contexts, we did not find any great differences in the usage of the profile in various areas. This development work and the profile format to which it has given rise are the subjects of this chapter.

The chapter is divided into three, according to the diagrams shown in Figures 8.2–8.4. The first part is concerned with the organisation of the profiling procedure itself; the second discusses the profile grid in some depth, in order to clear up some prevalent misunderstandings about it; and the third part takes a rather broader view in attempting to look into the future and see how various profiles might fit together. But as a preliminary, it is necessary briefly to outline the aims of profiling as set out by the City and Guilds.

The three aims which emerged were:

(a) to develop a system which would record students' progress within the curriculum;
(b) to promote students' maturity, in particular their self-confidence and their general awareness of their situation; and
(c) to generate a reliable profile report.

The City and Guilds' initial interest was in aim (c), and at that time we assembled a committee to try to decide on the content of this final report.

AN INFORMATION GAP

There have been various studies carried out in the past to find out what sort of information employers like to receive on job applicants (Stratton, 1983). What emerges is a clear information gap between academic results on the one hand and school references and private references on the other.[1] It was also clear that any additional information given to employers, such as a descriptive profile, must be credible and reliable. But producing a reliable report requires evidence to be generated to support it, and it was not long before the reporting system developed 'backwards', with the consequence that we are now in the slightly ironic situation—as are so many other profiling schemes—where the formative (counselling) tail is wagging the summative (reference) dog, rather than the other way round. Our main concern has been to get the balance right in the last year or so, and we are still doing work to this end.

For example, a follow-up study has been conducted on youngsters who went through the piloting stage of the profile, to find out what usage they have actually made of their records with employers (Beadle, 1984). We had already asked students in an earlier question-naire what they *expected* the usage to be, and about 70 per cent had said they expected to find it useful for one purpose or another. The current survey was carried out about six months after trainees and students received their final profiles. We experienced difficulty in locating the students in order to distribute questionnaires, so our sample—262—was not quite as large as we would have liked. Of this sample, 65 per cent replied, and we found that 60 per cent of those had already got a job before they got their final profile. This result under-lines the need to issue the profiles quickly, if their usefulness as references is to be maximised. Of the remaining 68 students and trainees, 49 had applied for a job, and 39 of these had used their profile either by sending it in advance to an employer or at an interview; 33 youngsters had had an interview and 32 of them showed their final profile at the interview to the employer. Although our evidence on employers' reactions is not yet fully analysed, from the smaller sample of students who were also interviewed it would appear that once the student shows his or her profile to a potential employer it does pro-vide an effective basis for conversation. We also know from such experience that where youngsters take their logbooks to interviews, employers are quite happy to dip into those as well, thus allaying fears expressed in some quarters about employers' hostility to lengthy reports. In all, 48 per cent of all respondents said that they had found the profile useful, while 39 per cent said they had not.

---

[1] These surveys referred to young leavers, whereas most of the City and Guilds' studies were conducted with youngsters already in or out of 6th form, so one should bear in mind that our own research results have to be translated down the age range.

ORGANISATION

I have already mentioned that the Institute initially saw its role very much as the issuer of final profiles, but that it was found necessary to develop a formative procedure to support this, which can be described with reference to Figure 8.2. Now the process of reviewing is the focus of the whole system. Regular one-to-one meetings between staff and students have become an essential and crucial part of the system. However, so that the participants can make informed decisions in reviews, both of them need to feed in information. The student side is straightforward; they keep a diary or log-book of some kind and use this as a reminder to themselves at the review of what they have done. In the log-book we recommend a dual system, keeping a factual record of what students have done on the one hand and keeping their reactions to what they have been able to do on the other.

Information flow diagram

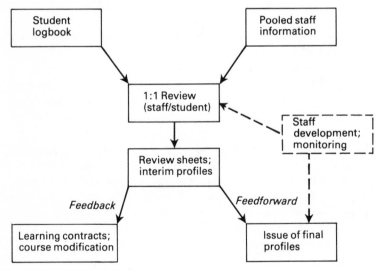

Fig.8.2 *Information flow diagram.*

Pooling the information from the various members of staff who have had contact with the student is more of a problem, and various ways have been used to deal with this, though it is inevitably somewhat time-consuming. Some centres use draft copies of profiles which individual staff can fill in and forward to the profiling tutor. Others ask the students themselves to undertake responsibility for the system, by obtaining corroboration from teaching staff of their main claims as they go. Although a variety of ways of tackling this problem have been tried, it is still not totally resolved. The most satisfactory solution depends a great deal on circumstances; for example, the student/staff ratio, the frequency of reviews, and so on. It is already evident that reviews work best when the student feels that the profiling tutor is in a position to know him or her reasonably well. A student is unlikely to have confidence in assessments made by someone who does not really know them, so it is recommended that one member of staff is responsible for profiling a youngster over as long a period as possible.

One effect of the system is to enhance the maturity of the youngsters. In fact, the description of the review process given in Figure 8.2 should have a further outcome box showing feedback concerning confidence and self-esteem. This is really a major effect. There are substantial indicators that students who are involved in this system, where it has been understood and run reasonably well, get enormous benefit out of personal contact with their tutors.

The more formal outcomes of a review are a progress profile and a simple learning contract. The aims of the review are to look over what the student has done and then to look for what the students and tutors might agree they should do in the forthcoming period. This amounts to a learning contract. The youngsters themselves feel that they do play a genuine part in the negotiating process, and as a consequence they accept personal responsibility for these outcomes. Sometimes there are criticisms of the course itself or of a particular teacher. If several students come up with similar points in this respect—for example where the course material has been gone through too quickly for them—use can be made of such feedback to modify teaching practices. That is the overall function of the review; there remains the detailed mechanism of completing the progress profiles.

It is suggested that reviews should take place fortnightly or thereabouts, and that the profiles be completed at approximately six week intervals. All these timings are very approximate and they are not critical. In terms of time resources, the results of the pilot studies suggest that the amount of time spent on reviews was between one-half and one per cent of staff time per student, depending on the frequency of the reviews. Ultimately this requires a value judgement as to whether it is worthwhile spending time in that way. The most promising approach is that used in the City and Guilds 365 course where profiling is treated as an integral part of the course. The pilot studies were less than optimal in this respect, as profiling was merely overlaid on existing courses, (such as 'O' levels, 'A' levels and BTEC courses), and so tutors had to make extra time for it. The fact that the process of reviewing worked reasonably well, even under these circumstances, would appear to augur well for profiling in the future when it is integrated into the curriculum. I would now like to turn to the profile grid itself.

PROFILE GRID

Figure 8.3 gives a list of the characteristics upon which the profile grid is based. The first of these characteristics is that the grid categories are the product of extensive development work and are now taken to be a fairly permanent selection. These categories, which generally come under generic headings such as communication skills and problem-solving, have been found useful both formatively and summatively. But despite the large degree of consensus about the kinds of categories that should be on the profile, differences have arisen about the choice of particular skill categories, such as the self-awareness category in the 365 profile. The point was made in a recent newspaper article (The *Guardian*, 1985) that 'self-awareness' was a rather ambitious thing to try to assess. Evans makes a similar point in his contribution to this volume. Thus it has been dropped from the Mark III profile. In fact it was dropped from the Mark II profile as well, for the practical reason that the examples of behaviour to do with self-awareness were either extremely vague, or, if more precise, tended to overlap with the last category which concerned the students assessing their own perform-ance. The reason it appeared on the profile in the first place was that it was part of the FEU's *A Basis for Choice* curriculum which had a number of objectives relating to student self-awareness. It has now become apparent that not all curriculum objectives can be carried over in a direct form on to the associated profile.

The next point concerns the grid band width (i.e. the achievement range it represents). The aim is to pick out examples of what the student has been doing which are relevant to these categories, and having picked these examples, to see what is merited in the way of a generalised statement of achievement. Part of the origin for this approach may be found in the FEU's interest in the notion of transfer-ability, which regards skills or abilities as generalisable beyond the contexts in which they were initially learnt and practised. Thus, one side of the profile gives an example to illustrate the context in which the skill was learnt, while the other seeks to generalise by selecting one

Notes on grid structure
1. Grid categories are stable (after development).
2. Band width of grid accommodates whole ability range.
3. Steps gradually increase in 'size' from l to r.
4. Steps increase in autonomy, complexity, variety of application.
5. Grid is essentially criterion-referenced.
6. Need to amplify with examples/criteria to overcome vagueness.
7. Grid rows are not commensurate.
8. Can replace grid by a structured checklist.
9. Grid must be supplied with a context.

Fig.8.3 *Notes on grid structure.*

of the grid statements (see Figure 8.1).

Another reason for this approach had to do with the sheer variety of schemes and courses involved in the piloting stage of the profile which prevented us from listing in advance all the relevant learning outcomes. It was not possible to generate banks of statements that related to each course or each scheme, although this might be possible in the future and I will come back to this later. Thus the City and Guilds was forced into relying on abstract, general statements of ability to provide a profiling framework.

Returning to the issue of the band width, Figure 8.1 shows that the Mark III profile has five and a half steps (i.e. it includes an overspill column). We found in our early trials with four-step profiles that we were not catering well for youngsters with learning difficulties, at one end, and potential 'A' level youngsters at the other end. So we expanded the range of the grid both downwards and upwards to try to cater for the whole student population. Thus all the descriptions, however basic they may seem, are the product of practical trials of what students can actually achieve. The aim was for the profile to act as a motivator so that even the least-equipped youngster should be able to achieve something at the outset and then see himself moving. At the same time, in order not to alienate the higher achieving youngsters, we had to stiffen the upper end and even provide an overspill in case the topmost step is exceeded. We feel that we have successfully researched this aspect and that the band width does correspond to the whole population range.

It is also necessary to point out that the steps gradually increase in size from left to right. The grid boxes are better referred to as 'steps', because mention of 'levels' and the like gives the wrong impression since this isn't really a grading system of any kind. These are just formative stepping stones. These steps are intended to motivate youngsters by enabling them to make progress at any point in a reasonable time. So they are pitched with that in mind, and at the upper end become rather large in order to accommodate the full band width. As you move from left to right on the grid, there is greater complexity of the sorts of tasks which are involved and a greater measure of independence is required of the student. Because of this complexity we cannot claim to have a logical hierarchy of skills statements. It is possible to check off a higher box, but not to have satisfied a lower one. This question was left open in the pilot studies to see if this would happen in practice, but we found very few gaps left on the profile and the conclusion must be that the profile identifies reasonable teaching–learning sequences.

The next aspect of the profile grid concerns criterion-referencing. Because of the empirical way in which the band width was adjusted until it was relevant to the whole population range, there is inevitably a kind of normative background to the grid, if a fairly weak one. It is certainly weak in the sense that the profile does not actually report any normative figures. There is no such thing as a purely criterion-referenced or a purely norm-referenced assessment; there is rather a spectrum in between. I would claim that the grid leans rather more towards the direction of criterion referencing. It is always amplified with concrete examples. By supplying these examples the grid statements are defined in a criterion-referenced sense. The practice has been to supply typical examples for each box, rather than try to spell out detailed criteria. As time goes on, it is likely that more and more examples will become available in a variety of contexts.

Yet another aspect is to look at the grid vertically. It is possible to add up the completed boxes vertically, find three in column one, three in column two, three in column three, and conclude that the procedure does not work because the spread does not allow the student to be graded. This is quite deliberate in that these rows are not equivalent; they are not comensurate. They are not comensurate in the demands that they make on students, nor are they similar in worth in each context. It is certainly undesirable that anybody should try to 'add up the system', as it were, to arrive at a figure. In fact, there is no reason for a grid at all, either at the formative or the summative stages. If the grid were turned into a structured check list, treating each head in turn, this would work equally well. However, the grid layout does have the virtue that it acts as a map for the students. They can see where they are and where they are headed. They like to see a map of objectives, but that is probably only a real virtue at the formative stage. It probably has no virtue at all at the summative stage. A further point to be made about the grid is to reinforce the fact that a context must be supplied so that the grid statements can be interpreted by third parties. This is best accomplished by referring explicitly to students' achievements.

Finally, it is well known that employers would like to see quite a lot about youngsters' attitudes as well as their achievements, and that in consequence some profiles volunteer information on attitudes directly. Table 8.1 gives a fictional (though representative) example of this type of profile. Its categories are fairly familiar territory, and include flexibility, initiative and commitment. Inevitably, many of the descriptors are highly negative, hence students are unlikely to show them to third parties—should they keep them at all! This is a good reason for keeping everything positive, and there should, by now, be no trace of a negative statement in the City and Guilds profile. The attitudinal information that employers would like is instead dispersed under a layer of talk about achievement and skill. The treatment of attitudes by reference to abilities is still controversial, but would seem to be an improvement. Thus we would reject direct statements of attitude altogether.

By way of illustration, I can refer briefly to a few examples from some genuine, but early, profiles. Fortunately these were formative examples and not summative ones. One of the categories was 'Talking and Listening', and one of the examples given for that was: 'Too much of the one and not enough of the other'. Obviously that cannot be translated onto a final profile. One of the problems, as with most other profiling schemes, is filtering the formative examples down for the summative record. How far this is possible depends a great deal on the quality of the formative examples as these are treated as a pool to draw from. In an open system of this kind, anything may be stated formatively with the youngster's agreement. Central to this is the total involvement of the youngster all the way through the system. A better example would be 'Can understand and explain safety rules in workshops', since it is reasonably concrete. The first, humorous one is simply inadequate. Another example seen under 'Calculating'—'Can't handle decimals'—does not tell you what the student *can* do in the way of arithmetic and demonstrates how easy it is to slip into a negative mode.

Everybody concerned needs to be a little more educated about the sort of statements which it is reasonable to make. If they had the awareness of adults, youngsters would not agree to some of the examples in the first place, but of course not all youngsters have that confidence or awareness at the present time. So there is a need to explain the system much more to them. A better example of 'Calculating' would be 'Can calculate hire purchase rates of interest to one place

Table 8.1 'Profile nasty' (fictional, but not untypical).

Relating to others	Uncooperative and disliked	Finds it hard to relate to others	Gets on all right with some people	Gets on well with most people	Gets on well with all sorts of people
Flexibility	Unwilling to adapt	Reluctant to try anything new	Fits in with changes	Accepts changes	Flexible and keen to learn
Initiative	Never acts off own bat	Rarely takes the initiative	Sometimes takes initiatives	Will usually act independently	Always enterprising and lively
Commitment	Puts in minimum effort	Less than adequate effort made	Adequate commitment	Has commitment for most things	Always puts in maximum commitment
Following instructions	Resents being given instructions	Often gets instructions wrong	Usually follows instructions	Carries out instructions adequately	Carries out instructions to the letter
Accuracy of work	Careless about work	Produces substandard work	Adequate quality of work	Good quality of work	Outstanding quality of work

of decimals given the relevant prices'. That is a good concrete example. Another kind of mistake, touched on earlier, is the tendency to grade or pseudo-grade. 'Examples' have appeared on formative profiles such as 'A very high standard'.

Finally a very common fault is vagueness. For example, when 'Obtaining Information'—'Can use reference books'. This is not only vague; it actually borrows phrases from the grid and thus cannot count as evidence. A better example would be 'Can use a telephone directory without help'. This illustrates the sort of examples envisaged in the profile, and demonstrates that they play a very important role in the City and Guilds profiling system.

A FRAMEWORK

Figure 8.4 is an attempt to bring together some of the main characteristics of any profiling system. I have indicated where the City and Guilds profile lies on the matrix. It is part of a 'family' of profiles which have several features in common. These are broadly, but not exclusively, pre-vocational profiles, although there is no reason why the usage of the profile should not spread across the academic and vocational as well as the pre-vocational parts of the curriculum.

Figure 8.4 refers to different kinds of profiling systems—open, closed and tied. These terms refer to the relation between the examples and the general statements. It would be possible to tie the general statements to specific educational objectives, in which case the former become redundant, and one might as well use the educational objectives. I refer to this fixed form of relation as a 'closed' system. At the opposite end is the system I've been describing, which is totally 'open', in that sources of evidence of achievement may be from curricular or extra-curricular activities, provided they are relevant to the grid. In between is what I refer to as a 'tied' system, in which some of the objectives of the curriculum which bear on each grid statement are identified, but there is also scope for others to be used should a student have done those activities. Thus the profile is left fairly open from the student's point of view, while making some reference to the general statement which in turn relates to the curriculum. It is likely that the City and Guilds will move towards this middle position of identifying particular activities within the curriculum that relate to particular parts of the profile. It remains essential to have the student fully involved,

A framework for profiling systems

Context	Academic	Vocational+	Pre-vocational*
Function	Formative (Counselling)	Summative (Reference)	Both*
System	Open*	Closed	Tied+
Participants	Student	Staff	
Content	Attitudes/ dispositions	General abilities*	Specific abilities*
Evidence	Formal tests+	Set work+	Observed activities*
Standard	Non-standard	Local standard	National standard*
Format	Free	Pre-specified check list*	Pre-specified grid*

* Current CGLI system
+ Likely future developments

Fig.8.4 *A framework for profiling systems.*

and for permissible evidence to come from any objective source where 'objective' means 'can be corroborated by at least one responsible person'. Evidence could be the result of a test, it could be the result of some kind of set work, or it could be some observed activity. In the profiling system currently in use, all these are possible information inputs.

Another important issue in profiling is the role of central bodies in relation to individual schools and colleges. In Figure 8.2 there is a box which refers to staff development and monitoring. These are very closely related activities in the sense that they reinforce each other. One element of the pilot schemes was to swap formative profiles between centres so that the recipients could see what other people were doing and comment on their profiles, and in return receive comments on their own profiles. It reassured the staff involved that they were not alone with the problems they faced and they could pick up ideas from what other people were doing. Such communication channels can provide a lot of mutual support when undertaking the new demands profiling makes.

Another important aspect is the need to create some degree of uniformity in the profiles, so that the final profile has as much credibility and recognition as possible. In order to achieve such status in the face of competition from other kinds of certificate, it is very desirable that the profile operates on a wider basis than the individual school or college concerned. The City and Guilds profiling system has adopted a 'process validation' approach. In effect, this guarantees that the mechanics of the system are being operated reasonably well, but does not guarantee every individual statement on every profile. That is up to the centre itself. So in that sense validation is a joint effort.

It is apparent from what I have said that, like other authors in this volume, I do not feel that the precise format of the various profiles is in itself critical, as long as it reflects certain principles. If, for example, there are different sources of validation, such as the City and Guilds itself, the school, and maybe the individual youngsters, then each of these elements should have different sections of the profile. Similarly there should be a further sub-division of the profile where radically different sources of evidence are being used. Thus, for example, test results which themselves have some sort of recognition should be treated in one section, and kept separate from statements of experience which should occupy another section.

One might anticipate the emergence of diverging models: a student-centred 'open' system for use where several curricula are being pursued in parallel (or, alternatively, where there is no curriculum as such), and course- or scheme-centred profiles based on specified objectives or programmes of work. These latter profiles may be independent or they may be secondary to an abstract profile of the type discussed above.

RECENT DEVELOPMENTS

Some of the foregoing suggestions about further developments in profiling are now taking tangible form. A student-centred general abilities profiling system is being piloted in schools. And a course-based profiling system has been devised for the Certificate of Pre-Vocational Education (CPVE).

Fourth and fifth formers are taking part in the schools' pilot, with termly and half-termly reviews respectively. The familiar logistical problems of scheduling the reviews have again surfaced as the principal barrier to successful implementation. However, two facilities being tried within the project show promise of minimising the paperwork aspect of reviews (though not the counselling aspect). Firstly, logbooks have been designed to be 'interactive' in that the students can analyse their entries for themselves in terms of the profile. Secondly, profiling software has been devised as a substitute for written records of progress. This software permits computer printout of profile reports based on 'best consistent performance'. It was intended that entries to the progress profiles be made jointly by student and tutor at a review. However, the interesting idea has been mooted that students should be able to make entries at any time and that the latter are merely edited at the review.

The formats of formative profiles and summative records of achievement are moving further apart, reflecting their differing functions. The grid (or checklist) style of profile serves to provide an effective map for plotting progress that is both motivating and orientating in its effects. By contrast the record of achievement picks out only the student's best consistent performance, thus eliminating a lot of redundant and possibly misleading information for third parties. Most importantly, each 'can do X' statement is followed by one or more concrete instances. The latter serve to interpret the former, so that these need no longer be regarded as standardised statements. Thus the formative grid becomes merely a piece of scaffolding which enables best consistent performance to be identified; the scaffolding can then be removed.

The CPVE provides a good example of current thinking in this respect. It embraces a fully fledged formative and summative profiling system based on both a personal reviewing system and a bank of summative 'can do X' statements. The structure of this bank reflects the ten core areas of CPVE. There will be a dozen or so statements for each area and these will be organised as several sets of hierarchically related statements, with some left over 'stand alone' statements. Thus each printed-out profile report will contain only those statements corresponding to best performance. These statements are intended to be standardised by linking them to key tasks in various contexts. Hence they could form the basis of grade-related criteria, should it prove desirable to discern 'levels' of achievement.

The profile of 'can do X' statements will be complemented by a separate Summary of Experience. This document will summarise a selection of items of work, details of which will be contained in the student's portfolio. The reviews will be used to monitor the portfolio and to identify progress in each core area by using the bank of statements as a checklist.

Clearly the CPVE profile is course-centred in that it reflects course objectives by means of standardised statements of achievement. This implies that the CPVE system will make additional demands on staff (compared with the student-centred approach described above), as tasks set for students must be analysed absolutely, rather than relatively, with regard to the profile statements. To ensure uniformity of interpretation of these standard statements, a considerable growth industry of moderation can be anticipated. This problem could be contained by limiting standardisation to those core areas most easily treated in this way. But this would risk devaluing the remaining areas. Again, it is possible that computer software could be of assistance. The CPVE bank could be considered to be a master profile, which may be translated wholesale into contextualised versions for formative use. It would be easier for centres to treat these more concrete versions uniformly. A microcomputer might then be used to summon up an appropriate version for each student; but such developments are still in the future.

LOOKING AHEAD

To conclude, there is a need to develop more streamlined solutions to the problem of generating reliable, descriptive records of achievement, whilst preserving considerable formative benefit. For student-centred profiling, this is likely to take the form of log-book-keeping combined with periodic updating (by students) of computer-based reports, and the issue of reports using custom-built software. For course-based profiling, there will be greater reliance on the preliminary analysis of selected tasks (or of entire programmes of work) in terms of a profile of learning objectives for that course or training scheme. In such cases, task sheets (containing the analyses) and computer software will provide for record-keeping and reporting respectively. Thus both types of profiling system might dispense with progress profiles as described in the body of this chapter, though reviewing would remain a central feature. Such streamlining can be expected to encourage the more widespread use of the types of profiling systems described above. Without it, the development of profiling is likely to be significantly impeded. Creative thinking about practicalities is no less important than the educational vision itself.

REFERENCES

Beadle, P. (1984) *How Young People use their Final Profile Reports*. London: CGLI.

Guardian (1985) Education Guardian, 24.1.85.

Stratton, N.J. (1983) *An Evaluation of a Basic Abilities Profiling System across a Range of Educational and Training Provision (Report for CGLI Profiling Project 3)*. London: CGLI.

The views expressed in this chapter are those of the author and not necessarily the policy of the City and Guilds of London Institute.

9

The Oxford Certificate of Educational Achievement

ALAN WILLMOTT

The Oxford Certificate of Educational Achievement has received perhaps more publicity than any other single 'records of achievement' initiative. It was one of the earliest schemes to combine exam board, local authority and university interests and it has introduced some radical new ideas into the 'records of achievement' debate. It is now one of the DES-funded pilot schemes. Writing from his position at the centre of OCEA development, Alan Willmott reviews the progress that has been made to date and some of the lessons that have been learned along the way.

—Editor

Only a few years ago the Oxford Certificate was not even dreamt of; only, perhaps, dreamt about. Many leading educationists had for some time been concerned that all five years at secondary school achieved for the vast majority of children was a recognition of failure. Many felt the examination system needed a major shake-up. But it was the combination of university, local authority and examination board interests which put flesh onto the bones of this dissatisfaction and led to the institution of the Oxford Certificate of Educational Achievement, late in 1982.

The Oxford Certificate of Educational Achievement (OCEA) consists of three different parts. The 'E-component' of OCEA consists of the record of results of external examinations, GCE, CSE, music grades, BTEC awards and so on. The 'G-component', which in the heady days of November/December 1982 consisted of graded tests, very rapidly became converted into graded assessments for reasons which I will go into later. The subject areas covered are English, mathematics, science and modern languages. Finally there is the 'P-component', which is a record of a student's achievements and experiences, formative during the years at school, and summative when leaving or changing school/college. It has been agreed that OCEA should be available from age 10–11, and also be available beyond age sixteen.

The collaborators in this development are the Oxford Delegacy (the University of Oxford Delegacy of Local Examinations—the Oxford GCE Board), the University of Oxford Department of Educational Studies, and four LEAs—Coventry, Leicestershire, Oxfordshire and Somerset. The real work of OCEA is being done by teachers seconded from the four authorities to work full-time on OCEA. The four LEAs each second one teacher to each of the five areas I have mentioned (that is, the four subject areas plus the personal component). We have, therefore, 20 teachers working full-time on OCEA.

OCEA is an initiative designed to offer a comprehensive response to the whole spectrum of achievement and experience in schools. It will be comprehensive because it will incorporate a description of the student's experiences, attainments, interests and skills; because it will offer a detailed description of achievement initially in the four key curriculum areas of mathematics, English, science and modern languages; because it will provide a record of external examination results achieved by the student throughout his or her school career, and because students will take an active part in the assessment and description of their own development.

THE 'G-COMPONENT'

Each of the four subject areas has a very different approach to the development of graded assessments. In English it has proved difficult to determine what graded assessment really means, and whether, indeed, such an approach is even possible in this subject. Pilot work is continuing an attempt to resolve these questions. The English group are developing 'features' on aspects of the English curriculum, and we will be looking at achievements within each of those features by means of criteria which are explicit descriptions of what each achievement entails within each feature.

In the case of science the curriculum, and assessments, will be concerned with skills and processes. The content of the curriculum of science education is seen to be the concern, as at present, of existing 16+ examinations. This emphasises a currently pressing problem, namely the co-existence of 16+ and graded assessments, both from the point of view of the Examination Board and (more specifically) as far as teachers in the classroom are concerned.

In mathematics, as in English, the idea is to have a number of 'features', perhaps at different levels. Individual features could be calculating, measuring, communicating information about data, communicating spatial information and so on. Again, the graded assessments would very much be based on a skills and processes, problem-solving type of approach, and not explicitly based on content.

In modern languages we thought the generation of graded assessments would be much easier because in our four authorities, Oxfordshire had OMLAC (the Oxfordshire Modern Languages Achievement Certificate), Somerset had the South-West Credit Scheme, Coventry was using the London-based 'Eclair', and Leicestershire was using the East Midlands Graded Assessment Scheme (EMGRAS) in modern languages. Actually, this diversity caused many problems, simply because of the amount of commitment to development which was very much from the bottom up, looking at the lower levels first. In modern languages, the approach was initially exactly the opposite and started with level 4, the top level. The reason for this was simply the need to work at something new, which could act as a unifying agent to bring the authorities together. More recently modern languages has, like English, abandoned the 'top down' approach in favour of an 'across the curriculum' approach. The emphasis is on the development of communicative competence in modern languages and, as far as possible, all assessment procedures should exclude activities with little resemblance to the use of a foreign language in a real life context.

THE 'P-COMPONENT'

The 'P-component' of OCEA is very different. All the other steering committees first met in February/March 1983, but the 'P-component' came somewhat later. The reason for this was quite simply that we thought it was the most important area; the most important and probably the most difficult also. For these reasons we wanted to make sure that we started off on the right foot. There was a great deal of discussion at this initial stage from which emerged agreement that the aims of the 'P-component' should be to allow students to talk about themselves using a wider term of reference than the examination-based curriculum allows. The 'P-component' aims to establish forms of continuous formative recording; to open up wider possibilities of curriculum structure, teaching methods and relationships between school and student; and to provide users with a wider description of the student's achievement.

There are a number of questions about the 'P-component' which need to be tackled. For whom is the 'P-component' intended? Certainly the student is one of the key people for whom it is intended, but this in turn raises the issue of the formative/summative link and the fact that the formative documentation is not the summative document. What should be the relation between them? Are both equally the OCEA 'P-component'? If it is the formative part then it is very much with the student and of course the teacher. If it is the summative part then there must be a wider audience. What should be the content? Experiences? Responsibilities? Interests? Aspirations? Competences? How should the record be made? Who makes the summative record? How is the 'P-component' going to be validated?

VALIDATION AND ACCREDITATION WITHIN OCEA

The position at the moment as far as the Oxford Delegacy is concerned is that with the graded assessments, the Examination Board will set up and run an appropriate system to moderate the assessments. Thus, if a certificate says a student has attained level 2 in mathematics, the board will be able to define what this refers to and describe the basis for assessment. Such an approach implies a certain amount of moderation on the part of the Delegacy. For the 'P-component' the intention is quite different. At the present time we are moving, like the scheme described by Burgess and Adams in Chapter 6, towards a system of accrediting centres and in this context a model such as that used by the CNAA has been suggested as one possibility. Such a system would indicate whether the institution had the appropriate mechanisms, and appropriate experience, to be able to set up and operate an appropriate recording system. The final certificate will report the information which is sent to the Delegacy by the school. Thus the Delegacy needs to be in a position to state that it has reasonable confidence that the information for the 'P-component' has been produced according to an accredited system. In no way can the 'P-component' be moderated in the same way as the graded assessments in the 'G-component'.

There was much discussion in the early days of OCEA about the relationship between the three parts: the E-component, the G-component and the P-component. In 1983 we agreed that, much as some might wish to see these three parts as being separate, basically they were three facets of the same thing. The student is a person and the certificate is a collation of the summative information about him or her. We are thus moving towards the position where we say that OCEA is a concept which is either taken as a whole or not at all. This would then not permit a school to participate and take, for example, just the graded assessments in mathematics. OCEA is increasingly regarded as a package in which schools will take the three components together.

The first pilot schemes for OCEA began in September 1985 in each of the four local authorities, involving a substantial amount of material available for each of the four 'G-component' subject areas and a trial of the 'P-component'. By September 1987, the scheme will be nationally available to any school which is interested.

THE IMPLICATIONS OF OCEA

Clearly this scheme poses some difficult questions. What are the implications of a negotiated curriculum and personal record upon student/teacher and student/adult relationships? How does any accreditation system achieve respectability with employers, parents and students? What are the INSET needs and how can a local education authority (LEA), best respond? It is significant that OCEA is a development based on an existing Examination Board. One of the things that Alan Evans comments on in Chapter 12 is the relationship between the committee structure of an existing board and the development that might take place on graded assessments or records of achievement. I can say that the OCEA team within the Oxford Delegacy has no links with formal GCE committee structures (e.g. the subject panels for 'O' level and 'A' level examinations). The development is LEA-led, teacher-driven, and is thus from the bottom up; for these reasons it is very healthy and this cannot be overstressed.

Another significant question concerns what the school accreditation criteria should be. Who says the school is, or is not, accredited? The LEA? The Examination Board? In one sense the answer to that question is obvious; it must be the LEA. In another sense the question is also obvious, it must be the Examination Board. Should OCEA begin in the primary school? Should out-of-school experiences be included? And what about the inclusion of aspirations? What about the relationship between the 'P-component' and 'G-component'? And how about the relationship between the 'G-component' and the 'E-component'? The latter is a major issue at the moment.

OCEA AND THE FUTURE

I would like to conclude this review with a description of at least one of our wildest dreams. At an HMI invitational conference held in 1984 to discuss the draft policy statement on Records of Achievement, Barry Taylor, the Chief Education Officer for Somerset said, 'The [curriculum] genie is now out of the bottle'. I wish to agree strongly with this statement. As this book testifies, developments similar to OCEA are happening all over the country and it is too late now to turn the clock back. There is a tremendous amount of interest and drive building up within the profession. I have used the phrases 'teacher-driven' and 'LEA-led'. In the Examination Board, we are conscious of the fact that we are, in a sense, in a very honoured position to be involved. As the curriculum genie runs out of the bottle, it brings about change that cannot be undone.

It is likely that, as a result of OCEA work in particular and other work in general, existing 16+ examinations will become increasingly irrelevant to the needs of students in schools. The teachers involved in the OCEA research and development groups are involved in curriculum change. They recognise that, for the last thirty years or more, at least as far as GCE is concerned, we have been paying lip service to the fact that examinations must follow the curriculum and not dictate it, knowing full well that what goes on in the schools must be that which is in the syllabus (at least in years four and five). What OCEA has done is to recognise that this situation cannot be changed but that methods of 'graded' assessment can be devised which will actually have a beneficial effect on what goes on in school. In other words, OCEA is quite unashamedly, an assessment-led curriculum development project.

It is also likely that relationships between teachers and students, and between teachers, will be changed for the better as a result of the need to increase communication and contact within the 'P-component'. As several of the contributors to this book have stressed, the teacher will have to know the student to be able to negotiate the student's personal record. Teachers will have to collaborate with each other much more in order to get some feeling of what is happening. And it is also true that students will be assessed when they and their teachers judge they are to be assessed. No longer will a student need to wait five years only to be told that he or she is a failure. With graded assessments taken when the student is ready, this could actually affect quite markedly the organisation of a school. A possible consequence—still a relatively new idea for OCEA—is that the school as an administrative learning unit may not in fifteen or twenty years' time be quite what we know and love today. The people who are involved with developing OCEA feel that this is in fact something that, unconsciously perhaps, they are working towards.

When starting out on a task which is difficult to achieve, fundamental in its concept, involves many interested parties, and is by its nature based on long-term development, it may be that if the job is worth doing it is worth doing badly in the first instance. OCEA is not perfect and will probably still be far from that when it is available as a national scheme in 1987. Nevertheless, we feel that the need for action is so urgent that it is worth having something which is not perfect as soon as is reasonably possible, rather than spending another ten years doing research and never actually grasping the nettle.

It is quite clear that resources are likely to be crucial to the successful implementation of OCEA. This may or may not mean extra money, but it certainly means in-service training. The three parts of OCEA have an integrity, and there are implications for in-service training especially when the 'P-component' is considered. What will be needed is an element of counselling, which is something that many teachers do not have experience of at the moment. Thus the provision of resources may mean some kind of organisational response to meet this need. LEAs may well feel it is not worth supporting the initiative in just one school, but where there are, for example, three schools not too distant from each other, it might be much more worthwhile to share the necessary training and resources.

Another important resource, at least in the pilot authorities, would be the teachers who have been involved in the development work. By the time we have been going for four or five years, our four authorities will each have something like 20 teachers who have been through the development process. They could be a core to provide in-service training. In addition, each teacher in each of the five areas—four subjects plus the 'P-component'—has behind him or her an authority reference group involving some 20–30 teachers from schools and colleges in the area. So, far from having just 20 teachers involved with development, we actually have something approaching 600 commenting on our work. This is a tremendously good base for getting feedback.

POSTSCRIPT

In this chapter, which is based on a transcript of a talk given in February 1984 at the University of Bristol, I have tried to describe the basis on which OCEA was founded and to look at current and future work. I have also explored what seem to me to be some of the implications of our work. Although OCEA is in a constant state of development, and has progressed considerably in the past two years, the basic structure has not changed since its initial inception. Increasing the P-component is being seen as the heart of an integrated approach to student learning. We now also have GCSE on the horizon with its criteria-related grades to replace existing GCE and CSE examinations at 16+; this will provide an interesting backdrop to current work on records of achievement, given that both initiatives enjoy explicit DES support. They may well prove increasingly contradictory as OCEA continues to grow and develop. The only thing that is certain at this stage is that constant change is here to stay.

10

Instituting Records of Achievement at County Level:

The Dorset/Southern Regional Examinations Board Assessment and Profiling Project

DAVID GARFORTH

This chapter describes another of the DES-funded pilot schemes on records of achievement. It is very different from OCEA, however, in that it represents the efforts of just one local education authority and its associated CSE Examination Board to institute a county-wide record of achievement. This model is likely to be much replicated in the implementation of profiling schemes in the future, and the approach adopted within Dorset, as outlined here by David Garforth (himself a leading figure in its design), has much to recommend it.

—Editor

Background to the Project

Dorset has been developing an interest in profiling over a number of years, and began drawing together exploratory initiatives in some of its schools with the secondment of a teacher from April 1982 to September 1983 to research into existing practices concerning the recording of student progress in schools and colleges on a national basis. As a result of this, a school-focussed INSET workshop manual was published

(Garforth, 1983), designed to assist individual schools in the design and implementation of schemes for recording pupil progress and achievement. The manual has commanded considerable attention both within and outside the Authority (the Dorset LEA).

Concurrently with the publication of the manual in September 1983, the Authority published its curriculum policy statement (Dorset LEA, 1983), which commended to schools a flexible approach to curriculum planning and recording pupil progress and achievement, in order to respond fully to the diversity of needs of individual pupils. County recognition of the potential value of profiling in realising these aims has led directly to the mounting of the Assessment and Profiling Project which is an essential pillar for the promotion of the aims of the County Curriculum Policy Statement in Dorset schools. In this project it is argued that curriculum and assessment objectives should be jointly planned, developed and evaluated.

OUTLINE OF THE PROJECT

The project is being mounted in collaboration with the Southern Regional Examinations Board (SREB). Over a period of four years from September 1984, all Dorset schools will be involved in the development of schemes for recording pupil progress and achievement.

The project is concerned with all four of the purposes identified in the 1984 Policy Statement on Records of Achievement (DES, 1984), namely to recognise achievement, to contribute to motivation and personal development, to encourage a review of curriculum and organisation and to produce a document of record. However, the Dorset scheme has as its main thrust the third of these, the review of curriculum and assessment.

As the Authority considers that this is properly the remit of individual schools, and part of the professional responsibility of teachers, one of the main features of the project is that the review of current practice and development of recording schemes is school-based. The interrelationship in the project between the review of curriculum and assessment, guided by the county's curriculum statement, and the development of profiling/records of achievement cannot be too heavily stressed. The variety of approaches that will emerge will be carefully coordinated through a 'cluster group' arrangement of schools working together, under the direction of a project director and small central team. From this, more general guidelines and criteria for developing recording schemes will be produced.

Such an approach should ensure that school individuality and diversity are accommodated, that all teachers are actively involved in and committed to the development, and that staff training needs are identified and responded to throughout the project.

The potential replicability of this approach is being tested within the project through a two-phase structure, whereby approximately half the county's secondary schools will be involved in the first two years, and their experience will form the basis for an extension to remaining schools in the last two years of the project.

BROAD AIMS AND OBJECTIVES

The overall aims are:
(a) to explore approaches to recording pupil achievement within the five curriculum areas of the Dorset curriculum policy statement (language; mathematics; science; personal and social education; aesthetic, creative and physical education), together with the areas of cross-curricular skills, personal and social skills and extra-curricular achievements and experiences;
(b) to explore the implications of records of achievement with regard to the learning and assessment process in schools, institutional structures and practices and examination board practice.

Main Issues

Within the aims, there are a number of key issues which the project is addressing:

1. *The potential of profiling and records of achievement as a tool for reappraising curriculum provision and assessment practice.*
2. *The effects and implications of introducing profiling and records of achievement on classroom practice.*
3. *The particular difficulties of recording personal achievements and qualities.* The project approaches recording in this area by separating personal and social skills from achievements and experiences gained outside the main secondary curriculum.
4. *The validation and moderation of records of achievement.* Echoing

some of the ideas Burgess and Adams set out in Chapter 6, the project involves the establishment of a validation board within each school to monitor the development and operation of profiles and records of achievement. Representation will include the practitioners, members of the governing body, the local education authority, the SREB, employers and parents. Evaluation of the effectiveness of this model of 'supportive validation', in terms of acceptability to users, will be part of the project.

5. *The potential of records of achievement in credit transfer within and between institutions and courses, particularly at 16+.* This involves the issues of storage, retrieval and transfer of data and the relationship of records of achievement to the secondary examinations system and to the GCSE national/general criteria and grade-related criteria as they are developed during the project's life.

   Use of the records in progression to and selection for post-sixteen provision such as GCE 'A' levels, CPVE, YTS and vocational courses will be explored.

6. *The relationship between formative and summative forms of recording progress and achievement.* This includes addressing the issue of relating internal school reports to periodic reports to parents.

7. *The potential of profiling and records of achievement in different parts of the education service* (e.g. their relative merits in secondary and further education, at 11+ and 14+, and in schools providing for those with special educational needs). These are issues which the diversity of institutions participating will allow the project to explore.

8. *The effects and implications of introducing profiling and records of achievement on institutional structures and practices* (e.g. on planning curriculum provision, on inter-departmental liaison, on organisation and staffing).

PROJECT PRINCIPLES

Each institution has accepted the following principles for the development of a profile and a record of achievement. (The term 'profile' will be used to describe the system of recording student progress during the learning process. The term 'record of achievement' will be used for the summative statement of achievements on completion of studies.)

1. The profile and record of achievement are for all students in the year group.

2. There is to be not only a record of achievement, which presents a picture of a student on leaving full-time education, but also a profile which assists the student in the learning process.
3. The student is to be fully involved in the process of compiling the profile.
4. The profile is to be developed in detail during the final two years of compulsory education, though the school needs to consider the assessment and recording and reporting procedures over the whole age range.
5. The profile will consist of:
   (a) subject assessments;
   (b) cross-curricular skills;
   (c) personal and social skills;
   (d) achievements and experiences.
6. Although the formative profile may be used for diagnostic purposes and may therefore identify both areas of strength and weakness, the record of achievement will consist only of positive comments.
7. The school will develop a validation procedure which will guide and monitor the development and operation of the work and will be a joint process involving the school, the LEA, the SREB, parents and employers.
8. The concept of a student's overall success or failure is to be avoided.
9. Although the student may make contributions to the profile and the record of achievement, the ultimate responsibility for their compilation remains with the school.
10. On completion, the record of achievement will become the property of the student.
11. The major potential users are to be actively involved in the development work in the schools.

THE DEVELOPMENT PROCESS

Over the four years of the project's life, from its inception in September 1984, there will be two major phases each characterised by a different development focus.

Phase One

This will last up to August 1986, and will involve 24 secondary institutions in one year of reviewing curriculum provision and assessment techniques and one year of piloting and modifying these.

An interim evaluation report will be prepared which will include the emerging key criteria for the development of profiles and records of achievement, together with problems encountered and lessons learnt. This will serve as the basis for Phase Two schools development.

Phase Two

Phase Two, which will run from September 1986 to August 1988, will involve the remaining 22 secondary institutions in the county in one year's planning and development, and a further year's implementation and modification. The experience and expertise developed in Phase One will be utilised in a 'cascade' effect by involving school coordinators from Phase One schools as 'accredited tutors' for Phase Two schools.

The strategy should ensure that there is a planned and phased authority programme which will use resources effectively to assist every secondary school in the design and implementation of profiles and records of achievement. The programme should ensure also that the proper emphasis is placed upon the development of assessment expertise of teachers in the schools through the provision of extensive in-service training (INSET) during the four years. This in-service provision is the key to the success of the project. The model makes it possible to bring together, into a unified INSET programme for the development of assessment expertise of teachers, all the different but related initiatives involving new forms of assessment, including GCSE and CPVE.

At county level an Advisory Committee will guide and manage the project during the development and evaluation stages. This committee has wide representation involving the Authority, the Examinations Board, practitioners in the schools, HMI, the careers service and industry and commerce. This committee will work in conjunction with a County Advisory Assessment team, which has been created under the management of the Project Director to provide assistance for schools during the development work and evaluation stages. The team carries a general responsibility for the overall design and development of the profiles and records of achievement but members carry a specific responsibility to develop techniques of assessment and recording for

each of the curriculum areas of the County Curriculum Policy Statement.

The schools are organised into four cluster groups. The strategy has
been designed to enable schools and colleges to develop mutual
support systems. Individual departments will be able to discuss and
develop their ideas with similar departments from other schools in the
cluster. The cluster is an in-service device designed to assist and
provide supportive expertise for colleagues facing similar problems. It
is hoped that the structure will facilitate the dissemination of good
practice. The development work in the individual school is directed by
the School Coordinator. The School Coordinator is released from the
school (encouraged by a small staffing subsidy to each school) on a
nominated afternoon each week to attend cluster meetings, in order
that experiences may be shared and information exchanged. Each
school has nominated in addition a Coordinator for each of the five
major curriculum areas already identified. These Coordinators generally form a development group in each institution.

The project institutions cover a wide range of experience and
background, and this enables an exploration of the potential of profiles
in a variety of contexts. The range of institutions include:

(a) a 5–16 Special School for children with moderate learning difficul-
     ties;
(b) a variety of single sex selective schools;
(c) a variety of comprehensive schools;
(d) a Tertiary College, and
(e) a College of Further Education.

INSTITUTIONAL DEVELOPMENT

The central feature of the project is that it is school-focused. The
responsibility of the Authority and the Examination Board is to
provide support to the school through an effective and dynamic
partnership at an operational level. This process is a continuing one
over the course of the project. As profiles are developed they are being
modified as a result of constant curriculum evaluation. Each school is
undertaking a similar programme of development, but the emphasis
and pace of the development varies from institution to institution. The
main features of this development programme are:

(a) a systematic programme for institutional self-evaluation;

(b) the development of key criteria;
(c) detailed planning of the constituent parts;
(d) an evaluation of the implications for the institution resulting from implementation;
(e) dissemination of information to all those involved in the development, and
(f) an evaluation of the scheme resulting in appropriate modifications.

The responsibility for the design of the profile and record of achievement lies with each institution, but both must contain the following four elements.

1. Subject assessment

This area is the key to the institutional development. It lies at the heart of the curriculum process in the classroom. The development operates at two levels, departmental and institutional. It is the responsibility of the institution to design the curriculum objectives and assessment objectives in such a way that they fulfil the aims of the institution. The departmental objectives need to be compatible with the overall institutional objectives. Relating the assessment objectives closely to the curriculum objectives enables the recording process to support pupils' learning, as well as assisting teachers in their evaluation of curriculum provision.

2. Cross-curricular skills

There are a number of fundamental skills which are common to learning in a variety of curricular areas. If a pupil experiences difficulties mastering any of these skills, learning difficulties are compounded across the curriculum. The inclusion of such skills in the assessment objectives should enable cross-departmental discussion to occur, which should benefit institutional curricular appraisal and individual pupil progress.

3. Personal and social skills

The promotion of these skills is commonly accepted as part of the educational process at a departmental and institutional level. They should form an important element in the discussion between teacher and pupil.

4. Achievements and experiences

Learning does not only take place in a classroom during specified periods but in many situations internally and externally, curricular and extra-curricular, planned and unplanned.

How these components relate to each other is for the individual institution to decide.

Monitoring and Evaluation

A programme of formative evaluation is seen as an integral part of the project's development work, to ensure that the lessons emerging from the first phase of the project can be fully utilised in the second phase, and to explore whether the development strategies can effectively be transferred to and replicated by other institutions. The evaluation programme will be important in order to provide evidence for effective dialogue with other Local Education Authorities and with other practitioners involved in national developments.

THE DORSET SCHEME IN RELATION TO NATIONAL INITIATIVES

The Dorset/SREB Assessment and Profiling Project has been selected as one of the DES pilot projects 'to provide information on how best to set about recording pupils' achievements and prepare the way for the establishment of national guidelines which can provide a basis for introducing Records of Achievement throughout England and Wales'.

During the development period, teachers will also be concerned with the planning and implementation of the GCSE. It is the intention of the authority that the GCSE and the development of records of achievement should be seen as complementary parts of one package. The existence of the criteria for the GCSE has already provided valuable insights into the issue of designing the criteria for the record of achievement, and teachers are already perceiving the possibility that the detailed recording of pupil progress during the learning process may provide important evidence for the teacher-assessed component of the GCSE.

The Dorset curriculum policy statement has attempted to resolve the issues of breadth, balance, relevance and differentiation of the curriculum at an institutional level; the development of effective profiles and records of achievement will assist the evaluation of the success of such a strategy at the individual pupil level. The strategy of jointly planning, developing and evaluating curriculum and assessment objectives should also ensure that there is progression, internal coherence and continuity of curriculum provision at institutional, departmental and individual pupil levels.

TRANSLATING PHILOSOPHY INTO PRACTICE

As the work of the project approaches the end of the first year, there are already several important issues which have emerged.

First, the Dorset initiative is a very radical approach requiring a re-appraisal of the fundamental aims, philosophies and objectives of the institution, collectively and individually. If the assessment objectives are not to be bolt-on components, unconnected to the curriculum objectives, it is essential that these fundamental issues are tackled and resolved. It is already clear that the preparatory design stage will take longer than one year. Indeed, many institutions may require two years of thorough review and detailed planning before they are ready to implement the scheme. It is, however, vital that the staff experience this process if the profiles are to have effective and lasting implications for the educational processes in our institutions.

Second, it is apparent that there are large-scale INSET implications for any similar initiative. Considerable enthusiasm from teachers has already been displayed, along with a willingness to tackle the issues. Teachers have readily exchanged views and experiences and have indicated a desire to learn. However, many teachers are not equipped with the skills needed to carry through the work. There is much to be done to assist teachers in terms of translating aims into curriculum objectives, specifying assessment objectives, developing assessment skills, designing appropriate methods of recording, and finally bringing all this together into a coherent pattern which achieves the institutional aims. These are all areas which require considerable support.

Third, one of the most obvious obstacles to change is the traditional structure of our schools. It is clear that more flexible organisational arrangements will be necessary if the aims are to be realised. This applies both at institutional level and at the level of classroom teaching.

Fourth, the issue of available time arises; this is related to the issue of structure. It will not be possible to introduce such radical changes in our schools in addition to existing practices. There must be a thorough review of existing assessment, recording and reporting practices for the individual teacher and in respect of the institution. The development of profiles must take the place of many existing practices. It will be important for the issue of classroom management to be considered in this context. There will need to be a reappraisal of the methods and frequency of assessment in the classroom.

The work completed to date has confirmed the Authority's view that the initiative should be principally school-focused. There are no ready solutions to any of these issues; they must be resolved individually within each institution. The work has also confirmed that the programme must be developmental and not static. But continuing to underpin the various institutional initiatives are the basic principles upon which the scheme as a whole is built, namely that the development of profiles and records of achievement must:

(a) assist the pupil in the learning process;
(b) assist teachers in an evaluation of the curricular provision at departmental and institutional level;
(c) provide information for other users.

These principles are unlikely to change whatever the next few years' development work reveals, for they constitute the core of the Dorset initiative.

REFERENCES

Department of Education and Science (1984) *Records of Achievement: A Statement of Policy*. London: HMSO.
Dorset LEA (1983) *Five to Sixteen: A Statement of Dorset Policy for the School Curriculum*. Dorchester: Dorset LEA.
Garforth, D. (1983) *Profile Assessment: Recording Student Progress. A School-focussed INSET Workshop Manual*. Dorchester: Dorset LEA.

11

Instituting Profiling Within a School

GLORIA HITCHCOCK

The final chapter in Part 2 is perhaps most characteristic of the profiles movement to date, since it concerns the implementation of profiling within individual schools without external support. Most of the momentum generated within the profiles movement has come from initiatives of this kind and the efforts made by individual institutions, sometimes linked together in consortia, to develop their own schemes. Whilst it is now increasingly the case that profile development is being supported by external agencies and external funding, without the commitment of individual teachers and institutions the movement has no hope of fulfilling the goals that are so clearly stated in the different chapters of this book. Thus Gloria Hitchcock's analysis of what can and must be done to facilitate this process at the level of the individual school provides a vital and timely concluding chapter to this part of the book.

—Editor

Profiles are the latest educational boom industry—one of the very few growth areas in a time of falling rolls, financial stringency, and contraction. Are they merely a bandwagon or are they here to stay? If they are here to stay, what are the implications for individual schools, and what has to be done in practical terms?

One thing seems certain: if profiles *do* gain general acceptance there are clear implications for the curriculum. For years the secondary school curriculum has been constrained within a straitjacket determined by the requirements of external examinations. Profiling offers the opportunity for teachers to look beyond these constraints to the whole pupil— to look not only at academic skills, but at practical, social and cross-curricular skills, and at personal qualities. When these areas are included in formal assessment the curriculum will inevitably broaden. It will be necessary to provide opportunities for young people to acquire and demonstrate qualities such as leadership, initiative, and perseverance. The very act of including in assessment a wider range of skills and qualities is likely to result in their being accorded a greater degree of importance within schools than ever before. Thus profiling, if taken on by a school, is likely to lead to major changes in curriculum and organisation. It is not something to be taken on lightly.

Before schools embark upon profiling, therefore, it may be helpful to ask three questions:

1. Why should we go to all the bother of introducing profiles?
2. What are the difficulties we are likely to encounter?
3. How might we overcome these difficulties?

WHY BOTHER?

Leaving aside the fact that the DES is likely to require all school-leavers to be provided with a record of achievement by the late 1980s, why should teachers in schools feel that it is worth the undoubted effort involved in developing a school profiling system for themselves?

Reasons advanced by teachers in schools which have already entered the field vary from the idealistic end of the continuum (self-development of the individual) to the mechanistic (better reports for job-selection). One of the most familiar motives for profiling is teachers' belief that every young person is entitled to a worthwhile leaving certificate at the end of eleven years of compulsory schooling. The claim for such a certificate has been advanced at regular intervals over the last seventy years, but it appears to be closer to realisation now than ever before.

The potential that profiles have to motivate young people is another persuasive argument in their favour. Many of those advocating the introduction of profiles into schools believe that pupils should be helped towards gaining greater self-confidence and a greater degree of self-assurance which will better prepare them for life in the adult world. With the growth in youth unemployment and the demand for ever higher qualifications, new ways of motivating young people are called for. The old tradition that 'if you work hard at school you'll get a good job' has lost credibility with many pupils, and teachers frequently face a difficult task in maintaining the interest and motivation of their pupils.

Profiles offer pupils the chance to experience and enjoy success, resulting from the recognition of their achievements. Such recognition of success is self-perpetuating, and hopefully as a result pupils will develop increased levels of motivation in school, leading towards their becoming more self-reliant, autonomous adults.

Allied to this increase in motivation is the role of profiles in placing assessment at the centre of the learning process, where it becomes an aid to diagnosis of pupils' strengths and weaknesses and the basis for dialogue between teacher and pupil. This dialogue is becoming more and more a fundamental part of the profiling process, and it is hoped that the consequent improvement in communication between pupil and teacher will frequently result in improved relationships.

The issues of motivation, reinforcing achievement, helping in diagnostic assessment, and improving communication and relationships are all incorporated within the function of profiles as part of the educational process itself. How they may be provided for within the individual school is illustrated by the case-studies which form the second part of this chapter.

It is clear that the pastoral system of the school has an important place in the development and implementation of profiling. Much of the existing work done in the fields of personal development and guidance can be subsumed into, and can reinforce, profiling, and the pastoral team can provide valuable skills and support for other staff who are less familiar with the kinds of interpersonal skills that profiling requires. On a more mechanistic level, profiles are also seen as being a doorway to improved recording and reporting procedures within the school. In most schools, much effort is currently being expended on the production of a variety of internal and external reports, which may be more effectively brought together under one umbrella. Many schools which have already introduced profiles were persuaded by the need to provide more detailed, more rounded reports for employers than had previously been the case. Many have worked with local employers in the design of such records. It is also hoped that both students and their parents will appreciate these fuller reports.

These are some of the main reasons why schools and colleges which have already embarked upon profiles took the decision. These reasons can be broadly divided into two main categories—those which are pupil-centred and those which are user-centred—each of which present their own challenge to the institution seeking to engage in development, as the next section sets out.

WHAT ARE THE DIFFICULTIES?

It would be naive to imagine that the introduction of profiling into a school will not be accompanied by difficulties. Some of the associated problems are commonly aired, others are less frequently recognised. One of the great dangers is that, in trying to take full advantage of the benefits outlined above, profiles run the risk of attempting to be 'all things to all people' and as a result become a compromise of elements which lack definition, satisfying no-one.

A problem which is less frequently recognised by either pupils or teachers, and which to date has been of greater concern to education theorists, is the potential danger of profiles acting as tools for the exercise of social control. As Hargreaves argues in Chapter 14, youngsters may be socialised into an acceptance of failure through a negotiated consensus. An individual damning assessment can be shrugged off by the pupil as being merely the opinion of a biased or unfair teacher. It can, however, seem as if there is no escape from a judgement reached as a result of views expressed by a number of people, including, perhaps, the youngsters themselves.

Allied to this danger, but more frequently recognised by teachers, is the issue of subjectivity. It is inevitable that we are all influenced by our own prejudices and attitude to life; the opportunity for these prejudices to adversely affect pupils' assessments is magnified by the degree of additional exposure of the individual's personality and character inherent in profiling. This danger is of particular concern in the sensitive area of personal qualities assessment. For this reason some teachers feel that any comment on personal qualities should be excluded from a profile. But this would, I believe, be over-reacting to an extent which is more likely to harm than benefit the individual pupil. For many youngsters, personal qualities assessment is likely to be their strongest attribute.

But, as Alan Evans suggests in Chapter 12, there is little doubt that in the eyes of many teachers the question of the time required for the effective implementation of profiling is of over-riding concern. There is a fear that teachers will be even more over-burdened than they are at present, and in a climate of teacher unrest and dissatisfaction with salary levels and awards, new and potentially threatening innovations are not welcomed by some.

Allied to, but not necessarily synonymous with, reluctance to embark upon profiling because of the time involved, are the problems raised by requiring staff who may not have the requisite skills to engage in either assessment or counselling for effective participation in profiling. In addition (and possibly as a result of this lack of skills), there are the problems caused by asking uncommitted teachers to undertake profiling. It is arguable that pupils who find themselves engaged in profiling with uncommitted teachers may emerge with a worse experience and certificate than they would have enjoyed under the existing system. They may also suffer from the comparison which is made between their profile and one which has been compiled under the guidance of an enthusiastic teacher committed to the concept of profiling. If profiling is to be a curricular element rather than simply a sophisticated form of record-keeping, some attempt to address this issue will be vital to the scheme's success.

Two other issues, which are not necessarily difficulties, will need to be considered by schools embarking upon profiling. The first is that of credibility. Will users grant profiles the degree of credibility required in order for them to gain universal acceptances? Given that profiles are only now coming to be used on any scale, there cannot as yet be reliable evidence on whether employers really will make use of such records. Certainly, as Mansell suggests in Chapter 2, there is evidence that employers will view profile reports favourably since they have, for some time, been calling for more detailed information on potential employees' attributes and personal qualities. It also might be argued that if profiles are intended primarily as tools for the self-development of the young person, such users' views are relatively unimportant. However, to say this is to remove one of the mainstays of the movement to date.

The second issue is concerned with ownership. In answer to the question 'who owns the profile?', most practitioners have already taken the stance that it belongs to the pupil, and the DES statement of July 1984 affirms this principle quite clearly. However, the issue is not quite as straightforward as this implies. There still remain problems associated with who physically keeps the profile during its compilation. To what extent should the material recorded in the profile be available to the school for possible use in references? Is the school entitled to retain copies of the profiles for its own internal records, and to what extent does the pupil control the copyright of material within the profile?

HOW CAN THE DIFFICULTIES BE OVERCOME?

There are a number of alternative strategies which may be adopted in order to ensure the successful development and implementation of profiling and to overcome some, if not all, of the difficulties outlined. I would advocate a combination of four of these strategies:
1. Consultation.
2. Identification.
3. Reorganisation.
4. In-service education.

Consultation

One of the first criteria for successful profiling is that the decision should be endorsed by the staff who will be expected to operate the system. This does not mean that 100 per cent of staff have to record their positive support for profiles—it would be difficult to find any initiative within a school which could command such universal approval. It *does* mean, however, that the steps taken towards profiling should involve teachers in consultation and in full discussion. There should be ample opportunity for teachers to advance suggestions, to air disquiet, and to incorporate the development of profiles within any curriculum development procedures which may exist within the school. Profiling which emerges as a result of an integrated curriculum and assessment policy is much more likely to be viewed by the whole staff as both viable and useful. Where profiling results from an imposed, top-down model, the chances are that the infant will be sickly and weak.

In addition to consultation covering the curriculum and the principles governing policy, consultation with staff could and probably should include factors such as how the timetable might be rearranged in order to accommodate profiling, what is to be included in any prospective profile, what is to be assessed, by whom and how frequently. Consideration of the ways in which the curriculum will need to be enriched and broadened, in order to provide opportunity for development of the skills and qualities to be assessed, also forms an important part of the consultative process. Such consultation should not merely include teaching staff; there is valuable experience and information to be gained from considering the views of parents, employers and the pupils themselves. Finally it can be helpful, as Stratton suggests in Chapter 8, to consult teachers in other schools who have already implemented profiling and whose expertise can be drawn upon in formulating the school's own policy.

As well as facilitating progress in the overall development of a profiling policy, this process of consultation should go some way towards solving some of the difficulties referred to in the first part of this article. For example, recognition of staff concerns, recording of staff suggestions, and the establishment of some consensus view on methods which may be employed to ensure that teachers' workload is minimised, should go a considerable way towards allaying fears about deteriorating conditions of service. Indeed the very act of involvement in the consultative process, whereby the advantages as well as the difficulties associated with profiling are aired, may help to convince uncommitted teachers of the benefits which can accrue, not only to the pupil, but to the teacher.

It would seem unrealistic to expect this consultative, preparatory process to take place over a time span of less than one academic year.

Identification

One of the most important steps following on from consultation is the identification of areas which the school considers to be of prime importance in the development of its profile. It may be, for example, that assessment procedures are deemed to be the area most vitally in need of improvement. Profiles are not, in themselves, methods of assessment—they are simply one way of recording assessment. However, it follows that if assessment within the school is unsound or inadequate, then the resulting profile is likely to suffer from the same defects. The school's assessment policy is inextricably linked with the profile.

It is often the case that when a systematic analysis is undertaken, it becomes clear that there is no clearly identified assessment policy informing teachers' judgements on pupils, either throughout the school or even throughout a department. Profiling can become the catalyst which leads to schools and departments becoming much clearer about such policy, whereby pupils are not only offered fuller, more detailed assessments of their work, skills and attitudes, but may be involved in contributing to those assessments, in discussing them, in taking advantage of the fact that more systematic assessment is taking place in order to diagnose strengths and weaknesses.

Dissatisfaction with its recording and reporting procedures is frequently the stimulus for a school to embark upon a profiling system. The underlying motive may be pupil-centred, in the desire to develop formative, developmental recording, or it may be associated with a more summative orientation in which the principal concern is to give young people a worthwhile leaving certificate; it may be user-centred, aiming principally to provide a better service to employers and other users. Whatever the original motive, the incorporation of existing assessment and reporting procedures offers the opportunity for both school and pupil to benefit from the keeping of fuller, more accurate records. This in turn leads to a more complete summative report. Whether the motivating force lies in the field of assessment itself, or in the recording and reporting of that assessment, it quickly becomes clear that assessment, recording and reporting are inextricably linked—it is for the school to identify the priority which it places upon any specific area.

When identifying areas of prime importance, it is likely that the school may choose a third option as the over-riding concern of the institution—that of the pastoral system of the school. Indeed, it would clearly be unwise to consider the implementation of a profiling system without close liaison with the pastoral team. Some schools take the pastoral system as the springboard for profile development, using a strong, well-structured system to mobilise support or to initiate the new venture. Certainly the role of the pastoral tutor in the guidance and counselling so necessary in profiling (and frequently in the collating of assessments) is likely to be crucial. In other instances it is the very lack of an adequate pastoral system and the identification of the need to improve or extend existing procedures which has prompted the school's involvement in profiling.

Following upon the school's identification of a rationale for introducing profiling is the need to identify those areas of existing practice which can easily be assimilated into a profiling system, and it is often surprising how many such activities are already taking place within the school, albeit in a more diffuse and ad hoc way. It is even more important to identify areas where there are glaring omissions, which need either major or minor rectification in order to produce a worthwhile profile.

The final important area is the identification of teaching staff who will have key roles in the implementation of profiles. These will need to be people who are able to lead other teachers in a belief that profiling is not only practical and feasible, but also beneficial; equally important will be teachers who will have responsibility for ensuring the efficient organisation and appropriate administrative procedures, facilitating the smooth running of the whole operation. It may well be decided that one person with overall responsibility should be appointed, together with a supporting team who will form a profiling working party.

In addition to clarifying the issues which are important to the school, and providing a framework within which to operate, one of the greatest benefits of this strategy of 'identification' is the establishing of clear aims. This in itself helps to mitigate the problems already described of profiles which try to be 'all things to all people'. It may also go some way towards persuading those uncommitted staff of the value of working within clear guidelines which link profiling with key areas of the life and work of the school.

Reorganisation

This section moves from discussion and planning into action. It is likely that any school embarking upon profiling will need to involve itself in some degree of reorganisation—in some cases this will mean minor readjustments, in others it may well mean major change. To a large extent this will depend upon:

(a) existing practice within the school—how far it is compatible with profiling; and
(b) whether the school decides to adopt a radical re-appraisal leading to major innovation, or whether it merely wishes to amend, adapt or extend existing practice.

One school which devoted considerable time to the development of a profile based upon employer liaison nevertheless wished to avoid major disruption. The necessary reorganisation certainly required commitment and a degree of 'pump-priming' from a number of key figures, but the additional work asked of teachers was offset by the expedient of senior management relieving staff for a certain number of tutor periods in order to free them for administrative work associated with profiling.

Another school, deeply committed to the whole philosophy of profiling, set up detailed administrative procedures whereby teachers were issued with a series of dates for completion of specific parts of the profile. This facilitated a rolling programme of assessment: the associated recording and reporting was reorganised and simplified. There was a major, whole-school reorganisation of the reporting system. Parents and pupils who previously received two major and one minor reports each year now receive one major and one minor report. It has been established that the time saved adequately compensates for the additional time spent on profiling.

A third school invested time and effort in developing a computer system which subsequently helped to reduce administrative chores for teachers, thereby freeing them for the more appropriate use of their skills in interaction with pupils.

A fourth school adopted a radical approach to the notion of profiling, completely reorganising their approach to assessment, recording, reporting, and even extending this to a complete reorganisation of the timetable. A clear relationship between profiling and the curriculum, profiling and assessment, and profiling and reporting was established at an early stage. It was recognised that in order for teachers to do justice to the concept of profiling within such a framework, a completely new look at the school's way of organising time was required. As a result, blocked timetabling, with considerable portions of time allocated to each period was proposed. This would afford the opportunity for teachers to engage in assessment, negotiation and counselling within their actual lessons, though tutors are also allocated a non-teaching 'profiling period'.

This approach reflects a perception of profiling as having important implications for the curriculum, and as being an integral part of the life of the school. This positive, vigorous attitude to reorganisation can have a dynamic and beneficial effect upon aspects of the school's life and work not originally envisaged in the intention to implement profiling.

Reorganisation is not lightly advocated as one of the four key strategies. It involves upheaval and change. But one of the main benefits to emerge from carefully planned reorganisation is the possibility of overcoming or ameliorating one of the over-riding concerns of teachers faced with implementing profiles: time. To some extent worries about the time involved in profiling become exaggerated by fear of innovation. There are, however, very real time implications, particularly in the early stages of development, before familiarity and increasing expertise speed the process. Some of the ways in which the time issue can be tackled are:

(a) to establish aims so that there is a clear idea of the direction in which the school is heading;
(b) to identify priorities;
(c) to initiate whatever reorganisation is necessary to make these priorities feasible.

This frequently means making a different use of existing time, rather than imposing additional time demands. A bonus accruing from this strategy is the psychological effect which is felt by teachers who are able to see that an attempt is being made by the senior management to recognise and take account of their disquiet, and to take practical steps to help alleviate the problem.

In-service education

This is a very important area. No profiling scheme can be implemented without adequate in-service education and training. The extent of available LEA support in terms of in-service days, increased staffing ratios which accommodate regular teacher involvement in INSET, or supply cover for occasional INSET activities, varies considerably. This factor will have implications for schools considering profiling. It may be that less fortunate schools will need to find time for in-service support largely within their existing provision; in other cases generous supply cover is made available.

Whether provision is generous or meagre, it will still be necessary to embark upon a programme of in-service education if a profiling scheme is to be successful. The quantity and type of such in-service work will vary from institution to institution. Some schools will feel that assessment is a priority, and teachers will look for help in assessment techniques related to both subject attainment and cross-curricular skills. Other schools will seek to develop their staff's counselling and negotiation skills, or even the straightforward techniques of reporting. A combination of approaches to INSET is likely to prove the most helpful. This will include the provision of externally provided courses offering information; the opportunity for teachers to draw upon the experience of practitioners from other schools and other areas; school-based in-service activities where the emphasis lies in answering the identified needs of the individual school; and faculty or department based workshops where attention is focussed upon the needs of a particular group of teachers. Many of those now involved in profiling have found that participation in practical exercises and activities has provided the most useful insight and preparation for their new role.

In-service education provides the key to many of the difficulties described above under 'Identification'. It can help to overcome the problem of subjectivity by encouraging teachers to look at what they are assessing, and at the factors influencing their judgements; it can help to obviate the dangers of profiles being used as tools for social control by raising awareness of the problem, and at least making teachers conscious of such records' potential for harm. To the extent that it allows untrained staff to be converted into trained staff, in-service education can help the teacher to make more effective use of the time spent on profiling.

WHAT IS IT LIKE?

In the final part of this chapter, I want to illustrate the general points I have been making by referring to three examples of schools in which profiling has been successfully introduced. These case studies are intended as spotlights focused on individuals and institutions attempting to introduce profiles. They are not intended as 'ideal types', nor are they chosen to conform to the model for implementation suggested in this chapter, though they may be interesting for comparison. They serve to demonstrate some of the strategies adopted in order to gain the best advantage from implementing profiling.

THREE CASE STUDIES OF PROFILE IMPLEMENTATION

Pen Park School is chosen to illustrate some of the step-by-step processes adopted by a school coming new to profiling, and seeking to implement profiling for all pupils, regardless of the course followed. Hayesfield School exemplifies profiling designed to relate to a specific course, in which curriculum development, assessment and pupil/teacher negotiation are inextricably linked.

Discussion of profiling often assumes that a major organisational change is unavoidable. The third case study is intended to show the progress which can be made even by one individual working within subject boundaries.

Example A: Pen Park Girls' School[1]—A Whole School Profiling Development

Background

Pen Park is a girls' 11–18 comprehensive school which is designated as a 'social priority' school. The target group for the introduction of profiles covers all abilities and all ages (with initial efforts being

---

[1] Pen Park is a pilot school participating in the South Western Profiles Assessment Research Project, which is a three-year project designed to discover the effects of profiling on a range of aspects of school life, including the effects on teachers, on pupils, on the organisation, on time and resources and other related issues. The author was involved with the school in the role of County Coordinator.

focused on the fourth year). The school has had experience of the Record of Personal Achievement, and later the Pupils' Personal Record schemes (see Chapter 7) since the early 1970s. This work was undertaken principally with those pupils who had not enjoyed conspicuous success in terms of academic achievement. Apart from this, there was no experience of profiling within the school.

The sequence of events in the development of profiling over a period of nine months was as follows:

1. The introduction of a profiling system was discussed at a general staff meeting with the Head. It was made clear that any system would be designed in such a way that staff would not be required to undertake extra work in their own time.
2. An in-school coordinator was identified.
3. A Working Party was established, consisting of the Head, Deputy Head, County Coordinator, In-school Coordinator and three other members of staff.
4. Aims relating to the needs of the pupils were identified.
5. These aims were submitted to the staff for discussion and amendment.
6. Each member of the Working Party met with Faculties to discuss and elucidate aims.
7. The aims of the scheme were amended in the light of this consultation and circulated to all staff.
8. The Working Party held regular, intensive meetings to identify needs for in-service training, and to prepare for a whole day, whole staff (together with representatives of parents, governors and employers) in-service exercise addressing the issue of assessment. It consisted of:
   . (a) a display illustrating a wide variety of existing profiles;
   (b) a practical exercise involving staff, which highlighted the need for clear aims in assessment, and the need to involve students in discussion of their own assessment and learning;
   (c) a presentation by a practising teacher with long experience of profiling;
   (d) Faculty meetings with a brief to begin identifying what should be assessed within the Faculty.
9. Working Party members collated the feedback from Faculties and prepared a report for the rest of the staff.
10. Continuing work on Faculty assessments including:
    (a) a talk on assessment given by the County Coordinator to Heads of Faculty.
    (b) individual discussion between the County Coordinator and

Heads of Faculty on approaches within the Faculty;

(c) Faculty meetings to continue the identification of areas to be assessed, and to look at ways of recording these assessments.

11. A team of volunteer tutors for the target year was established.
12. Every staff meeting contained a slot for a report on progress from the Working Party.
13. Preparation began for a second whole-school in-service day, to be devoted to:
    (a) negotiation and counselling;
    (b) tutor group meetings;
    (c) Faculty assessments.

This sequence reflects the progress made up to the time of writing. A further six months of preparation is planned before the first attempts to implement profiles are undertaken.

Example B: Hayesfield School, Bath

Background

Hayesfield School is an 11–18 comprehensive school of 1,356 pupils drawn from a mixed catchment area. Pre-vocational education has been recognised as an important ingredient within the curriculum since the first RSA Vocational Preparation course was introduced in 1979. Profiling has played an important part in these courses, and staff have built up expertise in using profiles as part of a formative process, as well as a means of providing pupils with a summative 'checklist' profile certificate stating what they have achieved.

The school has taken part in the 1984/85 piloting of CPVE, and staff have drawn upon their experience of profiling in order to facilitate its development within CPVE.

The sequence of events in the development of profiling for CPVE was as follows.

Preparation

1. Participating students and a team of volunteer teachers were identified.
2. The type of profile to be used in the formative coursework was identified. A criteria checklist approach, similar to the RSA profiles, was adopted. (A series of criteria are established, and

students are credited with a particular skill as evidence of mastery is displayed during the course.)

3. Teachers wrote the aims and objectives of the profile and established the pattern of activities to be carried out.
4. Each teacher within the team produced assignments, with team leaders showing the objectives which are achievable. Integrated assignments, covering all of the curriculum, were developed.
5. During this development process, assignment objectives were checked against the profile descriptors.

Implementation—the procedure in use

6. The objectives achieved by individual students (through the use of these integrated assignments) are circled.
7. These are then collated onto a profile grid through team meetings.
8. The student is issued with a course log-book, which is used in discussions with the course tutor to consider what has been achieved and what might be expected in future.
9. The structured allocation of time allows for student–teacher discussion and negotiation.
10. A separate work experience log-book is also kept by the student, as a record of experience, and as a medium for communicating with the work experience (WE) tutor.
11. Evidence drawn from the student's work experience is incorporated into the profile and collated through the team meeting.
12. Tutorials are time-tabled with the course tutor, and are available on demand with the WE tutor.
13. The profile is used as a continuing part of the learning and assessment process throughout the course.

The profiling format can be represented diagrammatically as in Fig. 11.1. In this example, it is possible to identify all four of the elements which have been advocated in the earlier part of this chapter:

(a) consultation (in establishing volunteer tutors, and in the design of the course);
(b) identification (of both staff and students, and of the clear aims and objectives of the course and the profile);
(c) reorganisation (in terms of both reorganisation of the curriculum and teaching strategies, and of the time-table, incorporating structured 'one to one' interview time and team meetings); and
(d) in-service education (the team collaboration in writing assignments is viewed as a valuable staff development exercise).

CPVE experience

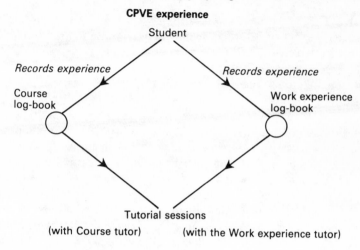

Tutorials with Course tutors are timetabled.
Tutorials with Work experience tutor are by appointment.

Fig.11.1

It is too soon to draw any definitive conclusion, but early reactions suggest that staff are gaining considerably increased job satisfaction from teaching and assessment, and that students exhibit a marked increase in motivation and attainment.

Example C: Gordano School—A single teacher, single subject approach to profiling

This case study is intended to illustrate the way in which an individual can incorporate the philosophy of profiling into normal subject teaching, regardless of the fact that the rest of the school is not involved in profiling. Ian Graves, of Gordano School, is the first to recognise that it is only a first attempt, but the significant aspects of his work revolve around:

(a) the separation of learning and assessment into separate categories;
(b) helping diagnosis;
(c) offering room for improvement in a specific area; and
(d) improving pupil motivation by discussion of progress and the ability to improve grades.

I have chosen to use Ian's own words for this case study, and whilst he has adopted his own format, elements of consultation (with pupils), identification (of aims and techniques), and reorganisation (of teaching method, and re-structuring of use of time within the class) which match the sequence given earlier in this chapter, can be easily identified.

'The class concerned is a mixed ability group of 26 fourth year pupils which I worked with for approximately half a term (14 one-hour periods). I wanted to do some work with the group on discursive and persuasive writing, encourage study skills, such as the use of reference materials, and boost discussion skills.

We spent a lesson talking about topics which contained enough disagreement to support a number of viewpoints, but which were capable of investigation. This led to a discussion of pressure groups. We followed this up with a lesson where we chose a topic from a list of suggestions provided by the group. I wanted one subject for all of us, but there was such a divergence of opinion that we decided to form two groups, one looking at Nuclear Weapons, the other looking at Drugs (see Figure 11.2).

FOURTH YEAR   NUCLEAR AND DRUG TOPICS

Aims
To collect information from a variety of sources.
To select and combine relevant information.
To detect and assess bias.
To be able to form a point of view supported by reasons.
To understand and appreciate others' viewpoint.
To be able to support a case in discussion.

Activities
1. Collect as much information as possible on your subject from a variety of sources. Always keep a note of the source so that you can find it again. Also keep your eyes open for any evidence of bias.

2. Make notes of most important points neatly on exercise paper. Group together points on the same subject, but include the source of information, as in 1 above.

3. Make a list of examples of bias in your sources, quoting where relevant and commenting on the bias shown.

4. List all information and opinion collected under headings of various viewpoints.

5. Write a speech in favour of the point of view with which you agree.

Fig.11.2 *Aims and activities relating to discussion topics.*

PUPIL ASSESSMENT FORM

TOPIC: *NUCLEAR WEAPONS*

Name: *Roger Williams*

This form will be completed by you and your teacher together – all grades must be agreed before they are entered.

This form must be carefully kept, as it will form part of your end-of-year report.

	E	D	C	B	A	Comment
1. Collection of information			✓	✓		(1) Limited variety of sources (2) Has added to information
2. Selection and combination of information				✓		Quite well arranged – too close to sources
3. Awareness of bias		✓				Has found a few examples
4. Forming reasoned viewpoint				✓		Drew out points well, and found reasons
5. Understanding others' views			✓			
6. Ability to argue case (oral)				✓		Spoke fluently, using reasons

Grades

A = As able at task as could be expected of age group/totally competent

B = Above average for age group/good attempt showing ability and effort

C = Average for age group/mixture of success and failure; moderate effort

D = Below average/needs assistance to complete task; lack of effort

E = Well below average/combination of problems understanding and completing task and lack of effort.

Fig.11.3 *Pupil assessment form.*

The next step was to get the group to write letters to groups and organisations (CND, Health Education Council, etc.) requesting information. I then decided to 'profile' the work, and produced the sheets illustrated in Figure 11.3, giving one to each pupil. We went briefly through what their meaning was and the reason for this form of assessment. This was generally well-received.

Since then the group have largely been working on their own at the tasks on the sheet. Circumstances have meant that we could not hold the discussion sessions envisaged as yet; they will be held after half-term. There has been a little input on a group basis from me (I showed them a cuttings file from the library, we have talked a little about the detection of bias) and there have been sessions when videos were on offer. In the main, though, the group has been working in pairs or threes on the topic, and I have played a consultant role, going round the class.

The reaction has been very favourable. None of the pupils have lost their assessment sheets; they regularly want me to fill them in and seem to have quickly understood that they can improve a grade by doing more. There has, as yet, not been a great deal of discussion of grades; I went round the class and sat down with each person to fill in the first category, Collection of Information. Only one person actually queried the grade I gave them. The second (and in some cases the third) section I filled in at home after reading the notes. The other three sections have still to be filled in. The oral assessment will be filled in by me during our discussion session, though pupils will be free to quibble later.

As might have been expected, the major problem is that the procedure is amazingly time-consuming, getting round to see each individual even once. This made me abandon my negotiative stance almost at once, while encouraging discussion of grades given.

The individual nature of the work and the realisation that grades can be improved upon has led to the group working for a long time at the first section; they were a bit too conscientious about finding material.

Because the first task was so simple everyone was able to get a good grade. I felt I was able to explain why I had given a grade and explain how the work could be better. Several pupils then improved upon their work and wanted me to raise their grades. The group felt that the system was fairer and easier to understand than just overall grades and want it to continue. Overall I detect an improvement in motivation which encourages me to attempt to profile our next unit of work, which will be based on using a Book box (thus literature). I shall also be attempting to use a profiling approach for language skills with my third year class.'

This case study does not describe any major structural changes in assessment policy. Nevertheless, it does show the changes in approach and teaching method which can be achieved even on an individual basis, and that a large input of time and resources is not always necessary in order to effect change.

Final Comment

This chapter has outlined some of the major concerns which schools and teachers considering the implementation of a profiling system are likely to have. For those still at the consideration stage, encouragement may be taken from the successes of a considerable number of schools in England and Wales which have devised and implemented their own schemes. Many of them are now sharing their experiences through the profiles information network Pearson describes in Chapter 3. Since the provision of records of achievement is now an explicit national policy commitment, all schools are likely to be involved in profiling in the near future. There is, therefore, a very good argument for ensuring that preparation and implementation is as thorough and effective as possible, in order that pupils will indeed receive the benefits from profiling which were outlined at the beginning of this chapter.

PART THREE

Critiques

Amid the euphoria currently being generated by the realisation that records of achievement are really on the policy agenda, there is also widespread realisation that many of the issues raised by this innovation are deeply significant. Some of the problems may indeed prove intractable. These issues range from the practical and pressing concerns of time and resources, mentioned by many of the contributors to this book, to the more technical but vital concerns of sustaining confidence in the accuracy of such records, and the most profound sociological questions about the interpersonal effects of new types of assessments. Although nearly all the contributors to the first two parts of this book raise some or all of these issues in general terms, the three articles in this final section address them in terms of a sustained critique. It is appropriate that a book which is principally concerned with identifying principles and describing progress should end on a warning note, lest in our enthusiasm for change we fail to notice the flaws that, unchecked, could turn the dream into a nightmare.

12

Pupil Profiles and Records of Achievement: an NUT Perspective

ALAN EVANS

In this chapter Evans echoes the widely-voiced concerns of many teachers about the implementation of profiles and records of achievement. Having given enthusiastic support to the concept of 'pupil profiles', the NUT, like the other teachers' unions, is now concerned to find practical and acceptable ways in which they might be implemented within the existing limitations of skill and resources. This very practical approach, which echoes some of the points Hitchcock makes in Chapter 11, is a vital feature in the potential success of profiling and thus constitutes an important element in the reflections of Part 3.

—Editor

Introduction

This paper begins by explaining why the National Union of Teachers supports the development of pupil profiles, and describing the major strands of its policy on this issue. I shall try to clarify exactly what the NUT understands by the term 'profile'; and to consider the different basic forms of profiling currently in use or being developed. I shall go on to consider some of the major issues arising for pupils, for teachers, and for the education service as a whole, from the development and introduction of pupil profiles. Finally I shall comment on the pilot schemes proposed by the DES and suggest a way forward for the teaching profession, and the other partners in the education service, with a view to furthering this debate and securing progress in the many important ideas and issues arising from it.

THE POSITION OF THE NUT

Like many other organisations, the NUT was a little late in raising the issue of pupil profiles as a major concern for schools and for the education service. The NUT was in the vanguard of the movement to establish a common examination at 16+, and tabled the first resolution to that end in the Schools Council in July 1970; but it was only towards the end of the 1970s that the NUT became increasingly aware that it would be inadequate and inappropriate to introduce such an important reform for only 60 per cent of the age group, and to have nothing of substance or value for the rest. So it was that, towards the end of the 1970s, the NUT began to do some serious thinking on the question of pupil profiles. Our commitment in principle to the development of profiles was enshrined as follows in a policy statement on examining at 16+ published in 1980:

> 'A truly comprehensive system of education demands a comprehensive system of examining—namely a system which, by design, caters for the whole range of ability. The Union recognises that such a system lies outside the scope of the feasibility and development studies carried out so far, but it nevertheless believes that considerable progress can be made towards it by the development of profile assessment techniques. The Union has for some time advocated that all pupils, whether or not they sit for external examinations, should be assessed by means of a 'profile', in the form of a record of personal achievement covering the whole of their secondary education. The need for such a profile is particularly crucial in the case of pupils for whom the examination system is inappropriate, and who at present leave school after five years of secondary education with no tangible evidence of their abilities and achievements.' (NUT, 1980)

Since that time the NUT has held two national conferences on profiles, as well as a weekend school and a number of seminars. It has entered into a dialogue with the Department of Education and Science and with local authorities, and through its representatives on the Schools Council in England and in Wales has been an advocate of pilot work in this area.

In May 1983, in order to further the debate, the NUT published a discussion document on pupil profiles (NUT, 1983). It deliberately used the term 'discussion document', for two reasons. First, it was not felt appropriate at that stage to produce a firm policy statement on the detailed aspects of profiling; and second it was realised that radical ideas could best be expressed through the medium of a discussion document. A policy statement can be a neutering exercise, or it can be as modest a contribution as the DES's own statement (DES, 1984). This discussion document was sent to the NUT's local associations and divisions and was debated at a local level. Comments were sent in, and the overwhelming majority of these were favourable. Reservations were expressed on some issues, the major one being, not surprisingly, staffing and resources; but it would seem that the desirability of developing and establishing pupil profiles in schools throughout England and Wales is a principle which now has the support of a very large section of the teaching profession.

Following the publication of the discussion document and the receipt of comments from our members, the NUT was in a strong position to respond to the draft policy statement issued by the DES in November 1983. In framing a response we took our policy on certain key issues a stage further than that which was expressed in our discussion document, and it was encouraging to note that some of our thinking found its way into the definitive policy statement published by the Department in July 1984.

Why the NUT supports the development of profiles

Two basic considerations underlie the NUT's support for the development of profiles. The first of these is the inadequacy of the public examinations system as a means of assessment. Examinations, as is widely recognised, can assess only a narrow range of skills or abilities; many are designed primarily to test knowledge acquired (cognitive skills), and are wholly inappropriate as a vehicle for assessing the wider range of skills, abilities and qualities which secondary schools seek to develop in their pupils. They provide no feedback to pupils or teachers, and no information other than the level of performance of a candidate in relation to other candidates. The NUT believes that the use of profiles would enable those skills, abilities and qualities which cannot be assessed by public examinations to be fully recorded and assessed, thus providing pupils with a more comprehensive, detailed record of their achievements; at the same time, it would provide users (such as potential employers) with more detailed and relevant information.

Second, the NUT attaches great importance to the principle that *all* the work of *all* the pupils in a school is worthy of being assessed and recorded. The public examinations system, which excludes by design almost half the age group, cannot fulfil this principle; profiles, if given the necessary status and importance by the schools and by users, would help to ensure that all pupils receive parity of esteem in terms of the professional time and effort devoted by teachers to the assessment of their work.

THE VIEW OF THE DES

The DES policy statement lists four 'purposes of records of achievement'. One of these, interestingly, is improving pupil motivation. Some have questioned whether pupil motivation would in fact be improved. From the discussions I have been involved in I would say that the majority of teachers believe that the use of profiles does increase motivation; and from the one or two schools where I have seen approaches to assessment that are far more sophisticated than those offered either in public examinations or in the profile studies to date, I have no doubt that pupil motivation is increased by such methods, and thus that this element of the policy statement is well-founded.

The DES also suggests that the introduction of records of achievement would help schools 'to identify the all-round potential of their pupils and to consider how well their curriculum, teaching and organisation enable pupils to develop the general, practical and social skills which are to be recorded'. I share this hope. Of course there is a possibility that, in the hands of teachers who are not thoroughly committed to the exercise, or who have not had the opportunity to discuss fully its purpose and implications, profiling could lead to a fragmentation of the curriculum—to 'teaching to the test'. This is a grave danger. But where teachers have been properly consulted and involved in the introduction of a profile scheme, and are fully committed to it, such a scheme could be a stimulus to schools to think far more sensitively about individual needs than they are encouraged or enabled to do within the constraints of external examinations, which are crude instruments which distort the curriculum and cannot be responsive to individual needs.

In the draft version of its policy statement the DES spoke of acknowledging 'the totality of what pupils have done and achieved';

the word 'totality' has, understandably, been dropped in the final version. Public examinations perhaps succeed in assessing as little as 30 to 40 per cent of pupils' achievements; if profiles can move along the spectrum towards 70 or 80 per cent they will have done well.

The fourth and final purpose advanced by the DES is that of providing a record 'which is recognised and valued by employers and institutions of further and higher education'. The NUT certainly concurs with the Department on this point, and indeed supports the general tenor of the document as a whole.

MAJOR ISSUES DERIVING FROM THE DEVELOPMENT OF PROFILES

Formative versus Summative Profiles

The NUT's discussion document states at an early stage that:

> 'A profile is not a method of assessment, but a *record* of information about a pupil, which may be presented in a variety of ways. It may include assessments of certain skills, abilities and achievements, as well as other elements which are not formally assessed or assessable. A profile is thus only as full and as varied as the information which it seeks to present.'

The document adopts as a basis for discussion the four 'profiling principles' first identified by Balogh (1982) in her survey for the Schools Council, namely:

(a) the recording of skills and personal qualities as well as traditional subject attainment;
(b) the presentation of roughly equivalent information for all pupils;
(c) the provision of an open document for school-leavers;
(d) the availability of the profile to *all* pupils.

The document then goes on to analyse the two distinctive types of profiles which may meet these criteria: *formative* and *summative.*

'Formative' profiles are diagnostic instruments: they are developed continuously over a period of time, regularly updated, and are intended to form an integral part of the learning process. As such they provide an opportunity for discussion between teacher and pupil, and for appropriate modifications to teaching and learning strategies in the light of strengths and weaknesses identified in the course of the assessment. 'Summative' profiles provide a final record and assessment of a pupil's achievement and abilities at the end of a course, available for the pupil to take away and use as evidence of attainment when applying for jobs or further courses. A summative profile might of course be based on a formative profile, but it is unlikely that a single document can perform both functions.

It is interesting that one of the most forthright and least cautious sections of the DES draft policy statement was that headed 'Compilation'; this has been amplified but in no way diluted in the final version under the heading 'Recording processes'. The DES document calls for schools 'to begin the processes of reporting, recording and discussion from the time when pupils enter the secondary phase and continue then on a regular and systematic basis throughout their subsequent time at school'. Clearly the policy statement is talking about both the formative and summative approach: it is a formidable task, which will require either substantial changes in the internal workings of secondary schools, or extra resources, or (more probably) both.

The DES states categorically that the summative record would not be a confidential reference. The NUT is far less categorical on this issue; although we have considerable doubts about the value of confidential references, they are clearly needed under present arrangements. We would hope that, if profiles were given due status and credibility, and were seen to be of value by employers and other users, they might lead to the phasing out of confidential references in the future.

Content

In line with most other profile schemes, the NUT's discussion document identifies four areas which might be assessed or recorded in a profile:

(a) skills and/or qualities besides traditional subject attainment, such as basic mathematical and language skills;
(b) cross-curricular skills, such as listening and problem-solving;
(c) practical skills, such as the ability to use tools correctly; and
(d) personal qualities, such as punctuality and initiative.

Of these four, the most controversial is undoubtedly the last—personal qualities.

The discussion document itself selects a part of the profile for the City and Guilds 365 course to demonstrate the dangers in attempting to assess personal qualities. The extract in Figure 12.1 is taken from the section of the grid devoted to the assessment of social abilities; the particular 'skill' being assessed is self-awareness, and the four boxes

Self-awareness	Is aware of own personality and situation.	Can determine own strengths, weaknesses and preferences with some guidance.	Has good basic understanding of own situation, personality and motivation.	Has a thorough understanding of own personality and abilities and their implications.

Fig.12.1 *Extract from pupil profile, CGLI 365 course.*

are intended to identify a hierarchy of skills within this category.

It is our view that even a mature adult would hesitate to claim 'a thorough understanding of own personality and abilities and their implications'; it is certainly highly questionable that teachers should be expected to relate statements such as these to sixteen-year-olds. It is apparent from the more recent City and Guilds work which Stratton describes in Chapter 8 that this view is now widely accepted.

The point I am making is that the area of personal qualities should be approached with great delicacy and sensitivity; I think that there would be considerable resistance, and rightly so, on the part of the teaching profession if they were called upon to assess their pupils' personal qualities by means as crude as ticks in boxes or norm-referenced grades. That is not to suggest that teachers should fight shy of this aspect of profiling, or that they do not have the necessary skills or sensitivity to tackle it. Certainly personal qualities are an important element in a profile; certainly employers are interested in such characteristics as reliability, initiative, willingness to work, cooperation with others. None of these qualities will be identified by the current examinations system. I believe that teachers have the capacity to make judgements in these domains, in a very positive way, and to indicate, by the masterly use of English understatement, that there are varying degrees of positive performance amongst pupils. I believe that the DES has struck the right note on this issue when it states that personal qualities should as far as possible be inferred from concrete examples of what the pupil has achieved or experienced.

The model profile developed by Jennifer Jones for the Schools Council in Wales offers an interesting approach to the assessment and recording of personal qualities in a sensitive and professional way. The profile evolved from four different pilot programmes, each adopting a distinctive approach. The first involved the grading of a range of skills, listed under headings such as written language and mathematics. The second used the same lists of skills, but required a written comment for each rather than a grade. The third was related to the first, using norm-referenced graded assessments of a range of skills; and the fourth used the hierarchical 'grids' developed by the FEU and the City and Guilds.

Having tested reactions to the four profiles amongst pupils, teachers and users, Jones found an overwhelming consensus in favour of the written statement and against grades or ticks in boxes. The national model that was subsequently developed is characterised by comments drawn from a computer bank and linked together to form statements of continuous prose (Schools Council Committee for Wales, 1982). Thus the sections on 'personal qualities' featured in the sample profiles for two mythical pupils, Sian Thomas and Huw Jones, are as follows:

'Sian is able to form and maintain very good relationships with adults and pupils, although some encouragement is needed in the first instance. If called upon she has shown that she can act as an organiser but she prefers not to take a leading role.
Even in the face of difficulties Sian's perseverance and application are notable and very little supervision is needed to enable her to complete work. Homework tasks are completed regularly and usually satisfactorily.
When encouraged Sian participates reliably and conscientiously in school activities and she has shown loyalty and commitment to the school on many occasions.'

Huw is described in the following terms:

'Huw is able to get on well with most pupils but prefers not to take a leading role. He needs constant encouragement to relate to others although he is well-mannered and courteous and is generally accepted by most adults.
Huw perseveres with most tasks although some encouragement is needed in the face of difficulties. Homework tasks are completed regularly and usually satisfactorily, but work is not always organised effectively unless advice is given. Although he tries to present work neatly he does not always succeed in doing so.
He is well behaved in class but has shown little desire to become involved in the extra-curricular life of the school. He takes part in the occasional school activity when his interest is captured but his main interests lie outside school.'

Although the use of 'comment banks' is still too deterministic for many teachers, these seem to me to be serious, credible and sensitive solutions to the problem of assessing or recording pupils' personal qualities. The use of the 'comment bank' is continuing in some of the schools taking part in the Government-funded pilot record of achievement schemes in Wales.

Who should make the assessments?

The general view of the NUT's membership is that the assessments should be a collective effort on the part of a number of teachers, but that the form tutor should play a central role in coordinating and (perhaps) moderating the assessments from individual teachers.

Form tutors are, or should be, in the best position to carry out such a role; they should be at the fulcrum of a network of information and comment about their pupils. They should be the mediators between the pastoral and the academic domains of the school, and in a position to know the most about the pupils in their charge.

There are difficulties in this area, however. Balogh (1982) and Goacher (1983) both cite pupils who contested the judgements made by their form tutors (and other teachers) because they felt that the teachers did not know them well enough to make those judgements. These difficulties arose mainly in the area of personal qualities, but also in cross-curricular areas. It is certainly asking a lot of the form tutors, and if they are to discharge this role adequately they will need adequate training and support.

Methods of recording assessments

The NUT discussion document refers to three basic assessment systems: 'normative', where a pupil's performance is compared with others, generally in the same year or teaching group; 'ipsative', where a pupil's level of achievement is compared with his/her own past performance; and 'criterion-referenced', where levels of performance are clearly defined in advance and pupils must show that they have reached the standard specified. Strongest support has been expressed for the last of these, criterion-referencing, while recognising that in practice there would have to be a balance between norm-referencing and criterion-referencing, between the subjectivity of the teacher's judgement and the objectivity of a refined assessment tool. Feeling is generally against the use of grades or ticks in boxes, and in favour rather of written comments, despite the fact that these are necessarily time-consuming to prepare. I have already referred to the idea of computerised banks of comments, as used in the Welsh profile scheme, that have been compiled by serving teachers and tested, amended and refined until they meet the need. Such comment banks may well represent the best and most sophisticated way forward, as long as the banks of comments are continually revised and amended in the light of experience.

Implications for the curriculum

I have already mentioned the danger that, in the hands of teachers who have not been properly prepared, profiles might fragment or act as a straitjacket on the curriculum. At best, however, the use of profiles should result in a refinement and improvement of the curriculum; formative profiles in particular should be diagnostic instruments, leading to curricular change and reform. Whether this comes to pass will depend on how well the teachers have been prepared for this task, and how well they are supported in it; it will depend also on the framework for curriculum evaluation and change within the school, and on how well it is able to promote or facilitate a response to identified needs.

Implications for teachers

Those teachers who responded to the NUT's discussion document were unanimous in their belief that profiles would involve a great deal of extra work. There is no doubt that, unless the introduction of profiles is accompanied by changes in the internal organisation of schools, there will need to be a massive increase in clerical, administrative and professional resources. Certainly it would be neither practical nor educationally desirable to stick profiles on as an appendage to the present system. It simply would not work. What is needed is for schools to re-examine their whole internal structure and practice—a point made forcibly by Burgess and Adams in Chapter 6. They must re-examine their pastoral and guidance systems, the role of the form tutor, and the relationship of those systems to the academic domain. They must also re-examine their systems for liaison with primary schools, with parents and with employers and further education.

The introduction of profiles raises profound implications for the internal organisation of schools. To be successful it must be accompanied by a redefinition of priorities within the school and a redistribution of teacher time and skills. There must be a change in the balance between pastoral and academic domains, especially in the amount of time and professional skill that is devoted to each, and to the assessment of pupil achievement in each. There must be a redistribution of the stock of assessment skills within the school: a more even balance between the affective and the cognitive, and between the formative, or diagnostic, and the summative.

Implications for local education authorities

These are major and complex professional issues, which offer a challenge not only to the teaching profession but also to the local education authorities. There is no way, in the second half of the 1980s, that sufficient new resources will be found to do profiles justice: chief education officers and their advisers will therefore need all the skill, imagination and resourcefulness at their command to offer teachers a package which will persuade them to enter into a dialogue about profiles, to make the necessary changes and undertake the extra work without a massive injection of new resources.

There are many teachers who would share this view. There are some who would say that it cannot be done. But, if people in positions of influence and authority throughout the education service are prepared to enter into a dialogue with the teaching profession on the lines I have suggested, then it can be done; if they are not, the reform will be stillborn. Certainly a handful of pilot schemes will not, on their own, succeed in changing practice in 5,000 secondary schools and among a quarter of a million secondary school teachers throughout England and Wales.

It is probably stating the obvious to say that a reform of this kind cannot possibly be introduced without full consultation with the teachers. If LEAs consult the teachers on profiles as little as they did on the first round of the TVEI they must expect total failure: there was virtually no teacher consultation where that initiative was concerned. Genuine consultation means a dialogue between both sides, and if necessary movement on both sides, in full recognition of the fact that in the end the local authorities are responsible for the delivery of the service to the community.

Second, there will probably be a need for extra non-teaching time for all staff involved, as well as the redistribution of time and skills which I mentioned earlier. Third, there must be adequate clerical and ancillary support, otherwise deputy heads, senior teachers and form teachers will be paid for undertaking clerical and ancillary work to the detriment of their professional duties. Fourth, there must be provision of adequate material resources, such as paper and reprographic equipment. Jones' work in Wales revealed that a very modest injection of funds brought surprisingly large returns (Schools Council Committee for Wales, 1983).

Fifth—and this is a major consideration—all staff involved must be given opportunities for in-service education and training. Given the nature and purpose of the exercise the bulk of this training needs to be school-focused or school-based, though some could be provided externally by colleges or by the local authority itself. Unfortunately school-based INSET tends to lack the status of externally-based courses. Nevertheless, the important thing is to invest time in teachers, to raise their horizons and increase their professional confidence.

Sixth is the need for guidance and support on the part of local inspectors and advisers. The problem is that most inspectors and advisers at the moment are heavily involved in the crisis management of the contraction of secondary schools—they do not have much time for promoting important and desirable reforms in curriculum and assessment. So there is a need to draw as well on the support and expertise of other professionals in institutions of further and higher education, and also to enable some teachers to have a period of secondment to support and promote the development of the necessary skills in their colleagues.

Validity, standardisation, and a national scheme

In England there is certainly as yet no consensus as to the practicality or desirability of a national, standardised system of profiles, nor has sufficient work been done to justify reaching such a consensus. In Wales, however, which is a much smaller and more cohesive entity than England (with only eight local education authorities) there is now a consensus on the framework for a national profile and on the key elements such a profile should encapsulate. These are: a statement of attendance; a personal comment by the form tutor; teachers' comments on the pupil's personal qualities; communication, practical and numerical skills; and a personal contribution by the pupil describing his or her interests and achievements and service to the school and community. Operational work on this model national profile began in September 1984 in secondary schools throughout Wales, and will be subject to detailed development and evaluation over the next three years. The main advantage of such a national scheme is its potential credibility with employers. Meanwhile it is necessary to carry out the pilot schemes, and learn from their very diversity what is required in terms of comparability of format and content, and how much variation there could be between schools.

THE PILOT SCHEMES

I have two major concerns about the DES-funded pilot schemes. The first is that those schemes which are associated with CSE or GCE examining boards should not become the creatures of those boards. The traditions of public examining are very different from the principles on which pupil profiles are based. Without decrying in any way the abilities and expertise of the officers of the boards and the teachers serving on their panels and sub-committees, I do not believe it would be desirable or appropriate to bring profiles under the control of the examining boards. What is required, both in England and Wales, is rather an independent, autonomous steering committee at local level, containing representatives of the CSE and GCE boards and of the teachers in schools, linked to, but not controlled by, those boards.

My second concern relates to oversight and control of the pilot schemes at national level. The Secretary of State has set up a national steering committee under DES chairmanship to oversee the monitoring and evaluation of the pilot schemes. It is crucially important, for the credibility of this committee and the success of the schemes, that the Secretary of State should appoint to this national steering committee a number of serving teachers, some of whom have a knowledge and experience of the theory and practice of profiling, and some of whom have no special expertise in this field but who have good judgement. In addition to representatives of the teaching profession there should of course be included representatives of the other partners in the education service—the local authorities and the institutions of further education—indeed all the diverse interests which have a role to play in making a success of the Records of Achievement policy. This is also true at local level, where there needs to be active and positive collaboration between the local steering group and all those involved in the development.

So far as the teachers' associations, including my own, are concerned, I hope and believe that we will be willing to participate in the pilot schemes both at national and local level, and that we would only consider withdrawing our support if a particular scheme was so bad that we felt it would be detrimental to the pupils. I think we owe it to a whole generation of pupils, and to future generations of pupils, to be as positive and supportive as we can; this in turn requires that the DES and local authorities accept this commitment in good faith and do not act in such a way as to make it impossible for us to give our support. Up to this point it has been first and foremost the enthusiasm of teachers which has made the profiling movement into a major platform for change. Without their continued commitment the policy cannot come to life.

REFERENCES

Balogh, J. (1982) *Profile Reports for School Leavers*, York: Longman for Schools Council.

Department of Education and Science (1983) *Records of Achievement for School Leavers: A Draft Policy Statement*. London: HMSO.

Department of Education and Science (1984) *Records of Achievement: A Statement of Policy*. London: HMSO.

Goacher, B. (1983) *Recording Achievement at 16+*. York: Longman for Schools Council.

National Union of Teachers (1980) *Examining at 16+: An NUT Policy Statement on Proposals for a Single System*. London: Hamilton House.

National Union of Teachers (1983) *Pupil Profiles: A Discussion Document*. London: Hamilton House.

Schools Council Committee for Wales (1983) *Profile Reporting in Wales: A Discussion Paper*. Cardiff: HMSO.

13

Profiles and Graded Tests: the Technical Issues[1]

DESMOND NUTTALL AND
HARVEY GOLDSTEIN

Some of the technical issues which Baumgart identifies briefly in Chapter 4 are here explored in considerable detail. Very few people have written anything about the technical problems that at least some of the approaches of profiling and records of achievement raise. Yet it is on these issues that the success of this innovation may well ultimately depend, for if the information in the records cannot readily be relied upon or used it will have no public credibility, and the whole edifice that so many people have been at pains to build in the last decade or so will crumble as completely as previous efforts to initiate such records have done. Whilst for many such minutiae may seem tiresome in comparison with the educational arguments involved, Nuttall and Goldstein demonstrate in this chapter that their resolution is an essential prerequisite to any system of recording achievement that aspires to more than a local focus.

—Editor

We shall review first, but briefly, what seems to be the current state of profiling; the aims and controversies which are being discussed. We

---

[1] This article is reproduced with the kind permission of the Further Education Unit who first published it in 'Profiles in Action', FEU, 1984.

shall then identify what seem to us to be the key technical issues which have yet to be solved before profiles can be accepted widely as satisfactory additions or alternatives to other forms of assessment. Then we shall describe and evaluate the graded test movement. Finally we shall link together graded testing and profile reporting and discuss the relationship between them. On all these topics we have been able to find little written about technical matters, and very little relevant empirical research, and in this article we therefore discuss the major technical issues in the hope of facilitating a more informed debate.

CURRENT ACTIVITY

The last few years have seen a considerable interest in profile reporting in education. An early report from the Scottish Council for Research in Education (SCRE, 1977) has stimulated a variety of others both at the school level in the work of the Schools Council (Balogh, 1982)— and even more vigorously at the FE level in the work of the Further Education Unit (FEU, 1982a and b), and the related City and Guilds of London Institute (CGLI) development work (Stratton, 1982a).

There is general agreement that the disaggregated nature of the information in a profile is of greater potential use to students, lecturers and employers who wish to understand the specific strengths and weaknesses of an individual, rather than some average assessment. There is also a general recognition of the need to distinguish formative profiles which are produced during a course from summative ones which represent a final assessment and are typically based on an amalgamation over time of the formative set of assessments. Formative profiles are designed to be part of the learning process, to be discussed by lecturer and student together, while the summative kind are designed for the outside world and selection for employment. These two broad purposes may be often in conflict and affect the need for comparability and reliability in the assessments, as we shall demonstrate.

There is also conflict among the motives of the advocates of profiles. At one extreme, in the words of Broadfoot (1982), herself a collaborator in the SCRE work, profiles provide a viable alternative to the powerful 'anti-educational' constraint of public examinations. At the other is the Associated Examining Board's new A-level Geography examination which provides a profile by means of a separate grade for each of four papers, to yield more information from existing examinations, a development reviewed in detail by Harrison (1983). In between, in the mainstream of development, is the FEU and CGLI approach and that of SCRE and many of the schools studied in the Schools Council work, which see their profiles as existing alongside centralised examinations. In the case of the pre-vocational courses stimulated by the FEU, the intention seems to be that profiles should become a dominant element in assessment, while in schools there seems to be a recognition that public examinations will remain the dominant element for some time to come.

One feature common to most profiles, in contrast to examinations, is their inclusion of personal and social skills alongside so-called basic skills and more conventional attainments. Sometimes the personal and social skills are reported simply as records of activity, without judgement, but often they are assessed and graded (by the lecturer alone, or by the lecturer and student in partnership). In the CGLI Vocational Preparation course (365), for example, there are four ratings for each of the abilities 'to be self aware' and 'to cope with problems', as well as for 'calculating' and 'reading and writing'. Simple rating scales of this kind are widely used; each point is accompanied by a description of the ability or attainment level it represents. While it is usually admitted that some of these ratings will be more 'subjective' than others, the common aim appears to be to remove this element as far as possible by providing careful verbal descriptions, training the assessors carefully and carrying out periodic 'quality control' checks on their work. Some more open-ended schemes use 'comment banks', consisting of comments whose placing on the scale has had prior agreement (Black and Dockrell, 1981).

This present article is largely concerned with some of the key technical issues which have received too little serious attention in the discussion up to the present. Such references as there are admit to the existence of problems of reliability and indeed validity, but fail to probe them in any depth (Macintosh, 1982; Harrison, 1983). In our view, however, there do exist serious technical problems and, unless these can be solved satisfactorily, profiles will rest on insecure foundations. We are concerned largely with the 'mainstream' developments, although we do recognise other strands to profiling.

NORM VERSUS CRITERION-REFERENCING

This article does not provide the space to present a detailed discussion of this issue, but some general remarks are relevant. This is because, for both profiles and graded tests, criterion-referenced assessment is commonly advocated. Further, since criterion-referenced assessment has often been regarded as not amenable to quantitative manipulation in the same way as norm-referenced assessment, there is the possibility that some important technical problems will be ignored.

Firstly, it is extremely difficult to imagine a criterion-referenced assessment that is totally independent of norm levels. If a criterion point is to be useful it must obviously distinguish between individuals, so that the possibility exists that some will reach it and others will not. We can know whether this is the case only by collecting data on how many individuals do so—thus estimating a norm. Since, in fact, 'cut off' points are a choice, if not actually arbitrary, this 'norming' information will typically be used in determining them, at least initially. The difference between criterion-referenced and norm-referenced tests lies in their methods of construction, intended use and interpretation. In terms of construction, criterion-referenced tests are designed consciously to avoid the psychometric models of norm-referenced tests, and in terms of use they employ fewer categories but ones which are designed to convey educationally meaningful information. In the case of profiles, the important issue is that of providing assessments that are both accurately related to the profile elements and comparable across individuals. This is not easy to achieve.

A central thrust of the profiles movement has been the attempt to relate assessment more closely to the curriculum than public examinations typically do (Mansell, 1982). Thus, teachers and lecturers have collaborated in the design and testing process, and assessments are intended to be made in the context of curriculum activities. If curricula differ, a comparability problem is immediately raised, since there is then no guarantee that consistent interpretations can be made. To overcome this problem, much effort has been put into an attempt to develop context-free assessments. The SCRE profile, for example, has one skill level for number which is described as 'Can handle routine calculations with practice', and the amplification is provided 'Fairly accurate but slow; is able to calculate percentages and money calculations etc.'.

The difficulty with such out-of-context descriptions is that they are too poorly defined to ensure comparability, and the more precisely defined they become the more rooted in a context they become. Thus the above definition would need to specify what was meant by 'routine' so that such a calculation could be recognised. It would need to specify the order of difficulty of the 'percentages' referred to and make much more precise the phrase 'Fairly accurate but slow', and so on. Eventually, for a high degree of comparability to be achieved, the description would have to be so precise that we would be very nearly back with the classical test situation where everyone is administered effectively the same set of items—i.e. a highly specific context for the assessment. Of course such tests need not be paper-and-pencil ones. They could be imaginative practical or work-related assessments, but still be context-bound, and thus would encounter the same problems as all traditional tests; namely not being equally relevant to each of a wide diversity of curricula.

It seems clear, therefore, that there is an inbuilt contradiction here that is not only unresolved, but also hardly discussed in the recent literature. Moreover, given the difficulty, if not the sheer impossibility, of achieving comparability between existing public examination boards because of the differences between the syllabuses and courses it is difficult to see a more satisfactory solution emerging for profiles (Goldstein, 1982).

If profiles are to be faithful to a curriculum, then they will presumably have to sacrifice the aim of comparability across curricula, and cease striving to become context-free. This raises the possibility that some (key) elements of the profiles will be 'centralised' and others 'localised'. In the circumstances it seems very likely that the former will come to assume greater importance than the latter. It is interesting to note that government policy on the 17+ is that in 'key' areas (English, science, maths) performance will be 'externally assessed or moderated' while at the same time the policy generally supports profiles (DES, 1982a). Whether the assessments are norm-referenced or criterion-referenced is secondary.

Before leaving this topic, it is worth pointing out that the skill descriptions used in profiles so far developed for the school or further education system presuppose, because of the context-free requirement, that there really are abilities or skills which can be applied equally within different contexts. Thus, in mathematics, skills are defined in terms of symbolic mathematical operations so that a child who can 'calculate a percentage', for example, presumably can do so in all practical contexts. What many researchers have realised is that such symbolically defined skills do not necessarily transfer from one situation to another, since performance depends upon disposition and motivation, for example, as well as competence, and indeed that the autonomous existence of a 'skill' is itself rather a slippery notion. It is arguable that this issue is fundamental to skill assessment and that if profiles ignore it their relevance will be greatly diminished.

This discussion has been mainly in terms of comparability, which is an attribute of assessment principally required by the selector (for employment, further or higher education) who wants to compare one individual with another. With formative profiles, comparison with others is less important; the record can then concentrate upon what the student has done, and under what conditions, so that the context is specified. The record can be cumulative, so that development of skills or their application in new contexts can be observed and discussed: the comparison is with the individual's own past and not with others' current performance. Reliance upon grades and grids is no longer necessary, and some schemes like the Record of Personal Experience (see de Groot, Chapter 7) consist only of the students' own accounts of their experiences (validated by an adult), without comment or judgement by the teacher.

In those schemes where a common framework is needed for the recording of judgements, valid, reliable and comparable assessment can be achieved only if assessors are trained to interpret the concepts used. Discussions of what is meant by the concept, the contexts or occasions in which it might manifest itself, and the evidence that would allow judgements to be made about the degree to which it is present, are all essential. Discussion followed by ratings of particular examples can generate a calibrated comment bank that will allow others to be trained more quickly in the use of a particular scale. Nevertheless, as pointed out above, once assessments are required to reflect learning contexts, true comparability becomes elusive. This will almost certainly happen if individual teachers or lecturers rate their own students.

There have been few studies of the degree to which the different scales in the profile are assessing separate attributes. In Scotland it was found that teachers were reluctant and often unable to make distinct assessments of personal qualities like honesty (SCRE, 1977), while Stratton found that improvements on one attribute were almost invariably matched by improvements on another (e.g. 'working with authority' and 'self awareness') though his findings were not consistent across his two samples of raters (Stratton, 1982a). While more studies of this kind would be useful, one must accept that lack of discrimination between attributes may arise through the 'halo' effect, that is, the tendency of a rater's overall impression (favourable or unfavourable) of the student to influence all the individual ratings. More training of raters, especially more discussion of specific examples of behaviour, may well reduce the 'halo' effect and so convey more real information.

SCALING OF PROFILE ELEMENTS

Whilst not all profile systems scale, if an employer or a teacher is offered a profile in which a number of disparate elements are each rated on a scale of 1–4 say, there is a clear invitation to compare the ratings. A student might be rated 1 (high) on 'planning a task' and also 1 on 'working with colleagues'. Yet if the former is applicable only to say 5 per cent of the population and the latter to 25 per cent it is difficult to see how the two ratings can be equated. Indeed, the only method of satisfactorily equating them is to define the ratings as applying to the same population percentages. Thus this would imply a direct 'norm-referencing' of the grades, and is again an issue which has been very little discussed. It is relevant to note the public examination boards' experience with equating grades in different subject areas. After some early work in the 1970s (Nuttall et al., 1974) the attempt was abandoned once it was realised that this could be done only on a strictly norm-referenced basis as described above, thus violating the principle that the grading systems should not be solely norm-referenced.

There seems to be no good reason why there should be the same number of steps for each element. The number should be determined through experience and discussion so that the lowest should be in reach of all, and the highest, neither a ceiling which all reach nor a level which few reach. In some cases, there may be room for several intermediate steps, in others for one or even none. The Scottish Vocational Preparation Unit has also drawn attention to the giant and uneven steps in many schemes, which could be avoided if the definitions of the scale points were generated by experienced practitioners familiar with the range of attainment in the population and using real examples of student behaviour.

Scaling done in this manner, leading to an appropriate number of steps for each element rather than forced into a uniform mould, might be less prone to invite inappropriate comparisons between ratings while, at the same time, leading to more attainable goals for students and lecturers.

WEIGHTING AND COMBINING PROFILE ELEMENTS

The grid type of profile tends implicitly to give equal weight to each element, leaving the user to choose the subset on which she or he wishes to concentrate. Once this subset is selected, however, there is still an implied equal weighting so that the user, in the absence of specific guidelines, presumably will attach equal weight to the selected elements. Yet, for a variety of reasons this may be inappropriate. Some elements may be measured with low reliability (see later), some skills may effectively appear several times in slightly different guises, some assessments may have stronger validity than others, etc. In other words, the user generally needs more information about the profile other than the profile itself, just as the traditional test user should have access to information on reliability, validity, norms, etc. Yet, given the already large quantity of data supplied in some profile systems, the provision of such extra information seems somewhat daunting. Some research to study users' needs and the way in which they are used the information supplied would be welcome.

The weighting problem becomes of crucial importance if a user is to aggregate all or a subset of the elements. Not only will the above considerations apply, but the user will have her or his own relative weights and some guidance would be useful. In the absence of such guidance, there is a danger that many users will, often inappropriately, average in some simple fashion the ratings, grades or scores.

Weighting and combining elements is particularly tempting if performance is recorded quantitatively, and the temptation to make inappropriate combinations might be less in schemes where numbers are not attached to the descriptions of behaviour or evidence. The temptation to weight and combine elements is also reduced if each element does not have the same number of scale points.

RELIABILITY

Quite a lot has been written about the reliability of grading systems, especially in public examinations (Wilmott and Nuttall, 1975) and it is now widely recognised that quite large measurement errors exist, so that there is a reasonably high probability that a student with a particular grade could have obtained a grade one or even two removed on a parallel examination, for example, one with a different set of questions or with a different marker. The reliability of the elements of a typical profile, often assessed subjectively or perhaps by means of a short skills test, could be very low, much lower than that of a public examination. Yet there is a negligible amount of serious effort devoted to studying this problem. Of course, as Macintosh says, validity is fundamental and we have already said something about that. However, if a very unreliable profile is interpreted too literally by a user, serious mistakes can occur. Consider, for example, the SLAPONS profile designed to communicate arithmetic skills to employers (Pratley, 1982). Each element has a 'score' of from 0 to 5, yet as with many conventional examinations, there is little indication of whether a difference of 1 or 2 or 3 score points between students or between elements is to be treated as meaningful or could be within 'measurement error'.

It is, of course, quite difficult to obtain estimates of measurement error (the standard error of measurement as it is known in the context of standardised tests) and the most popular traditional methods seem of little use (Ecob and Goldstein, 1983). The measurement errors can arise from a number of sources. There are differences between assessors or raters. There is a variation in the tasks on which students are judged and there is variation in the response given by the student from day to day or situation to situation. Also, in a profile, some of these measurement errors may be correlated and their effects thus compounded.

Stratton studied the agreement between raters by asking them to place examples of behaviour on the profile scale (Stratton, 1982b). There was consensus for 71 per cent of the examples, though for about a third of these the consensus may have been spurious. A sound consensus therefore emerged only with just less than half the examples. The raters were, however, inexperienced, and Stratton concluded that agreement might be much higher among trained, experienced raters. But this study shows the magnitude of error that may arise from just one source, and reinforces the need for considerable careful research in order to provide some indication of measurement error. For example, a set of confidence intervals, based on rough estimates, one for each element, could be devised so that judgement of differences would occur only for non-overlapping intervals. These could also, in principle, be incorporated visually onto a profile chart, as is often provided with standardised test batteries, and we would suggest that those who are preparing profiles pay particular attention to this possibility.

Drawing attention to measurement error is particularly important with summative profiles because of the importance of the decisions that might be made in the light of the information contained in them. With formative profiles, where irrevocable decisions can be avoided, lower reliability might be tolerated if an increase in reliability can only be achieved at the expense of validity. But it is likely that the techniques used to enhance reliability, like more training, the use of two or more raters or gathering more evidence, are also those that will enhance validity by promoting clarification and deeper understanding of each element in the profile. Thus we again return to the importance of collaborative development and operation of profile systems, in which training occurs through discussion and rating of examples, and where the possibilities and limitations of a profile system can be illuminated.

WHITHER PROFILES?

We have, quite deliberately, emphasised the current technical short-comings of profile research and implementation. We do so not because we wish to argue against profiling as such, in fact quite the contrary because we believe that profiles do have interesting potential. It is because we are concerned that a too ready acceptance of a technically weak system will ultimately be counter-productive when its deficiencies become apparent during use. As we have indicated, in the well-established area of public examinations there are still considerable technical problems to overcome and in the sophisticated area of statistical test theory and psychometrics these controversies over fundamentals continue to rage. In both these areas, part of the case against the assessment techniques has rested on technical inadequacies. We are quite clear that the technical problems surrounding profiles are just as difficult as in these other areas and to ignore them would seem to be folly.

In our view, it would be wise to spend time now reflecting on these technical matters before too widespread and too rigid systems are developed. From a research point of view there is no doubt that there are considerable challenges, and in the areas of reliability, scaling, weighting and studying 'skills' it should be possible to make useful progress.

GRADED TESTS

The graded tests movement shares many of the aims of the profiling movement, for example, a desire that education and assessment are seen as positive rather than negative experiences for all students, and a determination to put the curriculum first. Well-established in sport, music and other performing arts, graded tests are relatively recent arrivals in mainstream subjects of the secondary school curriculum, but have already made a dramatic impact upon the teaching and learning of modern languages and, in the Kent/Schools Council Mathematics Project, upon mathematics.

As Baumgart argues in Chapter 4, the basic idea of graded tests is not new and might be considered part of normal good practice. Phase tests in Technician Education Council (TEC) units, and indeed the TEC system of units at progressively higher levels (e.g. Maths 1, Maths 2, Maths 3), are straightforward examples of graded tests, where progress to the next level is contingent upon success at the previous level (a success that comes to most, if not all, students).

Yet graded tests have suddenly begun to attract a good deal of attention. The Cockcroft Report (DES, 1982b) has given graded tests— called 'graduated' tests there—further respectability and, in response to its recommendations, the DES has announced a substantial programme of research and development on graded tests in mathematics, principally for low attainers. Some of the modern language schemes are also designed principally for low attainers, but others are for the full ability range, as are most of the schemes in sport and the performing arts.

Perhaps the best known scheme (and certainly the oldest, founded some 100 years ago) is run by the Associated Board of The Royal School of Music. It attracted nearly 350,000 entries from the UK and Eire in 1980, an average of over 50,000 for each of the first five grades and sharply fewer (below 20,000) for the top three grades which involve a theory component as well as a practical. Each of the grades is designed to represent a defined standard of performance while the grades together form a progressive sequence of development in practical musicianship. The examination can be taken several times a year and the grades are not tied to particular ages, so that the scheme is tailored to the progress of each individual. Furthermore, as with sports, the choice of test items or pieces tends to be limited, with many elements, such as scales, known in advance.

Similar features, apart from the last, are characteristic of virtually all graded test schemes. In his review of graded tests Harrison (1982) encapsulates the essence of a typical graded test scheme in modern languages in three features: 'that it is progressive, with short-term objectives leading on from one to the next; that it is task-oriented, relating to the use of language for practical purposes; and that it is closely linked into the learning process, with pupils or students taking the tests when they are ready to pass.'

The curricular side of the schemes is especially significant in modern languages, where the movement is known as Graded Objectives in Modern Languages (GOML) to emphasise that the guiding principle is in the development of a well-defined progression of educational objectives (building from the bottom upwards) rather than in the tests themselves.

Advocates of GOML schemes (of which there were about 60 in 1981, according to Harrison) point to the increased motivation of their pupils, with tangible proof given by dramatic increases in the proportion of third-year pupils opting for modern language courses in their curriculum in the vital fourth and fifth years. They also report that pupils and parents value the certificates issued for each grade.

Nevertheless, in most of what has been written about graded tests (as about profiles) there is little dispassionate evaluation, and it is therefore difficult to analyse what the key ingredients of their success in motivating pupils really are. One is almost certainly the short-term nature of the objectives allied to the principle of mastery learning and testing by way of criterion-referenced tests, which more than 90 per cent will pass in modern languages (and more than 80 per cent in music): that is, positive reinforcement, coupled with a tangible reward, at relatively frequent intervals (in contrast to public examinations where reward is stored until the end of five years of secondary education, and then is granted to the few rather than the many).

Another key ingredient is the enthusiasm of the teachers, sparked off, it would seem, by the curricular innovations of GOML. GOML schemes tend to be local and the teachers using the schemes have the chance to be involved in the further development of the schemes and in the assessment of their own pupils. This professional commitment is reminiscent of the early days of the Certificate of Secondary Education (CSE) examination, and may well be dissipated (as many would say has happened in the CSE) as the schemes become routine or are taken up by those who have not been party to the original development. In Oxfordshire, HM Inspectorate judged that in many schools there was still far to go in thinking about appropriate objectives for the less able, which stresses how difficult it is to translate laudable aims into effective classroom practice (HMI, 1983).

The most common type of problem raised by GOML teachers in the survey conducted by Harrison was organisational, for example, a lack of secretarial help, additional demands on time or the organising of the oral tests themselves. But it is apparent that the organisational problems posed by individual rates of progress have largely been ducked by teachers, who have used the expedient of testing all pupils at about the same time. HMI are critical of this failure to meet what most would regard as one of the cardinal principles of masterly learning:

> 'On the whole, however, it [the use of Oxfordshire's graded test scheme] tends to be confined to the less able pupils who all take the test at the same time. . . . Even where groups have this measure of homogeneity it is clear that some pupils are being faced with too easy a test which for others is still too difficult. . . . Thus, while the original intention of a high pass-rate is achieved, the timing of testing is more often related to the age of the pupils than to their linguistic readiness.'

Sport and the performing arts tend to be taught either individually or in small groups not as closely linked to age as school year groups, and therefore avoid the problem of modern languages. But that problem is likely to be as acute in mathematics and other subjects for which graded tests are currently being proposed, namely science and English.

It is clear that the individualisation of learning, something that is likely to be accelerated by the microprocessor, creates organisational problems for an individual teacher or lecturer within the normal institutional constraints. Those concerned with whole institutions, such as principals, heads and LEAs, need to consider the implications of the widespread introduction of graded tests, and at least one Chief Education Officer has already welcomed the implied break with the tradition of grouping pupils by age and the possibility of grouping by attainment level or developmental stage instead (Brighouse, 1982).

THE CURRICULUM AND GRADED TESTS

Mansell remarked that 'profiling forces assessment into the learning process' (Mansell, 1982); the worry of many is that graded tests will force assessment into the learning process not in the constructive way hoped for by Mansell, but in a destructive way that will lead to an excess of testing and to a backwash effect throughout the secondary school or further education curriculum that will make the backwash effect of the much maligned systems of examinations at 16+ look mild in comparison. Curriculum-led assessment may be a splendid concept when the agreed curriculum commands enthusiasm and support, as it manifestly does in modern languages, but where there is no agreed curriculum or where the field of study is so vast that several different curricula are equally acceptable (as is the case of English), the particular subject curriculum that comes to lead the graded tests may be viewed by many teachers as a straitjacket. On the other hand,

Pearce sees graded testing acting as a stimulus to sort out some of the problems of curriculum diversity:

> 'Graduated testing on any scale would expose the flaws in our position with painful clarity. The real need is a machinery to enable teachers to negotiate agreed curricula and institutionalize those agreements with a necessary minimum of validation. That is what has happened with BEC, and to a different extent with TEC, with on the whole very encouraging consequences as well as the inevitable protests of those in whom the loss of their chains induces a state of terror' (Pearce, 1983).

One way to guard against the worst sort of backwash is to ensure that the assessment procedures validly measure the full diversity of curricular objectives. That requirement almost certainly demands an impressive array of oral, practical and written assessments, as well as course work, projects and other extended exercises so that we should talk of graded assessments rather than graded tests. Couple these assessments with the need for at least two formal occasions of testing each year at each grade level, and one arrives at a substantial assessment industry that is viable only if the teachers themselves accept a major role in the assessment of their own pupils.

The technical issues in assessment of pupils by teachers have been studied extensively (for example, Cohen and Deale, 1977) and can be summed up in the two concepts of reliability and comparability. With criterion-referenced graded tests, achieving agreement about the criteria for marking among all those involved might be simpler than it is within traditional public examinations, but the variation in the conditions under which the tests are given and the variation in the tasks from school to school, and occasion to occasion, may wipe out any enhanced reliability of marking. Since there is a ready opportunity to retake a graded test, it might be argued that reliability of assessment is not as important as it is within the public examination system but this will depend upon the significance of the decisions made as a consequence of the test result.

There is a further fundamental difficulty which arises particularly acutely when a test can be retaken, namely the opportunity to learn, or teach to, the test itself, so that the curriculum will become distorted. To avoid this problem, tests would have to be changed between administrations and a moment's reflection will indicate the enormity of the task of continually developing new tests and equating them with the old, where testing takes place two or three times a year. The investment of time and expertise that this process requires is well represented in Holland and Rubin (1982). We are not aware that this issue has been faced seriously by the advocates of graded tests.

If mastery is in fact essential before a student can successfully work at the next level, then a false positive (a pass given when a fail should have been) may be as damaging as a false negative, which denies a student who is ready to move up the opportunity to do so. The consequences for individual students, especially at higher levels, where the results are more obviously for external consumption, may lead to too great an emphasis on striving for high reliability. As with public examinations, the fear would then be that the demand for high reliability will override the demand for validity. This tension appears to be a common feature of assessment systems, and the direction in which it is resolved tends to be a function of the significance of the decisions made on the test results. Open entry to higher education, for example as in the Open University, would reduce the significance of A-level grades.

Similar concerns arise with the pressure for comparability. The more standardisation that is imposed in the quest for reliabilty and comparability, the greater the threat to the key features of graded tests. One area in which comparability might reasonably be sought is over the number of levels in a graded test scheme designed principally for the age range 11 to 16. Most of the modern language schemes have five levels, and the Cockcroft Report suggests between four and six. But in the first case, the five levels span the full ability range and five years of secondary education, while in the second the target is just low attainers from the age of 14 upwards.

DETERMINING GRADE LEVELS

What considerations are important in the choice of the number of levels and their positioning or spacing? Educational theorists are not in sufficient agreement in most fields to provide an answer, and so the choice will be guided largely by practical considerations such as balancing the value of frequent feedback to students with the desire to avoid excessive testing. How the grades of the graded tests might be linked to the grades of public examinations, most obviously those at 16+, if indeed such a link is either desirable or feasible, is also a matter for much discussion in the GOML movement as more and more schemes develop level 4 and 5 material (for more detail about these issues, see Harrison, 1982 and Kingdom, 1983).

Of more fundamental concern, as Baumgart also argues in Chapter 4, is whether the concept of progression from one grade to the next makes sense in many subjects of the curriculum. While almost all subjects are taught on a broad principle of progress, this progress is not tied to the linear development of an unvarying set of objectives and there are many different ways of progressing through the same sylla-bus. Mastery of the objectives at one level may, therefore, not be essential to the study of the objectives at the next level, and graded tests could easily become simply modular tests, that is, tests on self-contained content that can be taken in any order and whose material can be forgotten without apparent penalty after the test has been taken.

In practice, the lack of differentiation and individualisation in education (and the Oxfordshire modern language schemes are prob-ably typical in this respect) probably serves to make the graded part of GOML tests relatively insignificant: the important things are teacher enthusiasm and pupil rewards. A modular scheme might serve just as well. The most precious ingredient, therefore, becomes teacher enthu-siasm, which puts a premium on local self-determination and involve-ment and argues against making national or regional comparability so important that the development of graded tests becomes simply another centralised assessment activity.

Another issue is whether attainment of a grade or level, particularly when specified in criterion-referenced terms, can satisfactorily be determined at the gross level of a subject or has to be at a much more disaggregated level as we have discussed earlier in the case of profiles. In public examinations Orr and Nuttall (1983) argue that true criterion-referencing and aggregation are incompatible, and the same arguments would seem to apply to graded assessments. Harrison draws attention to the uneasy compromise between global certification and criterion-referencing that seems to be arising in some of the GOML schemes. Dealing with more narrowly defined skills or domains may help to make the progression through the grades more obvious, and allows for some skills to be put into cold storage at some levels while new ones are introduced, thus adding more flexibility in those cases where there is no single route of progress. At the same time, reasonably reliable separate assessments of many skills at each level may magnify the testing load unbearably, especially for the assessor.

PROFILES AND GRADED ASSESSMENTS

Thus there are a number of common, or very similar, issues facing profiles and graded assessments. In particular, the choice of the elements or dimensions that should be assessed deserves much deeper thought and investigation. At present, the dimensions have been chosen for sound educational (curriculum-led) reasons but without much subsequent exploration of overlap and redundancy. Sometimes a single dimension embraces multiple objectives that are better separated. More careful specification of the objectives and the evidence needed to determine whether they have been successfully or partially achieved would clearly be beneficial, and could be followed after the event by the straightforward analyses used by Stratton (1982a) to detect redundancy (or possible 'halo' effect).

Deciding upon the number of reporting levels and the size of the steps is also a shared problem. Its solution must be rooted in the experience of teachers and lecturers whose knowledge of the typical performance and the range of performance in the particular population of pupils or students is vital. But too great a reliance on the norms of the past should be avoided; both profiles and graded assessments have stimulated unexpected improvements in motivation and attainment, and the definition of the steps should therefore be carried out in action rather than determined in advance.

This leads to the suggestion that more needs to be established about the effects of profiles and graded assessments upon students and lecturers. It was suggested above that the notion of 'grades' or 'progression' might be relatively unimportant and that the key ingredients were public rewards for the students and the enthusiasm of the teachers, but this is still speculative. Investigations of profile schemes in action (following Goacher, and Stratton) and evaluation of the new graded test developments are essential. This is particularly important where graded test schemes are being devised only for the 'low attainers', since the dangers of labelling in this procedure are only too obvious; there are, in any case, considerable but rarely discussed problems in actually defining, for example, the 'lowest 40 per cent of the ability range'.

Both profiles and graded tests make the curriculum that leads them much more obtrusive than the system of conventional examinations. The consequence is that, if lecturers and teachers are to preserve their freedom in choice of teaching strategy and examples relevant to the local context, both kinds of developments must be local rather than national (though a national framework is, of course, not ruled out). The inherent limitations in the concept of comparability must be exposed so that the advantages of formative assessment can be permitted to flourish. But by putting emphasis on the local, the pressing need for training of assessors is also emphasised and made more urgent.

Although some profile schemes imply that each dimension is judged in the same way on a four-point scale, the evidence for the judgements can be of very different kinds, ranging from single subjective appraisals of personal qualities to cumulative test-based assessments of numerical skills. In the latter case, there is potentially a very obvious marriage of profiles and graded assessments.

It comes as no surprise, then, that profiles and graded tests are being brought together. The Cockcroft Report envisaged that performance in the graded tests might contribute to the kind of profile described above, an idea that has rapidly been taken up by a number of LEAs and examining bodies. For example, ILEA are proposing a 'London Record of Achievement', a portfolio containing details of examination passes, other achievements in school and a profile compiled by teachers, parents and the pupils themselves (see Mortimore and Keane, Chapter 5). The portfolio will also contain the results of graded tests in mathematics, English, a foreign language (European or Asian), science, and design and technology, though development work has begun only in mathematics, English and science.

Even more advanced are the plans for the Oxford Certificate of Educational Achievement (OCEA) which Willmott describes in Chapter 9, that will link a profile with graded assessments and examination results on one certificate.

The principal contrast between graded assessments and profiles (anyway, in their record form rather than the grid form) lies in their stance towards quantification and measurement. Graded assessments are firmly within the psychometric tradition of tests and examinations, while the advocates of profiles are often against measurement and the reductionism and trivialisation that all too often accompany measurement. So, in the union of profiles and graded assessments, we see the exciting prospect of bringing together the humanistic and quantitative traditions in educational assessment. From this could emerge a most fruitful collaboration that could give a new rigour to humanistic assessment while preserving the pre-eminence of validity and curricular relevance.

To achieve this, action research is essential, integrating the development with the evaluation, and analysing the processes of selection, judgement and interpretation in the development and use of the assessments within the context of the college, school and workplace. While the technical issues we have discussed also need to be studied, what is not needed is the sort of detailed technical research of the type that has been done for 50 years on existing examination systems, largely atheoretical and motivated by a desire to provide merely technical answers to essentially educational problems. Just as the accent in assessment moves to stress its formative value rather than its summative use, so the research should develop so as to be sensitive to such changes.

REFERENCES

Balogh, J. (1982) *Profile Reports for School Leavers*. York: Longman for Schools Council.

Black, H.D. & Dockrell, W.B. (1981) *Diagnostic Assessment in Secondary Schools*. London: Hodder and Stoughton for SCRE.

Broadfoot, P. (1982) 'The pros and cons of profiles', *Forum*, **24**, pp. 66–9.

Brighouse, T. (1982) *Education*, 24/31 December, p. 491.

Burgess, T. & Adams, E. (ed.) (1980) *Outcomes of Education*. London: Macmillan Educational.

Cohen, L. & Deale, R.N. (1977) *Assessment by Teachers in Examinations at 16+*, Schools Council Examinations Bulletin 37. London: Evans/Methuen Educational.

Department of Education and Science (1982a) *17+: A New Qualification*. London: HMSO.

Department of Education and Science (1982b) *Mathematics Counts* (the Cockcroft Report). London: HMSO.

Ecob, R. & Goldstein, H. (1983) 'Instrumental variable methods for the estimation of test score reliability', *Journal of Educational Statistics*, **8**, 3.

Further Education Curriculum Review and Development Unit (1982a) *A Basis for Choice*. London: FEU.

Further Education Curriculum Review and Development Unit (1982b) *Profiles*. London: FEU.

Goacher, B. (1983) *Recording Achievement at 16+*. York: Longman for Schools Council.

Goldstein, H. (1982) 'Models for equating test scores and for studying the comparability of public examinations', *Educational Analysis*, **4**(3), 107–18.

Harrison, A.W. (1982) *Review of Graded Tests*, Schools Council Examinations Bulletin 41. London: Methuen Educational.

Harrison, A.W. (1983) *Profile Reporting of Examination Results*, Schools Council Examinations Bulletin 43. London: Methuen Educational.

Her Majesty's Inspectorate (1983) *A Survey of the Use of Graded Tests of Defined Objectives and their Effect on the Teaching and Learning of Modern Languages in the County of Oxfordshire*. London: DES.

Holland, P. & Rubin, D. (ed.) (1982) *Test Equating*, New York: Academic Press.

Kingdom, J.M. (1983) *Graded tests*. Paper presented at an informal seminar at the University of London Institute of Education.

Macintosh, H.G. (1982) 'A 17+ package: a view from the school', in *Profiles*, FEU.

Mansell, J. (1982) 'A burst of interest', in *Profiles*, FEU.

Nuttall, D.L., Backhouse, J. and Willmott, A.S. (1974) *Comparability of*

Standards between Subjects, Schools Council Examinations Bulletin 29. London: Evans/Methuen Educational.

Orr, L. & Nuttall, D.L. (1983) *Determining Standards in the Proposed Single System of Examining at 16+*. London: Schools Council.

Pearce, J. (1983) 'The future of graded tests', *Education*, 17 June, 465–6.

Pratley, B. (1982) 'Profiles in practice', in *Profiles*, FEU.

Scottish Council for Research in Education (1977) *Pupils in Profile*. London: Hodder and Stoughton for SCRE.

Scottish Vocational Preparation Unit (1982) *Assessment in Youth Training: Made-to-measure?*. Glasgow: Jordanhill College.

Stratton, N.J. (1982a) *An Evaluation of a Basic Abilities Profiling System across a Range of Education and Training Provision*. Interim report for CGLI Profiling Project 3. London: CGLI.

Stratton, N.J. (1982b) *Reliability of basic skills profiles*. Paper given at the British Education Research Association 7th Annual Conference, St. Andrews.

Willmott, A.S. and Nuttall, D.L. (1975) *The Reliability of Examinations at 16+*. London: Macmillan Education.

14

Record Breakers?

ANDY HARGREAVES

*The question of whether profiles and records of achievement will
fulfil the hopes that lie behind so many development initiatives is
still open to question. Will such records help to provide a more
meaningful and thus motivating educational experience for the
majority of pupils? Or, as Hargreaves argues in this chapter, are
they accompanied by inherent dangers of subjectivity and intru-
siveness which could lead to far worse disenchantment than
anything we know at present? As will be apparent from other
chapters in this book, Hargreaves is not alone in this concern, and
his analysis provides a timely warning that such development
needs to be accompanied by sustained and impartial evaluation to
study whether the impact of the profiling process in practice really
does fulfil its avowed aims.*

—Editor

Introduction

In this chapter, I want to delve into some areas of difficulty and
ambiguity that seem to me to be contained within the Records of
Achievement initiative; to examine a number of issues and questions
which, in my view, could well break rather than make this important
new mould for educational practice if they are left unattended. My
contribution to this volume, then, is a critical one: it is a contribution

that is designed not to celebrate or persuade people of the importance of records of achievement—that task has been discharged very effectively elsewhere in other chapters—but to ask questions, some of them quite fundamental, which will point to areas of doubt and difficulty.

For some readers, especially those who are now broadly convinced about the desirability of records of achievement, this kind of approach might seem an untimely, pessimistic intervention in the present debate; a churlish attempt to clip the wings of an important innovation just as it is about to take flight. I should like to stress, however, that the chapter is written from a standpoint of broad sympathy towards and enthusiasm for many of the principles which records of achievement are designed to realise; for the processes of enhancing pupils' self-esteem and self-awareness, giving genuine recognition to the whole range of their achievements (not just academic ones), and bringing about a transformation of the teacher-pupil relationship so that a genuine dialogue which allows and encourages criticism and questioning of current practice *on both sides* can take place. It is precisely because of that kind of interest that I have written this chapter; out of a deep concern that unless certain ambiguities about the purposes of records of achievement are recognised, confronted and dealt with by those who implement them in schools, and unless various constraints on the actual practice of recording pupils' personal achievements and experiences are faced up to, managed and in some cases eased by teachers, heads and policy-makers; then many of those splendid principles and purposes of the kind I have just outlined may well be neglected, frustrated or undermined. What, then, are the dilemmas and constraints to which I refer, and how might they be resolved?

DILEMMAS

As I see it, those who participate or are about to participate in the Records of Achievement process—teachers, pupils and indeed parents—must, in their different ways, face and grapple with at least two important dilemmas of purpose and orientation that are bound up with this important innovation: dilemmas of *motivation versus selection* and *independence versus surveillance*. In either case, I want to argue, what is at stake is a fundamental choice: between a system which will define, declare and strengthen young people's identities and independence on the one hand, or a system which will trim and tailor those identities to the requirements of efficient employer selection and systematic social control on the other.

The motivation/selection dilemma[1]

In *Records of Achievement: a Statement of Policy*, the Department of Education and Science state that the Secretaries of State believe there to be four main purposes which records of achievement should serve. Among these, they list:

> 'Motivation and personal development: they [the records—AH] should contribute to pupils' personal development and progress by *improving their motivation*, providing encouragement and increasing their awareness of strengths, weaknesses and opportunities.'

> 'A document of record. Young people leaving school or college should take with them a short summary document of record which is recognised and valued by employers and institutes of further education. This should provide a more rounded picture of candidates for jobs or courses than can be provided by a list of examination results, thus *helping potential users to decide how candidates could best be employed, or for which jobs, training schemes or courses they are likely to be suitable*.'

> (DES, 1984, para. 11—my emphasis)

One of the dominant reasons for developing records of achievement, not just for the DES but also for many of those schools which have already produced their own home-grown schemes, is and has been to enhance pupils' motivation. In a review of visits to ten secondary schools where records of achievement were already in use—a review which, it was hoped, would 'serve to inform the debate on records of achievement' (HMI, 1983b:3)—Her Majesty's Inspectorate found that one of the two major reasons why they had been instituted was to increase motivation, particularly among less able pupils (p. 6). Similarly, in her relatively detailed study of nine secondary schools already using some kind of record of personal achievement, Janet Balogh (1982, p. 15) reported that 'the desire to improve pupil motivation by involving students in their assessment process or by making it clear that their behaviour and attitude could affect their leaving statement' was a very important factor in the development of such schemes. And in a follow-up study, carried out under the same auspices of the Schools Council, Brian Goacher (1983, p. 15) found that many schools partici-

---

[1] A more detailed version of this particular part of my argument appears in A. Hargreaves (1985a). Reproduced with thanks to P. Lang and M. Marland.

pating in a scheme to develop records of personal achievement did so because 'it was considered that pupils would benefit from improved motivation due to a better indication of what was expected as well as from more obvious indications of progress'. The Department of Education and Science, agencies like Her Majesty's Inspectorate and the (late) Schools Council who advise them, and (not least) a number of individual schools themselves, have therefore seen in records of personal achievement an important opportunity for boosting the motivation of those pupils who have so far had little else to gain from the secondary school system.

The school's capacity to realise these motivational goals is, of course, significantly limited by the discouraging press of economic realities on the hopes and aspirations of young people. That is to say, the problem of motivation, while encountered widely within schools, is not at all confined to them. Weakened motivation to work, to aspire, to conform is an increasingly pervasive feature of social life in modern Britain. With few prospects of work for many young people, depressingly little promise of any substantial improvement in overall living standards, and growing doubt as to whether hard-earned academic achievement will reap the once customary financial rewards, it is little wonder that bonds of mass loyalty to the present social and economic order should weaken, that indifference and dissent should increasingly prevail. It is not just problems of motivation in school that have to be faced therefore, but a deep-seated and far-reaching crisis of motivation, of loyalty and commitment to the present social order in society as a whole (Habermas, 1976). Only economic and social policies which offer young people realistic prospects of opportunity and improvement at least at the levels their parents had come to expect as usual, can ultimately deal adequately with a crisis on this sort of scale.

But if the economic context of educational reform is not particularly conducive to the very changes it requires, a second factor poses an even more immediate and direct threat to the motivational aims of records of achievement: the use of such records in the process of occupational selection, as a document that will be 'recognised and valued by employers' (DES, 1984, p. 3). I want to propose that these two purposes, motivational and selective, are fundamentally incompatible in important respects.

It is commonly assumed that employers will normally be among the major 'users' of a student's final (i.e. summative) record of achievement and of its personal record component in particular. As the Records of Achievement initiative has gathered momentum and gained a national impetus, the practice of including employers in the design of such records has therefore become increasingly widespread, if not yet ubiquitous. Within a political and educational climate where industrial values are attaining increasing force and respectability and where they make up an important part of the context of educational reform, it is easy to understand why educators are considerably more eager than they once were to encourage employer involvement in this and other innovations for the secondary age range, and why they are keen to design those innovations in such a way as to be 'user friendly'.

The move to involve employers and be mindful of their needs and interests concerning records of achievement is a politically astute one, then. Yet there is more to that move than sheer political opportunism. As I have argued elsewhere (A. Hargreaves, 1985a), employers have themselves grown increasingly dissatisfied with the present system of examination results supplemented by confidential references as a basis for selecting new employees. For a long time, successful performance in examinations has had to be interpreted by employers as an admittedly crude indicator of qualities of perseverance, commitment, motivation and so forth, when more direct information on such personal qualities would often have been preferred. Employers have thus begun to express cautious interest in a more extensive system of documenting pupils' personal achievements than most current forms of assessment allow (Goacher, 1984, p. 126).

Though there are clear arguments in favour of such a shift of attitude and orientation among employers towards a recognition of young peoples' personal as well as academic qualities, in practice such a move creates serious points of difficulty too. These are to be found at both the summative and formative stages of the recording process.

The Summative Statement

Schools and employers often have different views on the format that the final, summative record of achievement should take. Employers often prefer brief, summary descriptions of general pupil qualities (perseverance, punctuality, etc.) presented in the form of an easily-scanned set of numerical grades, ticked boxes or blocked-in charts (Balogh, 1982; Goacher, 1983; HMI, 1983b; A. Hargreaves, 1985a). Yet, what best suits the understandable needs for rapid processing of applications for the purposes of occupational selection does not necessarily best suit the needs of the individual pupil. Crude grades, especially where they are consistently low, may do little to enhance pupil motivation, as may an excess of negative comments (e.g. 'poor attendance') or other other slightly less obvious indicators of failure (e.g. 'can perform *simple* tasks'—Education Resource Unit for YOP,

1982). Cognisant of these sorts of difficulties and of their probable detrimental effects on pupil motiviation, it is not surprising that the Department of Education and Science have advised strongly against systems using 'ticks in boxes or numbers or letter gradings' or references 'to failures or defects'. (DES, 1984, p. 6).

One proposal which promises to circumvent these difficulties of contributing to occupational selection without prejudice to pupil motivation is for a final document which would take the form of a succinct prose summary involving 'sentences written for each pupil' (DES, 1984, p. 6). This, the DES argue, would be 'fairer to pupils' and 'less open to misinterpretation'.

Where this final statement is an open-ended one in which the choice of mentioned activities and experiences, the qualities they imply and the very words in which all these things are expressed are heavily influenced by the pupil, motivational ends could well be strongly fostered. The voice, the authorship of the documents will be largely the students' own; a matter which is as important for the longer term formative process, if not more so. As the contributors to a recent newsletter of the Oxford Certificate of Educational Achievement (1985, p. 3) indicated, the personal development and recording process should, in this respect, be very much 'about the student, by the student, for the student'.

Where the prose summary is more closed and entails less student involvement, however, the consequences for motivation are likely to be less positive. One such system of relatively closed prose recording is the *comment bank*. For reasons of cheapness and efficiency to which I shall return shortly, comment banks are currently being widely discussed as a serious optional form for records of personal achievement and I shall therefore devote a little space to them here.

Comment banks consist of pre-selected statements which identify beforehand the significant areas in which recordings are to be made, and the precise ways in which (indeed, the precise words through which) this is to be done. Thus, to take an example from the draft personal record sheet currently under consideration in one LEA, the tutor (in some cases with the student) rings or ticks an appropriate category under headings like 'attitude to people', 'attitude to activities' etc.[2] Under two sub-sections of 'attitude to people' for instance, the tutor must ring at least one of the following, adding any descriptive evidence as appropriate.

---

[2] The particular document cited here has been used only for trial purposes by the LEA involved, and that LEA has therefore not been identified.

P3A   He/she has a cheerful personality
P3B   Considerable concern for others has been shown
P3C   His/her confidence and assurance enable him/her to relate to other people well
P3D   The openness of his/her relationships enable him/her to solve conflict situations sensibly
P3E   He/she has shown himself/herself to be a responsible person
P3F   He/she is well mannered and courteous
P3G   He/she has a lively sense of humour

PD1   corresponds to a pupil who finds it very difficult to maintain relationships with (a) adults (b) pupils
PD2   corresponds to a pupil who refuses/is unable to relate to others despite encouragement
PD3   corresponds to a pupil who has formed no lasting relationships
PD4   corresponds to a pupil who is aggressive or lacking in self control
PD5   corresponds to a pupil who has shown neither an inclination, nor a capacity, for leadership.

What eventually appears as an open, continuous summative statement is in fact compiled from an assemblage of encircled, numbered categories. It is a disguised grid, no less. It is sometimes argued that systems of this kind have advantages for rapid systems of employer selection (though this assumes that the employers have access to the hidden 'codes' the comment banks contain), and for savings on teacher time by enabling them simply to encircle categories or punch them into a computer, rather than compile elaborate prose statements of their own. But these things are achieved at some cost; the cost of taking away the student's voice, his/her authorship, the stamp of his/her personal identity from the records of personal achievement and experience. In comment banks, student involvement is in effect reduced to making selections from lists of statements which, while they contain options, are not themselves negotiable and are not of the student's own making. While such sacrifices of personal involvement and authorship, such confiscations of the students' own voices and declarations of identity, might bring about certain short-term gains in organisational efficiency and employer relevance, the sacrifices made are probably quite damaging to the motivational purposes that records of achievement are intended to fulfil.

This is not to deny the need that schools may often have for some kind of guide, assistance or additional support for students and tutors involved in personal recording, especially where unskilled tutors and shy or inarticulate students are involved. Indeed, this argument is often put forward in defence of comment banks. But if it is starting points that are needed, or a list of possible areas to probe when discussion flags, then what is required is a supportive and suggestive 'prompt sheet', an optional tool to *stimulate* and *extend* the open-ended and two-sided process of recording students' positive achievements and experiences. The comment bank, however, constrains, contracts and closes down discussion rather than extending and enabling it.

The Formative Process

If the serious pursuit of motivational ends points to the open-ended prose statement as the most appropriate form for the summative document (with or without the assistance of prompt sheets), this still leaves unresolved the question of what kind of content that statement and its formative predecessors should contain. The difficulty for students and tutors here, in knowing just what to record, is that the kinds of qualities employers value and wish to see schools record are often not altogether the ones that schools themselves promote, or that some of their pupils deem to be important.

As long as the activities and experiences which pupils record and wish to record signal employability and all those synonyms for loyalty and obedience that employers value—they don't, contrary to popular belief, place much weight on initiative (Jones, 1983)—as long as their forte is with the piano, with scouting and guiding, or with the fishing club, then there is likely to be little conflict of interest or purpose between the pupil's own needs to declare and define his/her identity, and the interests of employers in identifying young people with qualities they regard as appropriate for employment. But where pupils' interests revolve around activities that suggest dissent (such as feminism or peace-campaigning) or where they imply deviance or nonconformity (such as Rastafarianism or breakdancing) then they and their tutors are placed in a real quandary: whether to define and declare interests and identities, however unconventional, even at the risk of prejudicing employment; or whether to edit, select, or even distort personal records a little so as to present a good impression to employers, but at the cost of concealing, suppressing or falsifying important aspects of pupils' own identities.

This dilemma—improve selection but weaken motivation, or boost motivation at the cost of selection— is a difficult one, and one that reaches right down to the finest details of the process of negotiating assessments between tutors and students. Ultimately, and most controversially, perhaps the most satisfactory solution to this would be to remove one of the parties engaged in this conflict of interest: i.e. to exclude the employers. If that seems an outrageous proposal— for it certainly flies in the face of all recent trends towards increasing employer involvement in curriculum development—it is as well to remember that very few young people now go directly into employment at sixteen (Raffe, 1984). And with the Chancellor of the Exchequer's recent proposals to extend the youth training system to two years, the documentation of pupils' personal records at sixteen will be still less relevant to employers in years to come. As far as employers are concerned, it is the report and recommendation of the most recent work-related experience of youth training that, aside from examination results (and increasingly now instead of them) will have the most direct bearing on their decisions to employ young people. Ironically, employers are scarcely *users* of records of personal achievement at all. Other than for reasons of political appeasement, then, there would appear to be few other grounds for their continued inclusion. Certainly, schools and exam boards and the like would do well to ponder the importance they attach to employer involvement, and the possibly negative implications of such involvement for the recording process and the motivational goals it is designed to achieve.

Short of strategies of exclusion of employers, however, the resolution of these difficult dilemmas, of these important value questions, will come to rest (as is so often the case) on the professional judgement of the individual classroom teacher as he/she participates with pupils in the process of negotiated assessment. Here, in making and having to make complicated philosophical and social judgements about what are acceptable and unacceptable activities for pupils to declare and record, teachers will need to be very much aware of the value questions that are involved to be able to reappraise their own values, to be aware of the dangers of stereotyping (Broadfoot, 1982) and to be able to monitor the effects of their own value assumptions on the recording process. For teachers—indeed for any human being—these are very challenging tasks to have to undertake, and if they are to be properly discharged they will demand the highest level of skill, awareness and sensitivity on the teachers' part.

As long as employer involvement in the Records of Achievement initiative remains, there will be no easy solution to this motivation/ selection dilemma: it is a matter of conscience and judgement with which teachers will continually have to wrestle on a one-by-one, individual pupil basis. It scarcely needs saying that a judgemental task of this magnitude and seriousness will require strong and continued in-service support, and sufficient time to treat it with the care and sensitivity it patently requires. This need for time and staff support clearly has important and unavoidable implications for the school context in which records of achievement are implemented. I shall return to these shortly.

The Independence/Surveillance Dilemma

A second major dilemma for Records of Personal Achievement concerns whether, intentionally or unintentionally, schools use them to increase pupils' independence and capacity for self-determination on the one hand, or to expand and refine schools' own capacities for maintaining surveillance, for instilling an unobtrusive but pervasive kind of discipline, on the other. Both these tendencies—the development of independence and the suppression of it—are contained within the Records of Achievement initiative. Either of them can follow as a widespread consequence of that initiative becoming established.

For many people who have been involved with records of personal achievement, such records hold out the hope of a radical departure from conventional secondary school practice. They offer—as many of the advocates of 'progressive' primary education in the 1960s did—the hope, the possibility of placing young people at the centre of their own learning, giving them increased responsibility for their own development and assessment, empowering them with the capacity for self-determination. Such principles were, for instance, central to the personal recording movement instigated by Stansbury (Swales, 1980). As de Groot argues in this volume, this was a movement which emphasised the student's autonomy, his/her ownership of and control over the process and product of recording. Here the role of teacher intervention was reduced to a minimum; the teacher's opinion and evaluation of what the student was recording was only offered if the student specifically wanted it.

In a document produced by the Management Group of one of the best known successors of these early schemes, PPR (Pupils' Personal Recording), this process is described as being:

> 'owned and controlled by the pupil and is made without imposition of ranking, rating, marking and censure. It is not something which develops merely as a response to teacher intervention. It can provide a framework for confident personal development in young people'.
> (PPR Management Group, 1984, p. 1).

That kind of development, they go on to say, is 'the highest aim in education'. It amounts to nothing less than 'the promotion of personal autonomy which will allow each person to make free, informed decisions as responsible adults and to exercise "a sense of personal power" ' (p. 2). Moreover, the group argue, successful PPR experience of this kind 'provides the bedrock for pupil participation in Records of Achievement' (p. 1).

Tyrell Burgess and Betty Adams, in Chapter 6 and elsewhere, have also advocated strong pupil involvement in schemes which record and assess their personal achievements, arguing that such involvement will help secure a basis for a whole new learning contract between teachers and pupils, based on principles of partnership rather than hierarchy. School-leaving statements which include records of personal experience and achievements that students have helped compile themselves, they say, would 'encourage young people to take charge of their own circumstances so that they leave school not only knowledgeable but also competent and independent'. This, they continue, 'will require teachers not to prepare for examinations by teaching to a syllabus, but to respond directly to what young people themselves need'. (Adams and Burgess, 1982, p. 1). As various practical examples in an earlier book of theirs indicate, the acceptance of pupils' rights to assert that sort of need carries with it an inescapable obligation to allow them opportunities to criticise the teaching and the curriculum they already receive, and to negotiate changes in it where appropriate (Burgess and Adams, 1980).

If the Department of Education and Science (1984) have not subsequently embraced these principles of 'pupil power' with quite that degree of enthusiasm, choosing instead to blur the issue of what form and extent pupil involvement should take—a strategy for which Burgess and Adams (1984) have criticised them heavily—developers of particular schemes at more local levels have been less circumspect. Another of the contributions to this volume describes the Oxford Certificate of Educational Achievement. In its draft handbook for pilot schools, OCEA describes the personal record component as aiming 'to involve students as active participants in their own development' and 'to open up possibilities for broader and deeper relationships between students and teachers' (OCEA, 1984, p. 4). And a glance at some of the Certificate Committees' working notes and memoranda would reveal pupil-centred statements of an even more forthright character.

Much of the grass-roots impetus behind records of achievement, then, is to do with the recognition and realisation of pupils' identities, with the development of their powers of independent judgement; that is, with the enhancement of their identity and independence as a whole. Nor are these things desired solely for their capacity to boost motivational ends; they are seen as something important and worthwhile in their own right.

Alongside these values, which place a premium on autonomy and independence, records of achievement also contain a set of possible purposes and consequences with different, indeed absolutely contrary, implications. The personal record component of records of achievement also has an extraordinary capacity to restrict young peoples' individuality, to discipline and control them through the power of a pervasive and intrusive pattern of personal assessment. I want to argue that this pattern, with its assessment and monitoring of affect as well as intellect, of personality as well as performance, according to a carefully graded schedule of systematised review, is in fact bound up with a more generalised trend towards the development and implementation of increasingly sophisticated techniques of social surveillance within society at large. In this respect, while records of personal achievement can certainly be used as part of a commitment to personal care, they can be employed equally well as part of a complicated apparatus of social and institutional control. What characterises this swing to surveillance, and what particular part might records of personal achievement be playing in this particular social development?

According to the distinguished French philosopher and historian, Michel Foucault (1977), attitudes to discipline and punishment have passed through three broad phases. At first, he says, punishment for serious crime was treated as a kind of vengeance where public torture provided a spectacle of retribution, in which the marks of that vengeance were applied to the body of the condemned person as a lesson in terror for all (p. 130).

In the second phase, punishment by vengeance was superseded by systems of correction designed to reintegrate offenders into society. Here, by opening prisons to the public and, through publicly visible signs of the convicts' dress, the chain gang, and such like, justice was *seen* to be done; a warning to others that it would be exercised on *them* if they should ever transgress in turn.

It is only quite recently, Foucault argues—mainly in this century— that the treatment of actual or potential offenders has entered a third and critical phase. Here, he says, punishment of whatever form has been gradually replaced or complemented by *discipline*. The purpose of this discipline is neither merely corrective nor even simply preventative, but is bound up with the very make-up of modern society and its concerns of control and efficiency (Broadfoot, 1984). Discipline, Foucault argues, is a finely graded, carefully regulated process of administrative control over both body and mind. As personification of this disciplinary process, Foucault cites Napoleon, a man who

'wished to arrange around him a mechanism of power that would enable him to see the smallest event that occurred in the state he governed; he intended, by means of the rigorous discipline that he imposed, to embrace the whole of this vast machine without the slightest detail escaping his attention'.

(Foucault, 1977, p. 141).

But this pattern of discipline is not merely exercised by particular individuals, by fascist dictators or even benevolent despots, but by and through entire administrative systems, where surveillance is perpetual and pervasive, intense and intrusive, continuous and remorseless in its application and effects.

At the heart of such systems of surveillance, Foucault argues, are two central principles: *normalisation* and *hierarchy*. Normalisation, or normalising judgement, involves comparing, differentiating, homogenising and excluding people in relation to assumed 'norms' or standards of what is proper, reasonable, desirable and efficient (p. 183). *Hierarchy* involves a process whereby power is exercised through 'a mechanism that controls by means of observation' (p. 170), where the powerful observe but are not themselves observed, where they see without being seen, where they judge, rank and rate, but are not themselves evaluated (p. 171).

Few processes, Foucault suggests, represent and embody this convergence of the principles of normalisation and hierarchy more clearly than the examination. For Foucault,

'the examination combines the techniques of an observing hierarchy with those of a normalising judgement. It is a normalising gaze, a surveillance that makes it possible to qualify, to classify and to punish' (p. 184).

All this, Foucault claims, makes it possible to establish and reaffirm the norm, and place people in relation to it.

In response to this interpretation of the role and function of examinations as instruments of surveillance, or normalisation and hierarchy, defenders of records of personal achievement might want to argue that they offer a pattern of assessment and a prospect for pupil's personal development which is quite different from and in many respects superior to the conventional examination system, with its principles of norm-referenced attainment. They would, I am sure, want to emphasise the non-hierarchical elements of partnership and negotiation involved in the personal recording process; they would want to stress the fact that pupils own and control the use of their final summative statement; and they would want to point to the distinctive contribution that self-assessment—assessment according to one's own set standards rather than to normative criteria established by others— makes to the recording of personal achievements and experience. A very good case indeed could therefore be made for saying that records of personal achievement are supremely equipped to mitigate and compensate for those very tendencies towards hierarchy and normalisation that are built into the conventional system of formal examining at 16+: that they can actually increase independence and suppress surveillance.

It is instructive to note, however, that when Foucault discusses examinations and their contribution to social surveillance, he by no means confines himself to conventional formal examinations with written papers, time limits and the like. For Foucault, the psychiatric examination and the case record assessment as applied in the prison service and social work are very much part of the same system. Indeed, it is in the case recording process that normalisation, hierarchy and all-embracing observation are at their most systematic.

Once upon a time, Foucault tells us, 'to be looked at, observed, described in detail, followed from day to day by an uninterrupted writing was a privilege' (p. 191); it was to have chronicled a biography of greatness and distinctiveness, to be part of a process of heroisation. But with the advent of disciplinary methods, he says, written description became 'a means of control and a method of domination . . . no longer a measurement for future memory, but a document for possible use'. In this particular kind of examination, Foucault goes on, each individual is simply made into a documented 'case'. It is a case which 'constitutes a hold for a branch of power', a case which describes, judges and compares the individual as someone who may now, or at some future unknown point need to be 'trained or corrected, classified, normalised, excluded, etc.'.

This building up of a dossier, of an extended case record, to be retrieved and referred to at any future point where the difficult work of institutional guidance and channelling, control and correction needs to be done, comes uncomfortably close to some aspects of the formative process of recording pupils' personal achievements. For instance, Broadfoot (1984) has noted how the system of continuous pupil assessment, of *orientation* in the French school system, already runs very much on these lines. And in Britain, comment banks seem as if they will be particularly well suited to the purposes of surveillance and control; ranking and rating pupils in relation to pre-selected (if thinly disguised) hierarchies of presumed institutional importance— according to the institution's criteria, not pupils' own—and in a form appropriate for easy and rapid processing and retrieval.

Moreover, the hooking up of personal records, particularly of the formative kind, to computer facilities in schools, as a number of schools are now planning to do, presents a strong threat to pupils' independence by enabling schools to keep hi-tech tabs on their pupils' emotional and behavioural whereabouts; to subject young people to and process them through a sophisticated technological apparatus of institutional control. In this respect, while very serious questions have quite properly been raised about who will be the users of a student's final summative record of achievement, we have scarcely begun to' discuss the equally important question of who will be the users of the *formative* records—pupils or teachers?—and for what purposes. Much of the decision that schools and their teachers will make in relation to the purposes of either independence or surveillance will hinge upon how this sensitive issue is resolved.

If the conversion of developing persons into easily processable cases is one surveillance-related danger inherent in personal recording, another is the development of a principle of observation and monitoring whose sophistication and comprehensiveness is virtually unsurpassed in the history of schooling. Foucault, following a hypothetical architectural structure of a perfect social and disciplinary observatory devised by Jeremy Bentham, terms this principle *panopticism*[3]. Panopticism is a principle of discipline in which power is exercised through an all-seeing but unseen observer, i.e. one who is so positioned to observe all those arranged around him without himself being observed. More than this, the power of panopticism resides not just in, observation per se, but in the observed never knowing whether they are being observed or not at any particular moment (Foucault, 1977, p. 201). For Bentham, this design was not just an architectural structure but an ideal abstract principle, a vision of how disciplined social relations could be sustained in society as a whole. Perfect surveillance!

The great advantage of panopticism is not only that it allows those in power to intervene at any moment, but that 'the constant pressure acts even before the offences, mistakes or crimes have been committed . . . its strength is that it never intervenes, it is exercised spontaneously and without noise' (p. 206).

In education, there have been few places where panopticism was more palpably evident than in the otherwise innocuous environment of the 'progressive' primary school. Here, despite a public and professional rhetoric which often stressed the collaborative quality of teacher–pupil relationships, and despite the superficial appearance of openness and equality which the architecture and internal organisation of 'progressive' primary schools tended to convey, teachers did not abrogate their control over pupils' learning and behaviour, but simply changed the mode of its operation. Control was no longer explicit and

---

[3] *Pan*—total, universal; *optic*—pertaining to sight.

overt but, to the 'outsider' at least, implicit and covert; quiet, detailed, unobtrusive in its operation (A. Hargreaves 1977). In making this shift to the implicit mode, teacher control did not diminish. On the contrary it became more comprehensive and more intrusive. In this 'invisible pedagogy' of the primary school, as Basil Bernstein (1975) called it, more and more of the child's life became open and subject to assessment. Not just performance, but emotions, behaviour, personal relationships—all were now subject to evaluation, appraisal and institutional intervention; to the teacher–judge's ever-watchful gaze. And if assessment now penetrated deeper into the child's personal and emotional being, it also extended across a wider range of his/her actions too. As the privacy of feeling became eroded, so too in principle did the realm of private space. Wherever children went, they were open to assessment. In the Wendy House they were watched, in the sand tray they were watched. In theory, no place was private; there was no hiding place from the teacher's relentless, if benevolent, pursuit.

In practice, however, surveillance was much less perfect, much less efficient than this. For strategies of teacher control and direction which are implicit and individualised, personal rather than public, also make exhaustive demands on teachers' time and energy where large pupil groups are managed on an individual basis in an open-plan setting. Under these conditions, personalised observation (the observation of eye and ear) is insufficient, and pupils often find that they are able to exploit the classroom's physical fluidity to escape the teacher's gaze and to avoid working. As some pupils I interviewed in a study of a 'progressive' middle school remarked,

> Teachers aren't often there to see you . . . With the teachers not being in the classroom all the time, they're all over the place looking after the other ones. All you have to do is stop dead and almost go to sleep.
>
> If you don't want to do it, there's nobody sort of jumping down your neck asking for it.
>
> Well you go into the toilets and you disappear and nobody really notices you until you're found later on.
>
> You can skive. They never know where you are, really.
>
> (A. Hargreaves, 1985b, p. 466).

The personalised, individualised observation of eye and ear in an open, large group setting is therefore necessarily limited in the degree to which it can realise the panopticist vision of perfect surveillance. Indeed, the recognition of those limits by teachers and heads in part explains why the use of written records has expanded in the primary sector in recent years as an aid to improving, monitoring and evaluating pupil progress.

But it is in the process of recording pupils' personal achievements and experiences that the combination of eye, ear and written word are potentially at their most powerful for fulfilling the task of social surveillance. Like 'progressive' primary teaching, records of personal achievement also review and regulate personal and emotional development, but they can do these things with far greater force and effectiveness. First, they carry with them the force of compulsion, of required pupil attendance in one-to-one sessions with their tutors, where it is virtually mandatory for emotions, feelings, and intentions to be exposed and subjected to scrutiny. Second, they bear the power of personalisation that is inherent in the intimate but imbalanced relationship between tutor and student, a relationship both intense and intrusive in the extent to which it allows the tutor to delve into emotional and personal areas that the student might otherwise wish to keep private. Third, they embody the continuous controls of periodic, regular reviews; a process which positions the pupil in relation to a document or computer-stored series of past reviews, marking his/her progress towards or deviation from 'normality'. This process, through the pupils' certain knowledge that there will be inescapable future reviews in an almost unending process of repeated and regulated assessment, suppresses 'deviant' conduct even before it arises.

The worst possible scenario for records of personal achievement, in which the principle of surveillance not independence is the dominant one, might be the 'ideal' system of modern penal treatment described by Foucault. Such a system, he argues,

> 'Would be an indefinite discipline; an interrogation without end, an investigation that would be extended without limit to a particular and ever more analytical observation, a judgement that would at the same time be the constitution of a file that was never closed' (p.227).

This is a nightmarish Orwellian vision of records of personal achievement, a vision in which all private alcoves, all means of escape from the all-encompassing gaze of permanent observation and assessment have been removed, a vision from which only the terror but little of the discipline of Orwell's OCEANIA (a name with an uncomfortably close resemblance to OCEA—the acronym for the Oxford Certificate of Education Achievement) has been removed.

If this vision is a depressing and frightening one, thankfully it is not by any means inevitable. The positive potential of records of personal achievement is very real: potential for independence, collaboration, criticism and questioning, for fostering genuine personal development and social awareness. But the dividing lines between care and control, independence and surveillance, are exceedingly thin ones. If I have devoted more attention to the possibilities for surveillance than for those of independence, that is because I regard the dangers and the imminent threat of increasing and intensifying surveillance in schools, as in society at large, as being very great: indeed, being no less than a threat to individual liberty, personal privacy and human diversity.

Schools and teachers, then, must recognise the choices that they have to make when they develop systems of recording pupils' personal achievements and experiences: choices between independence and motivation on the one hand, or selection and surveillance on the other. These choices are not merely academic; not just matters of theoretical nicety. They carry with them very serious practical implications. Systems which embrace the former (and in my view, more positive) set of values will require teachers who have a clear and agreed collective commitment to them, who are aware of the practical difficulties they entail in dealing with the more unconventional student, and who have the skills, sensitivity and professional courage to be able to foster qualities of independence and assertiveness on the part of their pupils, when the temptation to use the process of negotiated assessment as a mechanism of censure and control might be understandably greater.

CONSTRAINTS

If choice, commitment and awareness are essential to the business of implementing records of personal achievement in schools as a tool for enhancing personal development and independence, then schools and those who finance them must also recognise that teachers need time and opportunity to make these choices, to develop their skills and awareness. In this respect, I want to argue that if records of personal achievement are to be treated with the sensitivity and seriousness they patently require, then a number of other constraints that operate on teachers, that restrict their time and affect their educational commitments, will need to be attended to. Goodwill and exhortation will not be enough. In this final section, I want to explore four areas of constraint and pressure, whose management will in my view have important implications for the way in which teachers interpret and manage the personal recording process. These areas of constraint are time, subject commitments, examinations and what I call compound innovation.

Time

> In *Records of Achievement: A Statement of Policy*, the Department of
> Education and Science recognise that the processes of recording and
> discussion will make demands on teachers' time. The amount of time
> involved will need to be investigated. It will be essential to work out
> cost-effective arrangements for accommodating the processes of record-
> ing and discussion within schools' regular routines and to identify the
> scope for savings in other reporting systems and elsewhere.

(DES, 1984, para 41)

The problem of finding teacher time for records of achievement has
already been widely discussed in the literature on pupil profiles
(Balogh, 1982; Goacher, 1983; Broadfoot, 1982; Mortimore and
Mortimore, 1984) and is one that Her Majesty's Inspectorate have
also identified as placing major constraints on teachers' involvement in
innovation more generally.

In *Curriculum 11–16: Towards a Statement of Entitlement (Red
Book 3)*, for instance, HMI noted that teachers' existing time commit-
ments severely restricted the extent to which they could become
involved in processes of whole school curriculum reappraisal based on
HMI's classification of the curriculum into eight areas of experience.
They wrote:

> The work of the enquiry has demonstrated the difficulties of undertak-
> ing sustained evaluation and planning of the curriculum *and at the same
> time* meeting the pressures and demands of teaching and administration
> in a school . . . Problems of communication within the schools have
> been accentuated by the *limited time* which is available for this work in
> the normal context of school life.

(HMI, 1983a, p. 16).

In other words, unless teacher–pupil ratios are substantially improved
and non-teaching periods increased, one might expect, with DES and
HMI, that shortage of time over and above that allocated to ordinary
class demands will create major problems for teachers and schools in
the administration of records of personal achievement. And if as a
result the recording process comes to be handled within rather than
outside of the conventional class or tutor group setting, one might then
expect the distribution of teacher time *within* the class to be experienced as a major problem too, and to influence the kinds of teaching
strategies that teachers adopt there; perhaps pushing the rest of the
group into busy work while the more personalised business of one-to-
one assessment is being done (Sharp & Green, 1975).

Furthermore, if cost effectiveness and the making of economies in reporting systems are allowed to dominate unduly the management and operation of the personal record component of records of achievement, then teachers, schools, and LEAs may well find themselves drawn to systems which allow rapid and easy processing and which are quickly administered, easily stored and rapidly retrieved under these conditions. The comment bank and similar systems of pre-determined categories and criteria will look especially attractive, and teachers will be tempted and pressed into discharging the task of one-to-one negotiation in a swift and perfunctory manner, all at the cost of student involvement, of his/her own personal development and struggle towards assertive independence.

It is essential, therefore, that schools are provided with sufficient resources and teachers with sufficient time to administer personal recording with the sensitivity it requires; and that sufficient in-service opportunity is also made available on a continuous basis for teachers to recognise, clarify and confront the difficult social and moral value questions which are inextricably embedded in almost every moment of the recording process.

Subject Commitments

> 'The pilot schemes will need to address the implications of records of achievement for in-service training of teachers . . . In-service training is likely to have an important role to play in helping to equip teachers with *the skills needed* to make a success of the recording system'
>
> (DES, 1984, paragraph 41—my emphasis)

Curriculum and assessment innovations often carry with them requirements for change in teachers' pedagogy—the neutral chairperson in Humanities' Curriculum Project (Stenhouse, 1975), the organiser of collaborative group work in Active Tutorial Work (Baldwin & Wells, 1979), the non-interventionist teacher of PPR, and so on. One of the major areas of difficulty here is that the degree and kind of change needed in the development of new teaching skills often varies according to the teacher's subject. In *Red Book 3*, HMI noted that in general 'the organisation of secondary schools into subject departments . . . inhibits curricular reappraisal' and that 'this subject structure of the teaching profession exerts a particular kind of influence on ways of thinking about the curriculum' (HMI, 1983a, p.14).

In one sense this segregation of the teaching community into vipers' nests of vested interest seriously inhibits collective agreement on cross-curricular change. But in addition to this, a teacher's subject membership also affects his or her approach to pedagogical issues, be these concerned with, children's writing (Barnes & Shemilt, 1974), mixed ability teaching (Ball, 1981; Reid et al., 1981) or active tutorial work (Bolam & Medlock, 1983). Here, one might expect teachers of certain subjects to experience rather more difficulty than others in acquiring the interpersonal skills necessary for recording pupils' personal achievements and experiences. Physical science, mathematics and modern languages are three of the subjects that come most readily to mind here, subjects which have conventionally attributed little importance to the exploration and discussion of pupils' emotions and personal development (see Barnes and Shemilt, 1974).

The identification of such likely areas of difficulty are, of course, only loose predictions based on observation of how different kinds of subject teachers have responded to innovation elsewhere in the system. They are not hard and fast research findings—those are eagerly awaited. But they do suggest that schools might consider easing their teachers' long-standing subject loyalties a little by giving them a broader curricular role with younger pupils, encouraging them to offer unusual fourth and fifth year curricular modules outside their own subject in TVEI courses and the like, in order to widen their pedagogical experience and expertise. Such a policy would, of course, run directly counter to one major arm of government educational policy at the moment which, for complicated (and, in my view, somewhat misguided) reasons is currently seeking to tighten up the relationship between teachers' subject qualifications and the areas of the curriculum they teach in school (DES, 1983). It seems to me, however, that a policy of easing rather than strengthening teachers' subject loyalties may be extremely important for the successful implementation of Records of Personal Achievement.

Examinations

There has not yet been any serious proposition at the level of national policy that records of personal achievement should *replace* more conventional procedures of public examining at 16+. Many writers, including Her Majesty's Inspectorate (1979), have been asserting for some time that examinations exert a constraining, cramping effect upon the secondary school curriculum and upon the processes of teaching and learning that go on within it (Dore, 1976; D. Hargreaves, 1982; Goacher, 1984). Their restrictive effects on innovations within particular subject areas have been widely documented (Weston, 1979; Olson, 1982) and HMI have also noted how teachers' commitments to examination work make it difficult for them to embrace, or take seriously, proposed changes in their teaching which would seem to threaten their success in such work. In *Red Book 3*, HMI draw attention to the problems posed by 'society's requirement that young people should possess qualifications at the end of their formal education in the subjects of the conventional curriculum' (p.13). This pressure, they note, has if anything been heightened in recent years. They do not go on to say that in part this is actually a direct consequence of government policy requiring schools to make their examination results public, but, with a considerable sharpness of insight and subtlety of insinuation they imply as much when they say that:

> 'The schools see themselves increasingly *at the mercy of the market force of parental choice* in a time of falling rolls, and they judge their examination results to be among the major factors which determine the exercise of parental choice. This has led them to be understandably cautious in making decisions about the acceptability of change in the current curriculum, even when there has been considerable agreement about the desirability of such modification.'

(HMI, 1983a, p.14—my emphasis)

On the basis of these observations, we might predict that where examination-directed work and records of personal achievement make competing claims on a teacher's scarce time, then priority will be allocated to the former rather than the latter. Moreover, where most teachers' classes are geared to examination work we would expect those teachers to experience particular difficulty in conducting the processes of one-to-one discussion and negotiation with pupils in the spirit in which those processes were intended.

If public examinations at 16+ do indeed present a sizeable obstacle to the successful implementation of records of personal achievement —and it seems that these examination commitments will not only persist, but very likely *increase* with the advent of GCSE, whose introduction is planned to occur at the very same time that many schools will also be taking their first steps in relation to records of achievement—then schools might do well to consider ways of *easing* the weight that they attach to examinations and examination work.

Within the market system of parental choice, any school which *individually* decided to reduce its commitment to public examinations would, in effect, be putting itself into voluntary liquidation. But one strategy schools might consider as a reasonable and somewhat daring move, particularly where these schools are located in a coherent geographical area, would be to have a federation which agreed policy across a number of schools to lower examination entry ceilings at 16+ to no more than five or six subjects per pupil. This would bring about a de facto reduction in the competitive market influences of parental choice, reduce the prominence of examinations within the curriculum and create more space, time and alternative experience for the building up of other kinds of commitments. It is common to hear Heads extol the virtues of cooperation and collaboration amongst their pupils and their staff. It would be interesting and, as an act of innovative leadership, instructive to see what Heads could cooperatively achieve amongst themselves in this one important area at least. In the long run, the benefits to records of personal achievment might turn out to be considerable.

Compound innovation

The advent of the GCSE points to a more general problem for schools which have already committed themselves to or wish to commit themselves to records of personal achievement: how can they deal adequately with the requirement this innovation will make of them, when many schools are simultaneously being encouraged or (through the policy of 'earmarked' funding) enticed into taking on a number of other cross-curricular innovations too? How will schools respond to the records of achievement initiative when they have also committed themselves to, say, CPVE, TVEI or the Low Attainers Project, for instance, not to mention the de facto commitment to GCSE itself? How will schools and teachers balance these competing commitments on their time, energy and educational loyalties? What will be the implications of this climate of escalating pressure and constraint on the management and success of any one innovation, like records of personal achievement? What are the implications for in-service training and staff development; for teachers' very capacity to cope?

CONCLUSION

Few of these constraints are easily resolved. All are politically sensitive. Easing some of them could run directly counter to current government policy. Yet if the innovatory angels of curriculum development understandably fear to tread for too long in these earthly realms of politics and finance, of conflict and constraint, this may only mean that their high celestial principles achieve only the weakest degree of success when they are transported into the real world of schools. Time, resources, the easement of other competing commitments—these things are almost certainly essential to a personal recording process which is undertaken with the sensitivity and seriousness it deserves.

At the end of the day, the way in which records of personal achievement are interpreted and implemented will depend on the views and visions of social purpose they are seen to realise: independence, motivation and self-realisation on the one hand, or streamlined selection and intensified surveillance on the other. If it is the first set of values they are to realise and not the second, then teachers will also need the time, the space and the opportunity to develop and deploy the appropriate interpersonal skills and to deal with the difficult questions of social values. It is on these issues—the clarification of purpose and the conquering of constraint—that the success of a record of personal achievement which is personally liberating and not socially repressive will almost certainly depend.

REFERENCES

Adams, E. & Burgess, T. (1982) 'Statements at sixteen: an example', *Working Papers on Institutions No. 29*. London: North East London Polytechnic.
Baldwin, J. and Wells, H. (1979) *Active Tutorial Work Books 1–5*. Oxford: Basil Blackwell for Lancashire County Council.
Ball, S. (1981) *Beachside Comprehensive*. London: Cambridge University Press.
Balogh, J. (1982) *Profile Reports for School Leavers*. York: Longman for Schools Council.
Barnes, D. & Shemilt, D. (1974) 'Transmission and interpretation', *Educational Review*, **26**, 3.
Bernstein, B. (1975) 'Class and pedagogies: visible and invisible', in *Class, Codes and Control Vol. 3: Towards a Theory of Educational Transmissions*. London: Routledge and Kegan Paul.
Bolam, R. and Medlock, P. (1983) *The Evaluation of the Active Tutorial Work Project: An Interim Report*. School of Education, University of Bristol.
Broadfoot, P. (1982) 'Alternatives to public examinations', *Educational Analysis* **4**, 3.
Broadfoot, P. (1984) 'From public examinations to profile assessment, the French experience', in Broadfoot, P. (ed.) *Selection, Certification and Control*. Lewes: Falmer Press.
Burgess, T. and Adams, E. (1980) *Outcomes of Education*. London: Macmillan.
Burgess, T. and Adams, E. (1984) 'Records of achievement for school leavers: an institutional framework', *Working Papers on Institutions No.57*.
Department of Education & Science (1983) *Teaching Quality*. London: HMSO.

Department of Education & Science (1984) *Records of Achievement: A Statement of Policy.* London: HMSO.

Dore, R. (1976) *The Diploma Disease.* London: George Allen & Unwin.

Education Resource Unit for YOP (1982) *Assessment in Youth Training: made-to-measure?.* Glasgow: Jordanhill College of Education.

Foucault, M. (1977) *Discipline and Punish.* Harmondsworth: Penguin.

Goacher, B. (1983) *Recording Achievement at 16+.* York: Longman for Schools Council.

Goacher, B. (1984) *Selection post 16: the role of examination results.* London: Methuen Educational.

Habermas, J. (1976) *Legitimation Crisis.* London: Heinemann.

Hargreaves, A. (1977) 'Progressivism and pupil autonomy', *Sociological Review,* **25**, 3.

Hargreaves, A. (1985a) 'Motivation versus selection: some dilemmas for Records of Personal Achievement', in Lang, P. and Marland, M. (ed.) *New Directions in Pastoral Care.* Oxford: Basil Blackwell.

Hargreaves, A. (1985b) *English Middle Schools: An Historical and Ethnographic Study.* PhD thesis submitted to University of Leeds, March 1985.

Hargreaves, D.H.H. (1982) *The Challenge for the Comprehensive School.* London: Routledge and Kegan Paul.

Her Majesty's Inspectorate (1979) *Aspects of Secondary Education in England: a survey by HM Inspectors of Schools.* London: HMSO.

Her Majesty's Inspectorate (1983a) *Curriculum 11–16: Towards a Statement of Entitlement.* London: HMSO.

Her Majesty's Inspectorate (1983b) *Records of Achievement at 16: Some Examples of Current Practice.* London: HMSO.

Jones, J. (1983) *The Use Employers Make of Examination Results and other Tests for Selection and Employment: A Criterion Report for Employers.* School of Education, University of Reading.

Mortimore, J. and Mortimore, P. (1984) 'Secondary School Examinations: The Helpful Servants not the Dominating Master', *Bedford Way Papers No. 18.* University of London Institute of Education.

Olson, J. (1982) *Innovation in the Science Curriculum, Classroom Knowledge and Curriculum Change.* London: Croom Helm.

Oxford Certificate of Educational Achievement (OCEA) (1984) *The Personal Record Component: A Draft Handbook for Schools.* Oxford: OCEA.

Oxford Certificate of Educational Achievement (OCEA) (1985) *Newsletter,* Spring.

Pupils' Personal Records Management Group (1984) *Pupils as Partners: Pupils' Personal Records Handbook.*

Raffe, D. (ed.) (1984) *Fourteen to Eighteen.* Aberdeen: Aberdeen University Press.

Reid, M. et al. (1981) *Mixed Ability Teaching: Problems and Possibilities.* Windsor: NFER.

Sharp, R. and Green, A. (1975) *Education and Social Control.* London: Routledge and Kegan Paul.

Stenhouse, L. (1975) 'Neutrality as a criterion in teaching: the work of the Humanities Curriculum Project', in Taylor, M.J. (ed.) *Progress and Problems in Moral Education.* Windsor: NFER.

Swales, T. (1979) *Record of Personal Achievement: An Independent Evaluation of the Swindon RPA scheme.* London: Schools Council.

Weston, P. (1979) *Negotiating the Curriculum.* Windsor: NFER.

Postscript: The Way Ahead

This book reports on issues and practice associated with a number of attempts to develop profiles and records of achievement. It looks back to the early days of the movement and to the origins of some of today's most successful initiatives. Whilst it must be, first and foremost, an historical document, the book also provides a baseline from which to regard the future. If a similar book were to be prepared in two or three years' time, it is certain that both the experience reported and the issues identified would be radically different. The scale of development work now going on suggests that a 'critical mass' of experience has now been generated, sufficient to project the movement into a qualitatively different stage. Such a new stage might best be termed one of 'institutionalisation'.

This book deals with the first two stages of development in profiles and records of achievement. The first stage, from 1970 to 1980, might be termed the 'mission' stage, when a few disciples were involved in setting down the main principles of this new educational vision and in proselytising them to the rest of the world. The second stage, from 1980 to 1984, can be called 'disseminated development' since it is characterised by a large number of small-scale initiatives, cross-fertilising each other to produce five or six generic approaches to recording achievement (such as are reported here). The third stage in which we are now becoming involved is characterised by development work becoming increasingly large-scale. The efforts of individual institutions are becoming progressively overtaken by the more coordinated initiatives of local authorities and examination boards.

Characteristic of this new stage is the government's *Policy Statement on Records of Achievement* published in July 1984, which commits it to a policy of providing all school-leavers with such a record by the end of the decade. To make this possible, the DES is providing slightly more than £2 million over a three-year period to fund nine pilot 'record of achievement' schemes in England and Wales. The fact that three of the initiatives reported here—by Mortimore and Keane, Willmott and Garforth—are grass-roots developments which have now received major DES support, illustrates the kind of change I am describing. Such funding should make it possible to make more rapid progress with development work and, at the same time, convince potential consumers of the significance of the initiative as a whole. At the same time the DES has commissioned a major evaluation of this work which will look at all aspects of the design, implementation and resourcing of each of the nine pilot schemes.

However, whilst DES support and evaluation is likely to prove very significant for the eventual public acceptability of the new records being developed, equally important initiatives are being undertaken elsewhere. Many local authorities are joining together with examination boards to produce regional schemes. One of the first such consortia was that involving the Welsh Joint Education Committee (the Welsh Examination Board, which includes representation from all Welsh local authorities) and the Schools Council for Wales. This initiative resulted in a draft *national* profile for Wales, which has subsequently been taken up and developed in a number of individual schools and by consortia in Clwyd and Gwent. Now one of the DES/Welsh Office pilot schemes, Wales provides a most interesting pilot study for the implementation of records of achievement on a national scale. In another scheme, the South West Regional Examination Board has joined with six local authorities in the south west—Cornwall, Devon, Somerset, Avon, Gloucestershire and Wiltshire—to mount the South Western Profile Assessment Research Project. In the north of England, similarly, the local education authorities of Barnsley, Bradford, Calderdale, Doncaster, Gateshead, Humberside, Kirklees, Knowsley, Lancashire, Leeds, Liverpool, Manchester, Northumberland, North Yorkshire, Oldham, Rotherham, Salford, Sheffield, Sunderland, Tameside, Trafford. Wakefield and Wigan have joined with the examining boards of the Northern Examining Association to form the Northern Partnership for Records of Achievement development. The advents of the DES Lower Achievers Pilot Project and the MSC's Technical and Vocational Education Initiative and Youth Training Scheme have helped considerably to increase the involvement of examination boards in this movement, as local education authorities have sought new forms of assessment and certification to match these novel curricular approaches.

It is impossible to say yet whether the DES will succeed in bringing all such record of achievement schemes within its national guidelines when it has drawn them up in late 1988. It may be that individual examination board and LEA consortia will feel sufficiently confident in their own schemes and sufficiently convinced of their particular merit that they will not wish to be trammelled in this way. If national guidelines *are* successfully imposed, the effect may be to dampen the grass-roots enthusiasm so characteristic of the early stages of the movement and still vital to its proper implementation as part of the teaching–learning relationship. Even the existence of large consortia may have this effect in time.

Against this, record of achievement schemes which do not have a wide currency are likely to realise only a fraction of their potential impact. Without the public imprimatur of the examination board and the support in terms of resources and training that must be associated with such larger initiatives, grass-roots developments are likely to become increasingly demoralised and frustrated. It is to be hoped that some way will be found of controlling the escalation of activity currently taking place so that the spirit of the movement is not sacrificed for the undoubted benefits to be gained.

Perhaps the most important implication of the current 'institutionalisation' phase for records of achievement is also the least apparent. As the power of the movement to fulfil the aspirations of its progenitors steadily grows, so do the dangers of imposing an ill-conceived or insufficiently developed idea on a vulnerable educational world. The public examinations that were developed with such haste in the late nineteenth century, in response to both customer and consumer demand for a fairer means of assessment, are proving difficult if not impossible to remove despite widespread agreement that, for 16+ at least, their day has passed. The promise and the peril of profiles are even more critically balanced, and the stakes even higher.

The promise of profiling is that of an assessment system which can make a reality of the aims of education which we set for ouselves. It offers a vision of education which is characterised by democratic teacher–pupil relations; in which pupils have a sense of self-worth; in which they may voluntarily negotiate their own curriculum path; in which they develop the ability to be self-critical and thus to take responsibility for their own learning, and in which the competition is primarily with themselves and their own previous performance rather than with others.

However, it is readily apparent that such a change in educational processes cannot happen overnight, if indeed it can happen at all in the institutional setting as we know it. The relationship between teachers and pupils, and the relationship between the school and the society it serves, is to a very large extent determined by factors outside the control of the individual within the system. Teacher–pupil relations, for example, are very much a product of the sheer numbers within the system. Assessment procedures are very much a product of the selection imperative I mentioned earlier. It is widely accepted—and this is a point strongly made by Hitchcock and by Hargreaves—that teachers currently lack the skills and the facilities, if not the commitment, to change their way of working with pupils on a more than marginal basis. The pilot schemes currently being mounted in England and Wales are intended to explore just how far such a change is possible, where teachers are given the training and the resources they need to take such a new approach to curriculum, pedagogy, assessment and reporting. It does seem possible that if sufficient enthusiasm and vision can be generated to change the organisational structure of schools, which is itself largely a product of the advent of public examinations, that we could go some considerable way towards this new approach to learning.

At worst, the effect will be even more devastating than the worst excesses of public examinations. Subject to continuous, comprehensive scrutiny of every aspect of their life and work, pupils will be subject to an even more pervasive destruction of their self-image than they may be at present. Other pupils who, as they do now, early on learn to play the system, will quickly realise the values teachers espouse and will seek to present the appropriate front for such assessment. Still others will retreat from this nightmare of benign surveillance. If teachers operate the procedure insensitively, then pupils will be given well-meant advice which offers them no alternative to the route that benign guidance has mapped out. Those pupils who have hitherto been able to confound their teachers by showing in the relatively objective assessment of the examination that the teacher's stereotype was wrong, will have no such recourse in a system that depends totally upon more informal, formative modes of assessment. The result is likely to be a sense of powerlessness, of coercion, of intrusion and of even greater despair in the face of a hierarchy which is both impregnable and alien.

I have expressed the perils of this new system in strong terms, mainly to balance the euphoria that revolution tends to generate. The experience of revolution is all too often not liberation, and it is important at this early stage to consider the potential dangers of any such major change in our assessment system. It is also important not to regard such a system in isolation, but to see it as part of the configuration of economic, political and social pressures which are bringing about fundamental changes in the world of education at every level. Whilst the most cynical analysts see in such novel assessment moves an insidious trend towards greater social control, bound up with a more utilitarian and vocational emphasis within education as a whole, romantics see this as another manifestation of progressivism, the good effects of which are only held in check by a sterile and outmoded assessment procedure. Both views are represented in this volume. As usual, the truth is somewhere in between. Finding themselves tied to an external examination system which is inappropriate for the majority of young people in developing the skills and qualities they will need for their role in society, teachers and educationists generally are earnestly exploring alternative possibilities which promise better to meet these needs.

In this book I have been able to include descriptions of only a few of the current initiatives. Also, it would be necessary to consider the potential contribution of credit accumulation schemes, graded tests, and modular courses, as well as profiles and records of achievement, to get the total picture of the changes currently being explored. However, it is records of achievement which are obviously the most significant in threatening to break down the barrier between the cognitive and the affective domains in both curriculum and assessment terms; in threatening to change the whole basis of the educational relationship and, in so doing, offering the greatest challenge of the innovations currently being considered. As is so often the case, it is their very challenge that also makes records of achievement the most high risk initiative. Careful monitoring will be required to ensure that the rationale for the new procedure is indeed drawn out in its practice. The joining together of the diverse elements of our education system in common cause to bring about change is a sufficiently rare phenomenon that it demands most careful scrutiny. It also presents a most fertile ground for change. It is therefore imperative that the common cause now being established between assessment-as-curriculum and assessment-as-communication should not be allowed to result in what is at best a continued hindrance to the fulfilment of the whole range of educational objectives and, at worst, a system of surveillance and rejection far more total than that which exists at present. Public acceptability can no longer serve as a sufficient criterion for the acceptability of assessment procedures. The elevation of educational concerns to a position of prime consideration is long overdue. The contributions to this book have been written with this common cause in view. If, in the event, the papers are only of historical interest, the book will already have achieved its purpose.

P.B.

Glossary of Terms

Jargon is a much despised phenomenon which has a remarkable capacity to persist. Although every effort has been made to keep it to a minimum in this book, some readers may encounter terms with which they are not familiar. To this end, a glossary has been provided which defines some of the more ambiguous and important vocabulary that has evolved to accompany developments in the field of profiles and records of achievement.

The editor gratefully acknowledges the contributions of OCEA, the National Profiling Network and the DES Records of Achievement National Steering Committee Secretariat to the preparation of this glossary.

Accreditation

This is the process whereby a body, possibly established specifically for the purpose, grants its imprimatur to other agencies to undertake activities on its behalf. This tends to involve the licensing of an institution to operate an educational scheme and provide certification. The granting of a licence can be subject to rigorous conditions and involve inspection, and over the whole process hangs the power to revoke that licence.

Assessment

An evaluation of a student's achievement. There are many modes of assessment, each designed to allow for the best judgement of a student's performance in a given circumstance. An assessment may be pass/fail or graded or it may consist of verbal reporting.

Comment bank

A list of short statements, prepared phrases or sentences as objective as possible which may be coded and combined to give a prose description of a pupil's attitudes and achievements. The comments are usually designed to act as standard descriptors and so assist those completing and those interpreting the prose record.

Comparability

This refers to the extent to which the standards of an examination, or the examiners, are similar, e.g. from year to year, between different examiners or between different subjects.

Criterion-referenced

A system under which grades are defined and awarded in terms of standards of performance defined in advance and specific to the subject concerned. Candidates are required to demonstrate predetermined levels of competence in specified aspects of the subject in order to be awarded a particular grade. An assessment is said to be criterion-referenced when a student's performance is measured against explicit criteria; the student either achieves or does not achieve the criteria.

Descriptor

Words or statements describing skills, duties or tasks expected from a student or associated with a specific job are called descriptors. Also referred to as behavioural statements.

Diagnostic assessment

Assessment aimed at identifying students' progress, their strengths, weaknesses and learning difficulties and so being a guide to future action.

Formative and Formative recording

An event is taken to be formative if it serves to fashion the way or direction in which a student develops. Formative recording is a process involving some discussion between teacher and pupil, affecting both the course to be followed and the pupil's progress.

Generic skills

Behaviours which are fundamental to the performance of many tasks carried out in a wide range of occupations are called generic skills.

Grade descriptions

These descriptions are intended to indicate the levels of attainment likely to be shown by candidates awarded particular grades in a subject. Such descriptions should not be confused with criterion-referenced grading (see above).

Graded tests

> 'A graded test scheme is progressive, with short term objectives leading on from one to the next; task-orientated . . . and closely linked to the learning process with pupils or students taking the test when they are ready to pass.' *A. Harrison*

> 'A graded test scheme consists of a series of tests at progressive levels of difficulty . . . designed to be taken by students only when they have a high probability of success. Each test is closely linked to the curriculum for the relevant level . . . and which clearly specifies the task to be mastered.' *D. Pennycuick*

Graded tests appear to be one aspect, along with graded assessment and credit accumulation, of the concept of staged assessment. Modular courses may be assessed at various stages, but unlike graded tests they do not necessarily imply progression.

Moderation

Moderation is the procedure by which the results of assessments from a number of assessors (teachers, examiners, etc.) responsible for the assessment of their own candidates are aligned with an agreed, accepted standard. It may also involve aligning standards between different examinations or different components of examinations.

Modes

Originally defined in the context of CSE, there are three modes under which assessment can take place, as follows:
Mode 1 — board syllabus, board examination;
Mode 2 — school syllabus (approved by the board), board examination;
Mode 3 — school syllabus (approved by the board), school examination (moderated by the board).

Modes of assessment

There are a number of modes or methods by which a student's performance may be assessed. These may refer either to the way in which the instructions are given to a student or to the way in which a student responds. The main modes of assessment are: written, practical, spoken, course work, aural and project work.

Norm-referenced

A system under which grades are allocated to predetermined proportions of the candidate-entry for the subject concerned or of some other defined proportion such as the whole age cohort. The grade awarded to a student depends not only on the quality of the student's own performance but also on the quality of the other students' performance.

Negotiation

A process of discussion between pupil and teacher, either to draw out and nourish a view of significant experience and achievement in the past or to plan some future action, course or curriculum. A process whereby the aims, objectives, goals and content of a training programme are agreed jointly by tutor/trainee/student.

Negotiation presupposes open relationships between students and staff, where discussion of issues can come to mutually agreed acceptable conclusions without undue pressure or prejudice by one party or the other, and where due allowance is made for inexperience, lack of maturity or inarticulateness.

Performance

This is observable behaviour, i.e. the demonstration of a skill, the ability to use a concept, the exhibition of knowledge, the demonstration of a given attitude. This observable behaviour may not necessarily be assessable.

Personal record

A record initiated by the pupil describing experiences and achievements considered of value and significance to that pupil.

Profile

A profile is a method of displaying the results of an assessment; it is not a method of assessment. It is essentially derived from a separation of the whole of an assessment into its main parts or components.

A profile is 'a panoramic representation, numerical, graphical or verbal, of how a student appears to assessors across a range of qualities, or in respect of one quality as seen through a range of assessment methods' (Macintosh).

It is loosely used as a catch-all term for records and reports on pupils' achievements and experiences.

Profiling

A process of deriving information from pupils' experience and achievements in and out of school, which displays the results in the form of a profile. It may involve negotiation with students and could include a variety of assessments.

Profiling movement

An umbrella term which includes the diverse initiatives concerned with providing better, more detailed formative and summative reporting procedures. What this book is all about!

Record

A written statement on a number of facts and/or pieces of evidence concerning a pupil which do not involve a judgement.

Record of achievement

The term record of achievement is used to describe school-leavers' documents, which may include the results of a variety of examinations, graded tests and other assessments, and other information about a student, as well as internal records compiled by teachers and/or students and covering the total educational progress of the student.

Reliability

This refers to the consistency or accuracy of an examination component. A component is completely reliable if it would yield the same results when repeated by the same candidate under the same conditions.

Report

A formal statement (usually written) about one person to another person implying some degree of judgement.

Skill

A skill can be defined in terms of its features:

(a) it can be taught;
(b) it can be improved with practice and feedback;
(c) it can be applied in a variety of different situations;
(d) several skills are usually combined to form a smooth sequence of actions, directed towards a particular outcome.

A skill is a specific ability which can be enhanced by practice and through experience.

Summative or Summary record

A summative or summary record is a compendious statement of what students have achieved during their time at school or college, designed in such a way that it may be useful to prospective employers or establishments of further and higher education.

Validation

The process whereby approval is given to arrangements for the development of courses of study and their related assessment in accordance with an agreed set of rules and regulations. In a very elementary form it may mean the signature by someone (usually an adult) that a statement by a pupil is true.

Validity

The extent to which an assessment does that which it was designed to do. Since assessments are designed to do a wide variety of different things, their validity can be assessed in a number of different ways.

Appendix 1

Knowing our Pupils

An outline report of 'Pupils in Profile'
A joint study by the Working Party on School Assessments
of the Headteachers' Association of Scotland and the
Scottish Council for Research in Education[1]

THE INITIAL CONCERNS

> 'To consider the form and range of items of information needed to
> produce, for all secondary pupils, a comprehensive picture of their
> aptitudes and interests so as to enable responsible guidance staff to give
> them the best possible advice on future curricular and vocational choice;
> and offering them a common form of statement, which would be
> generally comprehensible and which would be available to them when
> appropriate.'

In simple terms, the aim was to develop a secondary school assessment
which would meet the needs of all pupils for self-knowledge, for
curricular and vocational guidance, and for a relevant and useful
leaving report.

The Working Party[2] was (and is) concerned especially about pupils
affected by the raising of the school-leaving age, who are at present

---

[1] © Scottish Council for Research in Education.
[2] The Headteachers' Association of Scotland's Working Party on School Assessment
was set up in 1972. The Scottish Council for Research in Education and representatives
of industry, education authorities, colleges of education, further education colleges and
Her Majesty's Inspectorate were also members of the working party.

leaving school at 16 without a nationally recognised certificate and for whom the O-grade is educationally irrelevant.

Before a year of feasibility work in schools, and the subsequent year of the pilot scheme and field studies, the following guidelines were agreed by the Working Party:

For all pupils **a**	The procedure would be applied to all secondary pupils.
Profile that would be	Pupils of differing aptitudes would have their various talents recognised by the assessment of a variety of abilities and qualities that at present are not officially noted. This would include not only achievement in learning at different stages of the curriculum but also of basic skills such as writing and numeracy and of work-related characteristics like perseverance.
Comprehensive and	There would be no assumption about what are major subjects, what minor; no division of pupils into preconceived categories such as SCE: non-SCE. Assessment would be made for all areas of school life, including activities such as community work or leisure activities to stress the value of positive qualities in all kinds of pupil.
Cumulative using	Assessments would support internal school guidance by continuing from year to year.
Appropriate techniques	A variety of assessment techniques would be employed, including examination and tests.
Balanced	The danger of over-assessing would be guarded against by assessing only those aspects of pupils' behaviour agreed as relevant to progress in learning or to further education or vocation.
Practicable	The assessment would require forms to be designed requiring the minimum of clerical work.
Flexible	These assessment techniques and procedures could be used by all secondary schools — no one type of school organisation, no single theory of curricular management would be assumed. Schools would be left the maximum freedom in

and

achieving the common objective of meaningful and efficient assessment.

Comparable

Moderation between schools would provide regional or national standards to allow the information to be of value beyond the school.

These aims are representative of a growing inclination in countries from New Zealand to Norway towards the recognition of school assessments as valid, reliable and useful criteria, and towards the recognition of teachers in school as the proper agents of these assessments. Recent Schools Council Examinations Bulletins and Working Papers illustrate this: for example, its Working Paper 53.

'To summarise our position, we believe that what are increasingly required in the 14–16 range of the secondary school are not so much terminal measures of achievement to be used for selection purposes as kinds of assessment which provide teachers, parents and pupils with guidance. We are particularly anxious that the examination system should not perpetuate a divisive curriculum. We believe that all pupils should be offered a documentary record at the completion of their secondary schooling. This record should be a balanced account of the pupil's attainments, interests and aspirations. The document should be externally validated and under-written by appropriate authorised bodies. We would see these bodies are offering a comprehensive assessment service which would in time supersede the present system of examining at 16+.'

RESEARCH AND DEVELOPMENT: PUTTING THESE IDEAS INTO PRACTICE

Over the last few years a research project carried out by the Scottish Council for Research in Education and funded by the Scottish Education Department has been conducted to develop a procedure to meet these aims. Various profile assessment forms which require teachers to contribute their individual knowledge of pupils to produce a detailed picture of each pupil in terms of his skills, achievements and characteristics were tried out in schools. Guidance for teachers making the assessments was offered in the form of subject guides prepared by panels of teachers. These were designed to help in defining the assessment categories and setting the standards for the five-point scale used. Problems were continually discovered during the field studies in schools, definitions were revised and alternatives tried. All aspects of the procedure—its aims and its content, reliability and validity— became the subject of enquiry.

Statistical analysis revealed those assessments which could be reliably assessed. It revealed crucially that teachers could and did 'profile' by giving pupils different grades for different skill levels. It provided the basis for revision and refinement in answering the question, what *could* be done. What *should* be done—an even more fundamental question—was the subject of extensive discussions with interested parties—the teachers involved in the field trials, pupils, parents, employers, colleges. Their wisdom, added to the practical experience of the school trials, forms the basis for the translation of the aims of the original remit into the practical procedures described in this leaflet.[3]

TEACHERS gave almost unanimous support for the schools being concerned with the 'whole child', and for the need for all pupils to have a leaving report. Two-thirds of teachers felt pupil profiles would help in this respect. This is a clear endorsement of the overall aim of the Working Party and of the concerns which led to its inception. Guidance teachers felt such a procedure would help them in their work by improving communication about pupils within the school, and by facilitating communication with the pupils themselves, with parents, and with outside bodies.

PUPILS generally felt their profiles were fair and welcomed the chance to be kept informed in a detailed way about their teachers' views of their progress and work-related characteristics. Most, especially those with little hope of external exam success, welcomed the idea of a leaving report for all pupils.

PARENTS welcomed such a profile record as a source of pupil self-knowledge and as a basis for their own understanding and support for their children although some stressed that a leaving report should not be prejudicial for any pupil.

EMPLOYERS welcomed the provision of valid information on basic skill standards and work-related characteristics for all pupils since many considered that these were more

---

[3] A full account of the research and the evaluation is available in the major report on the project 'Pupils in Profile' (1976), published by Hodder & Stoughton for the Scottish Council for Research in Education.

significant than subject attainments at the O-grade level.

COLLEGES felt such a report, if valid, would help their selection procedure to the extent that they were looking for qualities other than merely academic ability. Colleges of Education expressed a willingness to help in the training of teachers for such new assessment techniques.

CONCLUSIONS AND RECOMMENDATIONS

This research and evaluation study has led the Working Party to formulate the following conclusions:

Schools should be encouraged to develop and refine their techniques for assessing all their pupils.

1. These assessments should refer to general skills as well as to specific achievements.
2. Pupil assessments should be recorded for some work-related factors as well as for general skills and specific achievements.
3. Certain procedures for these assessments have been found practicable and should be offered to schools.
4. A common form of school-leaving report incorporating these features for all pupils should be instituted.
5. Further field study should be undertaken in order to produce, for each subject or activity within the curriculum, improved diagnostic profiles.

THE PROFILE ASSESSMENT SYSTEM

The profile procedure, developed, evaluated, and re-designed to meet these aims allows for teachers to enter on a class assessment form (see Fig. A.1) their assessments of those categories for each pupil of which they have knowledge, and includes blank optional categories which can be labelled as appropriate for each activity.

If computer-collation is used, each teacher's assessments are fed into the computer, which collects together for each pupil the report of all teachers by whom he/she is taught and prints them out against the

Fig.A.1 Teacher Assessment Form. The duplicate copy underneath is a single sheet (computer version) or partially overlapping individual pupil sheets (manual version).

S.C.R.E. PROFILE ASSESSMENT SYSTEM

CLASS ASSESSMENT SHEET

Pupil's Name

Class Group

Skills: Listening, Speaking, Reading, Writing, Visual understanding & expression, Use of Number

Performance: Physical Coordination, Manual Dexterity, Knowledge, Reasoning, Presentation, Imagination, Critical Awareness, Composite Grade, Perseverance, Enterprise

Subject/Activity

Teacher

Date

© Scottish Council for Research in Education 1976

pupil's name. If the manual system is used the same collation is achieved by having below the teacher's master-sheet a set of overlapping pupil sheets, onto the exposed edges of which the teacher's entries are reproduced by a carbon or similar process. These pupil slips can then be sorted and mounted for each pupil on a peg-board such that a profile of the pupil is built up from the various teachers' assessments displayed immediately adjacent one to the other.

The pupil profiles, produced perhaps once or twice a year, are designed to provide not only a comprehensive and cumulative basis for within-school guidance but also to provide the necessary information for a leaving report for each pupil, covering basic skills, subject achievements and personal qualities. This school-leaving report—a balance of comment and grades—aims to be brief, accurate, positive and useful to potential users and pupils. The format of the report is summative and does not include all the subject-specific categories useful for in-school purposes. It, too, has been the subject of a continuing process of development and evaluation, resulting in a recommended version, shown in Fig. A.2.

The report, given to the pupil when he leaves school, will be a summation and abbreviation of the internal assessment data. The contents of such a report will not be unexpected since a pupil will have been frequently advised by his guidance and subject teachers in their encouragement of self-assessment as he has moved up the school. This report has moreover been designed to be readily understood by those concerned with selection for employment or post-school education.

It is clear that different schools, and different teachers, will place different emphases on what they find most useful and most practicable to assess. It is also clear that the rationale of the procedure—detailed teacher assessment on a standardised format as a basis for guidance and certification for all pupils—has been generally accepted and the need for it fully endorsed through this enquiry.

All these materials are available including sample packs, from Safeguard Business Systems, Loomer Road Industrial Estate, Chesterton, Newcastle, Staffs ST5 7PZ. A user's manual, 'The SCRE Profile Assessment System: Manual' is obtainable, price 50p, from The Scottish Council for Research in Education, St. John Street, Edinburgh.

The financial support for the project given by the Scottish Education Department is gratefully acknowledged. The responsibility for the research and for the opinions expressed here is, however, the working party's alone.

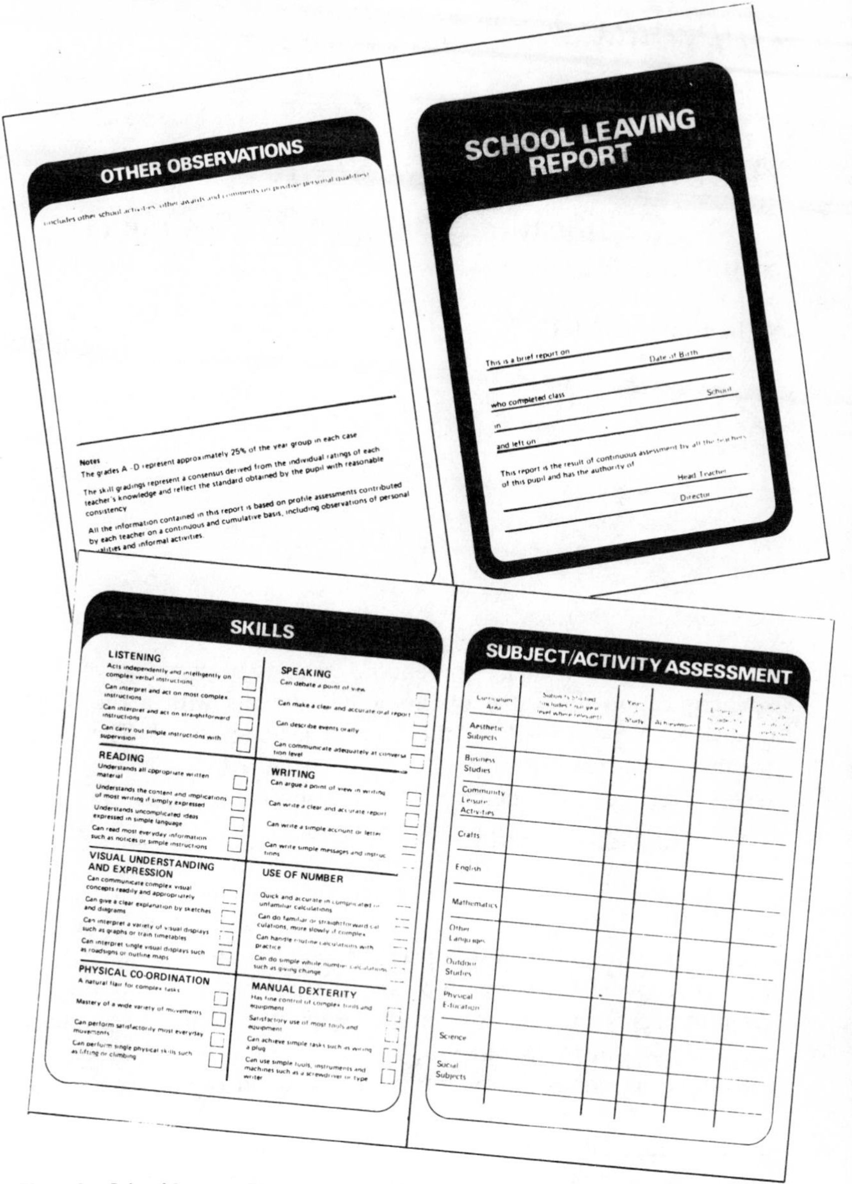

OTHER OBSERVATIONS

Notes

The grades A – D represent approximately 25% of the year group in each case

The skill gradings represent a consensus derived from the individual ratings of each teacher's knowledge and reflect the standard obtained by the pupil with reasonable consistency

All the information contained in this report is based on profile assessments contributed by each teacher on a continuous and cumulative basis, including observations of personal qualities and informal activities.

SCHOOL LEAVING REPORT

This is a brief report on

Date of Birth

who completed class

School

in

and left on

This report is the result of continuous assessment by all the teachers of this pupil and has the authority of

Head Teacher

Director

SKILLS

LISTENING

Acts independently and intelligently on complex verbal instructions

Can interpret and act on most complex instructions

Can interpret and act on straightforward instructions

Can carry out simple instructions with supervision

SPEAKING

Can debate a point of view

Can make a clear and accurate oral report

Can describe events orally

Can communicate adequately at conversation level

READING

Understands all appropriate written material

Understands the content and implications of most writing if simply expressed

Understands uncomplicated ideas expressed in simple language

Can read most everyday information such as notices or simple instructions

WRITING

Can argue a point of view in writing

Can write a clear and accurate report

Can write a simple account or letter

Can write simple messages and instructions

VISUAL UNDERSTANDING AND EXPRESSION

Can communicate complex visual concepts readily and appropriately

Can give a clear explanation by sketches and diagrams

Can interpret a variety of visual displays such as graphs or train timetables

Can interpret single visual displays such as roadsigns or outline maps

USE OF NUMBER

Quick and accurate in complicated or unfamiliar calculations

Can do familiar or straightforward calculations, more slowly if complex

Can handle routine calculations with practice

Can do simple whole number calculations such as giving change

PHYSICAL CO-ORDINATION

A natural flair for complex tasks

Mastery of a wide variety of movements

Can perform satisfactorily most everyday movements

Can perform single physical skills such as lifting or climbing

MANUAL DEXTERITY

Has fine control of complex tools and equipment

Satisfactory use of most tools and equipment

Can achieve simple tasks such as wiring a plug

Can use simple tools, instruments and machines such as a screwdriver or typewriter

SUBJECT/ACTIVITY ASSESSMENT

Curriculum Area	Subjects Studied	Years Study	Achievement		
Aesthetic Subjects					
Business Studies					
Community Leisure Activities					
Crafts					
English					
Mathematics					
Other Languages					
Outdoor Studies					
Physical Education					
Science					
Social Subjects					

Fig. A.2 *School Leaving Report. (Pages 1 & 4 above, pages 2 & 3 below). The entries on this record are derived from the series of profile records cumulated during the years preceding leaving.*

Appendix 2

A Comparative Case Study
School Certification: The Present Australian Situation

NEIL BAUMGART

Although there are many contentious aspects of certification, few would question the value of providing students with a record of achievement, particularly at the time of leaving school. The usual practices in the six Australian states and two territories have been to issue certificates to students at the end of Year 10 (corresponding approximately to the legal minimum school-leaving age) and the end of Year 12 (coinciding most often with admission to tertiary education). In recent years, with significant numbers of students proceeding beyond Year 10 but not completing Year 12, some systems have also made provision for the award of certificates to students completing at least some specified minimum course of study beyond Year 10.

The diversity of practices across the eight systems of secondary education in Australia with respect to provision of certificates for school-leavers means that exceptions can be found for most generalisations. A succinct account of practices at the Year 12 level in all systems may be found in the recent *McGaw Report on School Certification and Tertiary Admissions Procedures* (Western Australia, 1984a). In general, however, the following points can be noted about current Australian practices.

1. Certificates tend to be issued to students from both government and non-government schools by some form of board of secondary education, with membership representing tertiary institutions,

government departments of education and non-government schools.

2. Historically, the boards have evolved from earlier public examination boards, and notable in recent changes has been a marked shift away from dominance in membership by university representatives towards dominance by the schools sector.

3. Certificates typically summarise achievements in school subjects and some give information on competence in selected basic skills, but no attempt is made to report on personal qualities, practical and social skills, or interests and leisure pursuits.

4. The subjects studied and reported on certificates are frequently classified into two or more levels, according to the degree of control exercised by a board over the curriculum and over the assessment process.

5. In recent years, certificates at the Year 10 level (age fifteen or sixteen) have typically been derived from school-based assessment, with some systems attempting moderation across schools in selected subjects.

6. At the Year 12 level, external examination results form a part of the reported assessment in selected subjects in all systems except Queensland and the Australian Capital Territory, where no external examinations are held.

7. Particularly for Year 12 subjects categorised as relevant to tertiary entrance, various elaborate statistical moderation practices are used, with either external examination results or aptitude test scores as moderators, in an effort to achieve comparability across subjects, across schools and between school-based assessments and external examination results.

8. Some use is also made of other moderation practices, including visits by moderators and meetings of teachers aimed at consensus moderation.

9. Year 12 reporting is characterised by a tension between two functions—that of reporting achievements in secondary education and that of providing a basis for selection for tertiary entrance—and various attempts, both structural and procedural, to separate these functions have met with little success.

10. With the exception of Queensland where the *Review of School-Based Assessment* (ROSBA) (Queensland Board of Secondary School Studies, 1978) has led to attempts to evaluate achievement relative to defined performance criteria, all systems employ norm-referenced procedures to report results.

11. Quite different mechanisms are used to report achievement, including scaled marks, letter and number grades based on

divisions of standard score distributions or on percentiles, and descriptive labels.

12. In some systems, certificates imply if not define minimum levels of competence by distinguishing passing and failing grades, while in others the certificates simply express achievement relative to that of other students and hence avoid the pass/fail dichotomy.

13. In order to satisfy the demands by tertiary institutions for a tertiary selection score, all systems permit some aggregation of marks at the year 12 level in accordance with specified rules. However, such aggregates do not always appear on the certificate of secondary education.

Of course, a terminal school-leaver's certificate is not the only documentary evidence a student receives as testimony to the achievements of 10 or 12 years of schooling. All schools issue regular reports which could be retained by the student for future use. However, such reports are likely to be much less useful, for example, in seeking employment or entry to further education, than school-leavers' certificates for at least three reasons. First, the regular reports issued by schools have as their prime audiences parents and students, not employers or institutions of further education. Second, they are likely to provide formative rather than summative evaluation of student learning and hence to be diagnostic in their information and critical even if encouraging in their commentary. Finally, school-based reports, unless underwritten by some wider authority, will simply lack the currency of a system-based certificate. This is clearly to the detriment of students who happen to attend a school over-shadowed by a more prestigious school in the same locality.

Students may also receive a written reference on leaving school, sometimes on request but sometimes as a matter of routine school policy. While written references are useful, their major value probably occurs when the referee is asked to evaluate the suitability of a person for a particular position where a job specification is provided.

In summary, students leaving Australian schools currently receive limited formal recognition of their accomplishment. In spite of the diverse aims of schooling, system-based certificates of secondary education typically provide highly condensed information on achievement in academic subjects. Employers and others most likely to use such certificates for screening applicants are thus encouraged to value global academic prowess above specialised skills or other personal qualities. On a national perspective, variations in the source of information provided, the different ways marks are scaled and interpreted, and the numerous modes of presentation contribute to a complex picture.

A major review of reporting practices is therefore timely. Since reporting the outcomes of education has been a topic of lively debate in the United Kingdom in recent years, it is opportune to ask what this debate can offer to Australian policy-makers.

Index